STUDIES IN THE GOSPELS AND EPISTLES

STUDIES IN THE
GOSPELS AND EPISTLES

By
T. W. MANSON

EDITED BY
MATTHEW BLACK

THE WESTMINSTER PRESS
PHILADELPHIA

Printed in Great Britain

PREFACE

By MATTHEW BLACK

THE idea of collecting and publishing in a single volume a selection of the late Professor T. W. Manson's Rylands Lectures was one which had occurred to several of his friends long before his death ; and it had been suggested on more than one occasion to their distinguished author himself. After his untimely death in 1958 it seemed the first and obvious step to take to help to perpetuate his memory.

The proposal commended itself at once to the Rylands Librarian, Professor Edward Robertson, a friend and former colleague of Professor Manson in the University of Manchester. Permission was granted for republication by the Governors of the John Rylands Library, and, with the co-operation of the Manchester University Press, the present volume is the result.

These famous lectures, delivered over a number of years to audiences in the John Rylands Library and published regularly in the Library's *Bulletin*, contained some of Manson's finest scholarly work, done during his tenure of the Rylands Professorship of Biblical Exegesis, and on the subject which he professed with such distinction.

As a selection had to be made, it seemed appropriate to confine the contents of the volume to two longer series of Rylands lectures, given between the years 1943 and 1953 : the first series appeared under the general title *The Life of Jesus: A Study of the Available Materials*. The second series dealt with the Pauline Epistles ; four were entitled *St. Paul in Ephesus* ; these were followed by *St. Paul's Letter to the Romans and Others, The Problem of the Epistle to the Hebrews*; the last two lectures, *St. Paul in Greece*, dealt with the Thessalonian correspondence.

Is it possible to write a Life of Christ? That is the question the first series of lectures sets out to answer, and it does so by subjecting to a careful scrutiny the actual materials available for such an enterprise. The profound theological scepticism which had set in, in this connection as a result mainly of the researches of Schweitzer and the school of Form-criticism, was met by Manson with a reasoned and tempered optimism. For Manson the ministerial practice of Jesus was vastly more important than any apocalyptic or eschatological theory attributed to him (a hitherto unpublished story of F. C. Burkitt, told at page 10, furnishes an excellent illustration of Manson's firmly held views on this controversial topic).

The second series on the Pauline Epistles will take their place among the best recent attempts to deal with some of the basic problems of history, background and development in St. Paul's writings.

These two series are now published, as Part I and Part II respectively of this volume, under their original titles. The first Part on *The Life of Jesus* is introduced by a lecture, which was originally entitled *Recent Work on the Leben-Jesu Forschung*, given as a Commemoration Day Address at Westminster College, Cambridge, in 1949. This lecture had never been published; it contained so much that was characteristic of Manson's work that it seemed appropriate to include it as an introduction to the longer series, though it could equally well have stood as a conclusion to the series.

We are grateful to Dr. R. D. Whitehorn, Principal of Westminster College, for his kind permission and encouragement to publish this notable Commemoration Day Address of one of Westminster's most distinguished *alumni*.

Professor Emeritus H. H. Rowley, a close friend and former colleague of Manson for many years in Manchester, has contributed a Memoir to the volume.

St. Mary's College,   M. B.
University of St. Andrews
14th January, 1960

CONTENTS

CONTENTS

T. W. MANSON: AN APPRECIATION

By H. H. ROWLEY

RECENTLY there has been some discussion on the qualities to be looked for in the appointment of a university professor. Should he be primarily a gifted teacher or a brilliant researcher? Or should he be one wise in counsel and skilled in administration, able to take his share in the increasingly complex work of running the university? In all of these ways and in many others besides Thomas Walter Manson was outstanding, and by his death on 1 May 1958 not alone the University of Manchester and New Testament scholarship throughout the world were impoverished. In many places at home and abroad and in many ways his influence was missed, and a wide circle of friends in Europe and America mourned the loss of a man whose gentleness matched his strength, and whose charm was equalled only by his integrity and learning. To do justice to this many-sided man is quite impossible, and all that can be attempted here is to pay some tribute to the memory of a very great man.

It is unnecessary to review the course of his life, since this has been done by Principal Matthew Black in the Obituary Notice published by the British Academy.[1] Manson was born in Tynemouth on 22 July 1893, and was proud of being a Tynesider. At the same time he always remembered that his roots through both his parents were in the Shetland Isles. The story of his early education and his debt to his parents and his minister, and of his brilliant career as a university student in Glasgow and Cambridge, has been recounted by Principal Black. Not always is the promise of a student fulfilled in after days. In Manson's case it was more than fulfilled. Whatever he did he did well, and there were few things relevant to the career he followed which he did not do with supreme distinction.

[1] Published in the *Proceedings of the British Academy*, xliv, 1958, and obtainable separately from the Oxford University Press.

He was trained for the ministry of the Presbyterian Church of England, and he was never diverted by the claims of scholarship from his vocation as a Christian minister. He had charge of the Jewish Mission Institute in Bethnal Green and then of a congregation at Falstone in Northumberland for but a few years, though during the Second World War he combined the charge of St. Aidan's Church in Manchester with his work in the university and in the city. In 1953 he served the Presbyterian Church of England by becoming its Moderator, and gave himself unstintingly and beyond his strength to the service of the Church throughout the country, while he was still carrying his full load of work and responsibility in the university. Nor did he serve his own Church alone. In 1944 he was invited to become the President of the Manchester Free Church Council, at a time when its then President resigned under embarrassing circumstances. For ten years he continued to hold the office, and on countless occasions he represented the Free Churches of Manchester. At the same time he had the respect and affection of all those in the Established Church with whom he came into contact. His Free Churchmanship was never something angular or negative. He brought a positive contribution to the total Christian witness, and while sure of his own position and ready to speak with forthrightness on occasion, he never stepped beyond the bounds of Christian charity. He also shared in the work of the Manchester and Salford Council of Churches, of which he was for several years a Vice-President. As a preacher he was welcomed in the pulpits of churches of various denominations. His voice was not powerful, and wherever he went he compelled attention by the substance of what he had to say. At the same time his diction was choice and there was finish of form in every utterance. It was fitting that after his death a memorial service was held in Manchester Cathedral, when his friend the Bishop of Manchester gave the address. For Manson belonged to Manchester and to all the churches, and was God's gift to more than the Presbyterian Church.

As a theological teacher he served as a Tutor at Westminster College, Cambridge, for three years before his ordination. Then, after seven years in London and the north, he became Yates

Professor of New Testament Greek and Exegesis at Mansfield College, Oxford.   Many of his friends had hoped that he would be called to serve as Professor at Westminster College.   When the Assembly of the Presbyterian Church of England decided otherwise, Mansfield College quickly showed its discernment by inviting him to succeed C. H. Dodd, when Dodd moved to the Rylands professorship in the University of Manchester.   Manson's qualities as a teacher were soon in evidence in Oxford, and when a few years later Dodd went to the Norris-Hulse chair at Cambridge, Manchester invited Manson to succeed him a second time.   For more than twenty years he continued in the Rylands chair at Manchester, despite approaches from other universities, and here his main work was done.

He was a superbly good teacher, who took infinite pains both with his lectures and with the direction of the research of post-graduate students, and few university teachers have been held in higher esteem than he.   His fame spread far and wide, so that students came to him from other universities and from other countries.   All who came under the spell of his influence were not merely instructed, but inspired.   He was never a dull purveyor of information, but one who communicated to his students a sense of the meaning of that whereon they were en-gaged.   He was always exacting, and as he did not spare him-self, so he expected his students to be unsparing of themselves. True education can never be onesided, and its fruitfulness depends on the response it evokes from the taught no less than on the ability and toil of the teacher.   From many of his students Manson found an eager response, and from all he won affection. For they knew that he was interested in them, and that all the varied tasks and responsibilities that fell to him did not for one moment make him forget what he owed to them.

His service to the university did not end in the classroom.   In the Faculties of which he was a member and in the Senate he was regularly in his place, and when he spoke he always had some-thing to say.   He could speak with vigour and strong conviction when any academic principle was at stake, and was formidable in debate.   He served on innumerable committees, where his judgement was always treated with respect by his colleagues, even when they did not share it. His qualities as a Chairman were very high, and when once the Theological Faculty had seen him in action as Dean, it did not want to change him for another. The result was that instead of the Deanship of this Faculty being held by various members in turn, as had been the custom previously, he continued to be re-elected and served as Dean for eleven years, until he was chosen to be Moderator of the Presbyterian Church of England and was compelled to ask for release. When the Faculty celebrated its Jubilee, it looked to Manson to write the review of its history, and this was published as an Introduction to the little volume which contained the three public lectures which were delivered to celebrate the occasion.[1]

For four years Manson was a Pro-Vice-Chancellor of the university. In this capacity he had to chair many committees, as well as represent the university in a variety of ways. To every task he brought the same efficiency that he brought to his teaching work. For twenty years he was the official Presenter for honorary degrees, and for this his skilful turn of phrase and never-failing wit were invaluable. His colleagues came to Founder's Day with high expectation that was never disappointed, and many an honorary graduate of the university must treasure the little gem of a speech with which he was presented to the Chancellor.

I knew a university professor who on more than one occasion observed : " I never read books ; I write them." That was not Manson. He had a large and well-chosen library, and he loved good books, as every scholar should. But his thought was not of his private collection alone. He served on the Library Committee of the university, and on the University Press Committee, and of both of these bodies he was Vice-Chairman for a number of years. In addition he was a Governor of the John Rylands Library, and regularly attended the meetings of the Governors and served on the Library's Book Committee. He was also a feoffee of the very ancient Chethams Library in Manchester.

The Teacher Training Colleges of the city and its neighbourhood, now gathered into the University School of Education, claimed much of his time, and for several years he served as their

---

[1] Published under the title *Theological Essays* in 1954.

External Examiner in Religious Knowledge and as the Chairman of the subject committee. He will also be remembered by many in Manchester for the work he did for the Extra-Mural Department of the university. The Faculty of Theology was for long housed in the same building as the Extra-Mural Department. It was probably less due to this fact than to his readiness to serve wherever he could that for years Manson regularly delivered extra-mural courses, which commanded widespread interest in the city of Manchester, and which he gave up only when the inexorable pressure of commitments beyond his strength to carry compelled him to give them up.

One of the most valuable features of Manchester University is Staff House, where members of staff of all grades and of all faculties meet together, particularly after lunch. In the life of Staff House Manson took an active part, and usually joined a group that contained members of several faculties—Science, Arts, Law, Theology, Medicine, Economics—as well as members of the administrative staff. Here a lively conversation on a wide range of topics took place, and many good stories were told. Manson was himself a good raconteur, and his richly stored mind and ready wit enabled him to contribute to the discussion on most subjects, whether they concerned general affairs or the life and work of the university. He was always excellent company, and whether the conversation were grave or gay his versatility ensured him a part in it.

Beyond the bounds of the University of Manchester Manson served as a co-opted member of the Faculty of Theology of the University of Wales, though his attendance at its meetings was less frequent than he and the Faculty could have desired. His help was sought for the new translation of the Bible now in preparation, and he was a member of the panels charged with the translation of the Apocrypha and the New Testament, and served as the draft translator of some books. The Institute of Christian Education valued his aid, and he was the founder and chairman of the Manchester branch of this Institute, and regularly gave of his time to its service. After his death the Manchester branch wished to commemorate all he had done for it, and did so by presenting to the Faculty of Theology and to the John Rylands

B

Library framed photographs of him, which now hang in the main lecture room of the Faculty and in the room of the Library where the Book Committee holds its meetings.

Mention should be made of Manson's services to his country. In the First World War he interrupted his studies to enlist in the Royal Field Artillery, and served in France, where he was wounded. In the Second World War he served as Operations Officer in the North-West Regional Headquarters, in the War Room of the area that covered the north-west of England from Chester to Carlisle. During some of the worst bombing raids this region suffered Manson was on duty. He also served as Captain in the Home Guard. Memories of the lighter side of his experiences in both wars sometimes enlivened his conversation, but neither in this connection nor in any other did his friends hear him speak of the things he had done. His modesty was an integral part of his greatness.

As a reviewer of learned books he was much in demand. He contributed regular articles to the *Manchester Guardian*—as the paper continued to be called until after his death, when it became *The Guardian*. Many of these articles were devoted to the appraisal of books. Beyond this, his advice was often sought in the planning of special Religious Book Supplements. For the *Times Literary Supplement* he wrote frequent reviews, as well as for a number of learned journals. When *The Times* issued a special Supplement on the Bible, afterwards published in book form,[1] Manson's advice was sought as to the assignment of the articles. Many publishers turned to him for advice. When the Society for Old Testament Study was asked to advise on the preparation of a handbook to the Bible, it recommended that this work should be entrusted to the editorship of Manson, and the widely used *Companion to the Bible* was the result. To every task he brought meticulous care, and those who knew best how many tasks he undertook were constantly filled with wonder that he found time to execute them all.

He was much in demand for lectures in other universities and before learned societies, as well as before religious bodies. He was welcomed as a lecturer in foreign universities, and especially

[1] *The Bible Today*, 1955.

in America, from which country he received far more invitations than he was able to accept. In the years 1943-5 he delivered the Grinfield Lectures on the Septuagint in the University of Oxford. Frequently the B.B.C. sought his services, and twice he consented to appear on television. Moreover, every year he delivered a lecture in the John Rylands Library, and these were eagerly looked forward to by those who could be present to hear them and by those less fortunate who had to wait until they appeared in print in the pages of the *Bulletin of the John Rylands Library*. Some of these lectures are gathered together in the present volume. Manson played an important part in the formation of the Studiorum Novi Testamenti Societas, and served as its President, in addition to being the Chairman of the Editorial Board of its periodical, *New Testament Studies*.

Many honours came to him, but not more than he deserved. Honorary doctorates were conferred on him by universities in Great Britain and abroad. The two universities of which he was a student, Glasgow and Cambridge, both honoured him in this way, and in addition Durham, Dublin, Strasbourg and Pine Hill (Halifax, Nova Scotia) conferred doctorates on him. He became a Fellow of the British Academy and served for some years as the Chairman of the Biblical and Theological section. He was also awarded the Burkitt Medal for Biblical Studies. The American Society of Biblical Literature and Exegesis elected him to Honorary Membership, and the Akademie der Wissenschaften of Göttingen honoured him with election to a Corresponding Fellowship.

Of the quality and range of his scholarship only very inadequate mention can be made here. In Cambridge he sat the Oriental Languages Tripos and was placed in the First Class. He therefore came to his acknowledged front rank in New Testament studies via the study of the Old Testament. He could have filled an Old Testament chair with as much distinction as a New Testament chair. In Manchester he was Professor of Biblical Criticism and Exegesis, though in fact his teaching and research were almost entirely confined to the New Testament and the Early Church. His knowledge of the Old Testament always enriched his teaching of the New, and the acquaintance with Rabbinical Hebrew which he gained in his student days was never allowed to be forgotten. His expert knowledge of Syriac was, of course, constantly drawn on, and in addition he acquired an intimate knowledge of Coptic. He was thus well equipped to continue the great work of editing the Cambridge Larger Septuagint, which he had undertaken. It was his hope that he could devote much time to this after his re-tirement—which, alas! he did not live to see. By his early death future generations of students of the Septuagint will be impoverished.

His contributions to scholarship may be judged in part by the list of his publications which will be found in the volume which was planned as a *Festschrift*, but which became a Memorial Volume.[1]   But the quality of his work was more impressive than its quantity. He was ready to learn from all his colleagues, but to surrender his judgement to none. There was a rare balance in him. He brought his own original emphases in New Testament study, and never touched any subject without illuminating it and bringing something new to it. Yet he propounded no revolution-ary view and was not ready to be swept off his feet by those who did. While he was essentially a liberal in New Testament scholarship, he was never a radical, and he believed that liberal scholarship took a wrong turn early in this century and that it was necessary to go back to where it went astray and pursue a different line.

His most important work is still his first, *The Teaching of Jesus*, in which he put forward the view that on the lips of Jesus the term " Son of Man " was originally a collective term, as it is in the book of Daniel. By this he stood substantially to the end, though there was some modification in detail and the recognition that what Wheeler Robinson called the concept of " corporate personality ", whereby thought could pass to and fro between the community and the individual who represented it, or embodied it in himself, entered into the use of the term. To many *The Sayings of Jesus* is the most useful of his works, while the smaller volumes, *The Church's Ministry* and *The Servant-Messiah*, are full of good things. Scholars will value the essays collected in

[1] *New Testament Essays*, published in 1959 by Manchester University Press.

the present volume, in which many original contributions to New Testament study will be found. Yet they are found in lectures which were prepared for an audience of very varied character. For Manson was always able to present the fruits of his study in such a form that they had meaning not alone for his peers in scholarship—of whom there were but few—but also for a wider circle. He was no believer in the profundity of obscurity.

A few years before his death he moved from Manchester to Milnthorpe in Westmorland. His friends were sure that he had long overtaxed his strength, and felt that he was wise now to husband it and to reduce his many commitments, and he himself was well aware of this. Manson was a keen angler, and not far from his new home were waters he had often fished, where he might find pleasure in less arduous hours than those he had so long known. His wife, a woman of spirit and energy that matched his own, who had taken an active part in public and denominational life and who was a Justice of the Peace, sparing herself no more than Manson had spared himself, needed also to reduce her commitments and to conserve her strength. How much Manson owed to her he alone knew. How much those he served so well owed to her they can never know. Her pride in all that he was and all that he did was very deep, and no selfish thought ever stood between her and his work. In her own service she found some compensation for what she gave up of him, and both had served with over-generosity. So the move was welcomed by friends and colleagues, even though they regretted that it meant that they would see less of their distinguished colleague, and that many of the things he had long done in the university would have to be left to others. But alas! the move came too late to bring relief, and there were periods when he was not able to continue his teaching. Bravely he continued his work so far as might be to the very end, with his thought ever of his students and the university he loved so well and served as few have served it.

Many will remember him as a man of great learning and of strength and grace of character, a Christian gentleman in every sense of the term, a man of the highest integrity and loyalty, and a friend from whose spirit they have drunk and for whom they thank God.   For myself, it was the prospect of working in close association with Manson that brought me to Manchester, and I count it one of the highest privileges of my life to have done so. His memory is for a blessing : and most blest are they who knew him best.

PART ONE

MATERIALS FOR A LIFE
OF JESUS

1.

THE QUEST OF THE HISTORICAL JESUS
—CONTINUED

A Commemoration Day Address delivered at Westminster
College, Cambridge, in 1949

THIRTY years ago this term I performed one of the major
wise acts of my life by entering this College as a student.
Let me begin by saying a word about the men who taught here in
those days. Even after thirty years I still feel that it would be
something of an impertinence for me to praise them ; but like
Marcus Aurelius I may begin my meditations by casting up my
debts :

To John Skinner and Charles Anderson Scott the proof that
exact and thorough scholarship can be linked with a deeply-
rooted faith in such a way that scholarship is delivered from mere
antiquarianism, and faith from obscurantism.

To John Oman the sure conviction that in theology we are
not hanging on to the remnants of an inherited and almost
bankrupt estate, but exploring a whole continent stocked with
inexhaustible treasures ; and that the only thing to be feared
is cowardice, the only thing to be despised insincerity.

To Carnegie Simpson the assurance that Church History is
by far the most important kind of history, and that it has to be
made as well as learned : indeed that all our learning of it is
little worth unless we come out better fitted to make it.

And to Islay Burns the example of how much loyal and devoted
service can be given to God and man without making a great stir.

It was under these men that the day-to-day tasks of a theological student were done. It was by their example and encouragement that more ambitious projects began to be framed ; and it
is of one of those projects, after thirty years still unfulfilled,
but still not abandoned, that I should like to speak today.
It was a Westminster man, William Montgomery, who by a

3

stroke of genius translated Schweitzer's matter-of-fact title
" Von Reimarus zu Wrede " into " The Quest of the Historical
Jesus ". That is the title I take today with the addition of one
word : the subject is " The Quest of the Historical Jesus—
continued ". We may surmise that Schweitzer himself would
hardly approve the addition. One of the main theses of his
book was that there could be no sequel to it. Rightly understood
the history of the attempts to write the life of Jesus was the record
of a process leading by inexorable logic to the grand disjunction :
" Either Wrede or Schweitzer ; either thoroughgoing scepticism or thoroughgoing eschatology " ; in other words, either you
accept Schweitzer's solution of the problem or you give up the
problem as insoluble. *Tertium non datur.* But if a disjunctive
proposition is to stand, it must exhaust all the possibilities ; and
time has shown that Schweitzer's disjunction does not. It is,
therefore, legitimate to say " The Quest of the Historical Jesus—
continued ".

There is, however, this much in Schweitzer's statement of
the case, that progress in this study since the Quest was written
has been, in the main, a continuation along the lines of which
Wrede and Schweitzer were the termini a generation ago. If
we consider the two most outstanding developments of our own
day, Form-criticism and Realized Eschatology, I think we may say
that the first suggestions of Form-criticism are already present
in the work of Wrede [1] and others : and that Realized Eschatology
is the logical sequel to Johannes Weiss and Schweitzer.

After thirty years it is possible at least to attempt an appraisal of
Form-criticism ; and it is becoming increasingly evident that it
will have to be a rather drastic writing down. Strictly, the term
" form-criticism " should be reserved for the study of the various
units of narrative and teaching, which go to make up the Gospels,
in respect of their form alone. It is concerned with the structure
of these units ; and it is at least interesting to know that there are a
number of anecdotes in Mark, Matthew, and Luke, in which a
brief statement of time and place leads up to a short conversation between Jesus and someone else, which is terminated by a

[1] Messiasgeheimnis.

dogmatic pronouncement from our Lord.   It is interesting but
not epoch-making.   So far as structure goes, similar stories
can be found in Boswell's *Life of Dr. Johnson* and many another
place.   We can list these stories in the Gospels.   We can label
them—once the Form-critics have agreed on the terminology of
their science.   But a paragraph of Mark is not a penny the better
or the worse as historical evidence for being labelled, " Apo-
thegm " or " Pronouncement Story " or " Paradigm ".   In fact
if Form-criticism had stuck to its proper business, it would not
have made any real stir.   We should have taken it as we take the
forms of Hebrew poetry or the forms of musical composition.

But Form-criticism got mixed up with two other things.   One
was K. L. Schmidt's full-scale attack on the Marcan framework ;
the other was the doctrine of the *Sitz im Leben*.   Schmidt's
thesis really asks us to believe that Mark was produced by
putting together a random assortment of disconnected anecdotes.
Those dealing with the Passion clearly had to come at the end
of the collection ; but the rest were just fitted together by the
evangelist to the best of his ability.   Such a theory makes too
large demands on our credulity.   It is clear that by the time
Mark was written (say, 58-65), there were people who wanted
more than disconnected anecdotes : they wanted the story of the
Ministry as a whole ; and *Mark* is the supply to meet that demand.   But if the outline had then to be created *ad hoc*, it can
only be that for the thirty years between the end of the Ministry
and the production of *Mark*, Christians in general were not
interested in the story of the Ministry and allowed it to be forgotten.   One would like to know why the first generation were not
interested while the second generation demanded a continuous
narrative.   More than that, we need some explanation why it was
possible for the details of the story to be remembered and the
general outline forgotten.   It is not the normal way of remember-
ing important periods in our experience.   I should maintain,
therefore, that Schmidt's hypothesis has a very high degree of
a priori improbability.   More than that, I am increasingly
convinced by prolonged acquaintance with *Mark* that it is *not*
a patchwork-quilt, but that in the main it presents an orderly and

logical development. In short, the title of the Marcan framework to be regarded as respectable historical material is as good
as that of any detailed story in the Gospel.

Sitz im Leben introduces a new set of considerations, which
again have little or nothing to do with Form-criticism in the
strict sense of the word. It is undoubtedly a good thing that the
Gospels should be studied in the context—so far as we can know
it—of the interests, problems, and practical needs of the people
who first used them. No doubt the particular stories and sayings
were useful to missionary preachers of the first century : no
doubt they gave guidance to the early communities on questions
of faith and conduct. But we are travelling much too far and
far too fast, if we infer from that that they were created by the
community to serve these ends or to meet these needs. In
most cases it is equally possible, and a good deal more likely,
that the tasks, problems, and needs of the first century church
affected the selection of what went into the Gospels out of a much
larger mass of material. But even that may not be the whole
truth of the matter. It is at least conceivable that one of the
chief motives for preserving the stories at all, and for selecting
those that were embodied in the Gospels, was just plain admiration and love for their hero. It is conceivable that he was at
least as interesting, *for his own sake*, to people in the first century
as he is to historians in the twentieth.

That, however, is a consideration that hardly weighs with
the most ardent explorers of the *Sitz im Leben* ; and the result
is that they tend to explain more and more in terms of the *Sitz
im Leben der alten Kirche* and less and less in terms of the *Sitz
im Leben Jesu* or the *Sitz im Leben des jüdischen Volkes*. So
Professor Bultmann's *History of the Synoptic Tradition* is an
account, not of how the life of Jesus produced the tradition,
but of how the tradition produced the life of Jesus. And when
the work of the tradition has been undone, there is very little
of Jesus left. I may remark in passing that the disseminated
incredulity of Bultmann's *Geschichte der synoptischen Tradition*
has its nemesis thirty years later in his *Theologie des Neuen
Testament*, in which a perfunctory thirty pages or so is devoted to
the theology of Jesus himself, while a hundred or more are

occupied with an imaginary account of the theology of the anonymous and otherwise unknown " Hellenistic Communities ".

There is a simple test that can be applied to theories that suggest that the tradition about Jesus is in any considerable degree the creation of the Christian community. We possess a fair selection of the written works of one of the most influential figures in the Church during the period in which the Gospel tradition took shape. St. Paul's letters were all written before the earliest Gospel. The Roman community—the traditional home of St. Mark's Gospel—possessed the Epistle to the Romans before it possessed the Roman Gospel of Mark. The Pauline letters abound in utterances which could easily be transferred to Jesus and presented to the world as oracles of the Lord. How many are? None. It seems a little odd that, if the story of Jesus was the creation of the Christian community, no use should have been made of the admirable materials offered by one of the most able, active, and influential members of the community.

To speak candidly, I find myself, after a good deal of labour in this field, being gradually driven to the conclusion that much that passes for historical study of the life of Jesus consists not in asking of any story in the tradition : " Is it credible in itself ? " but : " What motive could the Church have had for telling this tale ? "—which can easily become the question : " What motives led the Church to invent it ? " The danger is that what is entitled " Life of Christ " or the like should turn out to be in fact a psychological novel about a large number of anonymous members of the primitive Church. And, what is worse, that this brand of fiction should enjoy a greater credit than the Synoptic Gospels themselves. Anyone who doubts this has only to consult the voluminous life of Jesus written by the late Professor Guignebert. Present M. Guignebert with a couple of verses of Mark or Q and his mind at once became a prey to doubts and misgivings of all kinds : present him with a couple of pages of M. Loisy's imaginative reconstructions of what " must have happened " in the early Church—what *must have happened* commonly designates that for which there is no evidence except the writer's inclination to believe it—and he will swallow the lot at one gulp.

I venture to think that this kind of thing has gone on too long. It may be granted that the stories in the Gospels have forms. It may also be granted that the early Church found the stories useful for all kinds of purposes. It may even be granted that the Church *might* have invented them. But it is a long way from what the Church might have done to what the Church in fact did; and there is a good deal to be said for abandoning the study of the branch of fiction known as Überlieferungsgeschichte in favour of an unbiased examination of the evidence supplied by the Gospels. This is not to suggest a return to fundamentalism: it is merely to ask that the Gospels should be taken for what they profess to be: not theological treatises or manuals of behaviour, but information about an extremely interesting and important person known to his Jewish contemporaries as Jesus bar Joseph of Nazareth, to the Roman authorities as Jesus, domiciled in Nazareth, Pretender to the Jewish throne, and to his followers as Jesus the Messiah and Lord. The career of such a person must have an interest of its own and for its own sake; and the openings of all three Synoptic Gospels seem to me to suggest that this interest was the most effective motive behind both the demand for and the supply of Gospel material. I submit that what is long overdue is a return to the study of the Gospels *as historical documents* concerning Jesus of Nazareth, rather than as psychological case-material concerning the early Christians.

I turn now to the progress of thoroughgoing Eschatology. Schweitzer's interpretation is vulnerable at many points. It can be urged against it that it depends on a thoroughly uncritical use of the Gospels, particularly the First. It can be urged that, in spite of the moving eloquence with which the story of Jesus according to Schweitzer is told, there is no escape from the conclusion that its hero is a deluded fanatic. But those are not the points that seem most impressive. The real answer to thoroughgoing eschatology was given by one of our greatest New Testament scholars, who was himself deeply influenced by Schweitzer—F. C. Burkitt. In the Epilogue to his book, *The Earliest Sources for the Life of Jesus* (pp. 130 f.), he says: " There is a sense, on the eschatological view, in which it is true to say that Jesus had radically changed the messianic ideal. He had changed it, not by ' spiritualizing ' it, but by adding to it. The ideal of King Messiah, coming in glory on the clouds of heaven to judge the world and vindicate the elect of God, he left untouched, but he prefixed to it a Prologue. He prefixed to it not a doctrine about Messiah, but the actual course of his own career. We call it his *Ministry.*—Why? Because his view of the office of the Man who was predestined to be Messiah was that he should ' minister ' to the needs of God's people (Mark x. 45). According to Mark, Jesus went up to Jerusalem to die, to be killed, believing that thereby the Kingdom of God would come. And his great resolve has to be judged in the light of its amazing success."

Along with that, let me put a personal reminiscence. Burkitt came to Wesminster in my student days and read a paper to the College Theological Society on this subject. In the course of the debate that followed the point was made that if the life of Christ is construed on the lines of thoroughgoing eschatology it can only be described as a gigantic mistake. Burkitt's reply was in effect : " Mistake or no mistake it has sent Schweitzer himself to Africa as a medical missionary."

Put those two things together, and it emerges that the thing that really matters in the story of Jesus is not the eschatological theory but the ministerial practice. The Prologue in fact makes nonsense of the expected sequel ; so much so that it is no calamity but a positive relief that there is no Parousia of the conventional Jewish pattern. Similarly the thing that really matters for Schweitzer, the thing of eternal import, is the thing that on his own theory he ought to call *interim Ethic.* The work in Africa that commands our unstinted admiration and respect is a con- tinuation of what Burkitt calls the Prologue. In a word, the most significant thing about the Jesus of the eschatological theory, the permanently effective thing right down to the life of Schweitzer himself, ·is the non-eschatological, even the anti-eschatological element. The interim Ethic is the permanent moral force : the Prologue has become the whole drama.

That, I surmise, is the foundation fact upon which the theory of Realized Eschatology must be based. For the essence of this position is that we say : " the ministry of Jesus is not a prelude to the Kingdom of God : it *is* the Kingdom of God." And if it is, we have to begin revising our ideas of the Kingdom in the light of the Ministry. And that means that once more we are driven back upon the task of treating the Gospels as historical documents, using all the resources of exact scholarship and strict historical method for the task. We need not ask that the documents should be exempt from any of the tests that are applied to other ancient historical texts ; but we must ask that they should be taken seriously as evidence for the events they purport to describe ; and in the first instance as evidence for *those events* rather than for the states of mind of first-century Christians.

I suspect that this will mean retracing our steps in some directions and reopening some questions that had been thought to be completely closed. Thirty years ago, for example, Schweitzer was able to write off the Fourth Gospel completely so far as history was concerned. D. F. Strauss had disposed of it once and for all. Today we are not so sure. There is a growing body of evidence that the Fourth Gospel enshrines a tradition of the Ministry which is independent of the Synoptic tradition, of Palestinian origin, and on some points quite possibly superior to the Synoptic. The question of the historical value of the Fourth Gospel is wide open again.

We may well rejoice that it is necessary to continue the quest of the historical Jesus. True, the rejoicing will not be universal. There are those who watched the thoroughgoing historical scepticism of Wrede become more thoroughgoing still in Bultmann and Guignebert and said in their hearts something like : " Well, that's that. I take refuge in the Councils of the undivided Church." Unfortunately for that policy the councils of the undivided Church had already assumed the general reliability of the Gospels as historical documents. They cannot be used to solve the historical problem, only to bypass it. Others seek theological safety in a revived or modified Calvinism. Bultmann himself seeks to escape from the consequences of his ruthless criticism by insisting that quite apart from any question of historicity the figure of Christ in the New Testaments presents men in every age with the challenge to make their decision

(Entscheidung), i.e. their submission to God. That is all very fine and it speaks of things that truly belong to the Christian religion ; but Entscheidung is not the differentia of Christianity. It is something which Christianity shares with Islam. The really characteristic things about Christianity are the things that have already been liquidated by Bultmann's critical work. So he finds himself in the awkward position of having to maintain at one and the same time that the God of the true religion is a God who reveals himself in history, and that the truth of the Christian religion can never be based upon the results of historical enquiry.

But if God does reveal himself in history, it is there if anywhere that we must find him. If God spoke through the prophets it is vitally important that we should ascertain as exactly as possible what was said to them and what it meant. If God spoke through the life and death of Jesus it is vitally important to know as fully and as accurately as possible what sort of life and death became the medium of God's revelation. There is no escape from the historical enquiry. And there is no occasion to be pessimistic about it.

After many years of work at the problems, I confess that I am increasingly convinced that in the Gospels we have the materials—reliable materials—for an outline account of the ministry as a whole. I believe it is possible to produce such an outline and that, when produced, it will dovetail into the rest of the picture, that it will fit with what we otherwise know about contemporary Jewish faith and life in Palestine. It will also make sense in the context of Roman imperial policy in the Near East. And it will give an adequate explanation of the existence of the Church. We shall not be able to fit in all the details. The life of Jesus of Nazareth lasted between thirty and forty years ; and his public career was hardly less than eighteen months and may well have been a good deal more : and all the records we possess can be read in a few hours. The gaps are enormous. But we have *some* details ; and I think it is true to say that these short stories, parables, sayings, poems, and so on, which go to make up the Gospels themselves, epitomize the whole story. Each of them is, as it were, a little window through which we can

c

view the ministry as a whole ; a vantage-point from which we can take a Pisgah-view of the authentic Kingdom of God.

There is very much work still to be done here. I believe that as it progresses we shall find that the ministry of Jesus is a piece of real history in the sense that it is fully relevant to the historical situation of its own time, to the hopes and fears, the passionate convictions and the gnawing needs of our Lord's own contemporaries. And just because it was so relevant to their life, we shall find it relevant to our own today. I believe that we shall hear less and less—and I shall not be sorry—about the Urmensch and the rest of the Religionsgeschichtliche menagerie. I believe that we shall have to do some drastic revision of the notions we have inherited from R. H. Charles—and when we do it we shall have to use materials which we owe almost entirely to Charles's learning and scholarship. There is a vast deal to be done and it is infinitely well worth doing. The quest of the historical Jesus is still a great and most hopeful enterprise.

Even the most tedious discourse must end sometime ; and as this one began with thanks for the past, let it end with hopes for the future. I speak for all here in expressing the hope and prayer that all good may attend the College in the days to come ; and very high among the blessings I wish this College is that she may continue to foster and encourage this great enterprise and continue the quest of the historical Jesus.

2

THE LIFE OF JESUS:
A STUDY OF THE AVAILABLE MATERIALS.
(1943)

SOME time ago I published [1] a short article on the question, Is it possible to write a Life of Christ ? That article indicates the main lines along which I propose to tackle the problem before us ; and I begin by giving a brief summary of its main points.

First, it must be admitted that it is not possible to write a Life of Jesus, if by that we mean something like Boswell's *Life of Johnson* or Morley's *Life of Gladstone*. The reason is simple : the materials are not available. Not a single chronological point can be fixed with certainty. The life of Jesus lasted probably between thirty and forty years : concerning at least twenty-eight of them we know precisely nothing at all. What information we have is mostly concerned with the public career of Jesus, that is, with the last period of his life, a period whose length is uncertain, but probably not less than one year nor more than about three. But there is not even enough material for a full account of the Ministry. It lasted at least a year—I should say a good deal longer—and all we know about it, including duplicate narratives, can be read in a few hours.

Secondly, there is the question of the reliability of the evidence at our disposal. This touches both the individual narratives and sayings and the order in which they are presented. Did the events narrated in the Gospels really happen just as they are described, and did the actual sequence of events correspond to the sequence of narratives ? What allowances must we make for the editorial activities of Evangelists and the compilers of the sources which they used ? How has the material

---

[1] *Expository Times*, liii (May, 1942), 248-251.

been affected—perhaps even created—by the practical needs of the Early Church ? These and other questions cannot be evaded, and our materials are subject to all the varieties of criticism—textual, synoptic, and, of course, form-criticism. What is left when they have done their work depends, in any particular instance, on the scholar who is handling these tools ; and we get all kinds of results from the rigidly conservative to the rigidly radical. Yet in spite of the extravagances and fads of individuals, there is a steady, if slow, progress in the scientific sifting and weighing of the evidence, and it can fairly be claimed that we are in a better position to-day to assess the evidence and make the best use of it than any previous generation of students of the New Testament ; and I, for one, do not believe that further progress is barred.

That brings us to the third point, the problem of how to use what materials we have to the best advantage. My own opinion is that we must work on the lines laid down by Eduard Meyer, and set the stories about Jesus in the larger context of the history of Religion and Civilization from about 300 B.C. to about A.D. 300, from Alexander the Great to Constantine the Great, from the days when the tide of Hellenistic civilization began to flood over the East till the days when the counter-currents of missionary Christian religion swept irresistibly westwards over the Roman Empire. Within those six centuries lies a shorter period, from about 168 B.C. to A.D. 135, the period of the Jewish struggle, from the revolt of the Maccabees to the revolt of Bar Cocheba, from the Ḥasidim to R. Akiba. Here the tide of Hellenism was checked, and here for the first time the world was presented with the phenomenon of the martyr. Within this narrower period lies the actual turn of the tide, the first decisive movement appearing in the missionary activities of St. Paul. Right at the critical point lies the ministry of Jesus, at the very centre where so many conflicting ideals and ambitions clash. It seems to me that the task of the historian is to try to place our pieces of evidence in their proper setting in this great context in the hope that so placed they will shape themselves into a clear and convincing portrait of Jesus and at the same time illuminate the whole period.

So much by way of introduction : now we turn to the closer examination of the materials. The first and obvious division is that between information supplied in the New Testament (primarily, of course, the Gospels, but also the other books, in particular, Acts and the Pauline Epistles), and that found in Christian, Jewish, and pagan writings outside the New Testament. It will be convenient to deal with the extra-canonical material first.

From the Christian side we have a considerable and increasing mass of Apocryphal Gospels and Agrapha.[1] The former present some very interesting features. First of all, their scope : this can be most vividly seen if we consider the contents of Walter Bauer's great book on the subject.[2] Bauer set out to see what sort of a life of Jesus could be written, using the Apocryphal Gospels as the material. His narrative, so composed, occupies 279 pages. Of these the first hundred are taken up by the parentage, birth, and childhood, and the last hundred and twenty with the Passion narrative ; nine pages are occupied by the ministry of John the Baptist ; and the whole public ministry from the Baptism to the Entry into Jerusalem and the Cleansing of the Temple occupies pp. 110-158 —forty-nine pages. The disproportion is most striking : it reflects the peculiar interests of the Apocryphal Gospels, concentrated on the birth and death of Christ or, in theological terms, the Incarnation and the Atonement. The concentration of interest on these two points is the continuation of a process which is already at work in the Canonical Gospels ; for when, for example, the narrative material peculiar to Matthew is examined, it is found that the greater part of it is concerned with the birth and infancy of Jesus and with the Passion.

This limitation of interest is accompanied by peculiarities of taste. Many of the incidents related in the Apocryphal Gospels are incompatible with what is given in the Canonical Gospels. Stories are told, which are merely grotesque when

[1] Most of the more important of these are given in English in M. R. James, *The Apocryphal New Testament*, pp. 1-193. A very full collection of Agrapha is that of Resch, *Texte und Untersuchungen*, N.F. xv, 2 ed. 1906.

[2] *Das Leben Jesu im Zeitalter der neutestamentlichen Apokryphen*, 1909.

they are not actually revolting. I would add that the peculiar quality of these Apocryphal tales is not uniform : sometimes it appears to be a throwback to the primitive fascination by and dread of the supernatural ; sometimes the story seems to have a definite theological axe to grind. There is all the difference in the world between the horrid stories told about the supernatural little bully of the *Gospel of Thomas* and the carefully constructed narrative of the *Gospel of Peter*, narrative composed with one purpose—to support the Docetic interpretation of the Incarnation and the Passion. But they have one thing in common : they are fiction.

The Agrapha are on a different footing. The most important of them are sayings attributed to Jesus, which have been preserved outside the accepted text of the Canonical Gospels. They vary in the quality of their attestation and in inherent credibility. Probably the best known and best attested is the saying attributed to the Lord in Acts xx. 35 : ' It is more blessed to give than to receive '. Almost equally well known is the one spoken to the man working on the Sabbath, preserved in Codex Bezæ at Lk. vi. 4 : ' Man, if indeed thou knowest what thou doest, thou art blessed ; but if thou knowest not, thou art cursed, and a transgressor of the law '. There are a good many more not so well known : for example, this one reported by Origen in a Homily on Jeremiah : ' The Saviour himself says : " He that is near me is near the fire. He that is far from me is far from the kingdom ".' [1] It is a task of no small difficulty to decide about some of these sayings. *A priori* there is no reason at all why genuine sayings of Jesus should not have survived outside the four accepted Gospels ; and when some of those that offer themselves are examined there seems to be nothing against them. Others again do not commend themselves at all ; and there is a third group which defy decision.

We turn to the Jewish accounts. These include statements in the Talmud and later Jewish literature, and three passages in Josephus, of which one concerns John the Baptist, one Jesus,

---

[1] Codex Bezæ = Resch No. 23 ; Origen, *Hom. in Jer.* = Resch No. 150.

and the third James the Lord's brother.[1]   The Talmudic and later Jewish pieces resemble the Christian Apocryphal Gospels in being tendentious : they differ only in the nature of their tendencies.   That of the Jewish writings is definitely hostile. Whereas many of the Christian apocryphs fabricate miracles as evidence of the supernatural character of their hero, the Jewish writings explain all the miracles claimed by the Christians as works of magic and sorcery which Jesus had learned in Egypt. While the Apocryphal Gospels continually add embroideries to the story of the Virgin Birth, the Jewish writings turn the whole thing into a scandalous tale of an intrigue with a Roman soldier.   Clearly we cannot hope for much in the way of reliable data from sources of this character.

One point is worth noting : it is that the farther we go back in the Jewish tradition the more scanty the references to Jesus become.   The later Jewish romances are of some size ; the Talmudic references are considerably less in extent ; and, when we come to the Mishnah, there are no direct references at all.[2]   It may well be that this paucity of references is just what we ought to expect.   Both the Church and the Synagogue were well aware of the value of silence and neglect as weapons against persons, movements, and doctrines that were not approved.   There is a most instructive passage in the *Ecclesiastical History* of Eusebius quoting Dionysius of Alexandria on the subject of heretical literature.[3]   The great Bishop of Alexandria says :

' But as for me, I read both the compositions and the traditions of the heretics, polluting my soul for a little with their abominable thoughts, yet all the while deriving this advantage from them, that I could refute them

[1] The Talmudic texts are edited by Dalman as an appendix to Laible's *Jesus Christus im Talmud* ; the later Jewish writings are published and fully discussed by S. Krauss, *Das Leben Jesu nach jüdischen Quellen.*   There is a large literature grown up around the Josephus passages : the best statement and discussion, in my opinion, is that of H. St. J. Thackeray in his book *Josephus the Man and the Historian*, pp. 125-153.   Cf. F. C. Burkitt in *Theologisch Tijdschrift*, xlvii. 135-144.

[2] There are a few possible veiled allusions but nothing that can be regarded as an absolutely certain reference to Jesus.   The passages usually quoted in this connexion are *Yebamoth*, iv. 13 ; *Aboth*, v. 19 ; *Sanhedrin*, x. 1 f.

[3] Eus. *H.E.*, VII, vii. 1-3. (Lawlor and Oulton's translation.)   Cf. De Labriolle, *Les Sources de l'Histoire du Montanisme*, Introduction, pp. ix-xv.

for myself and loathed them far more. And indeed a certain brother, one of the presbyters, attempted to dissuade and frighten me from becoming involved in the mire of their wickedness, for he said that I should injure my own soul ; and said truly, as I perceived. But a vision sent by God came and strengthened me, and a word of command was given me, saying expressly : " Read all things that may come to thy hand. For thou art able to sift and prove each matter ; which thing was originally the cause of thy faith." I accepted the vision, as agreeing with the apostolic saying addressed to the stronger : " Be approved money-changers ".'

It may well be the case that the Jewish authorities in the earlier period thought that oblivion would be a better ally against the new religion than any polemical propaganda they could devise.

Here we may pause for a moment by the pagan materials. The remarkable feature here is the minuteness of the quantity. If we except the brief notice in the *Annals* of Tacitus [1] (published in the second decade of the second century), there is little or nothing of consequence. One inference may be drawn from this silence. If Jesus had, as some have imagined, actually staged a revolt against the Roman Empire, we should doubtless have heard more about him from the Roman historians. Their silence may be taken as good evidence that no such rising took place : that the Cross was a preventive rather than a punitive measure.

The famous and much-disputed *Testimonium Flavianum* runs as follows in Thackeray's translation : [2]

' Now about this time arises (or "is born "—γίνεται) Jesus, a wise man, if indeed he should be called a man. For he was a doer of marvellous deeds, a teacher of men who receive the truth with pleasure ; and he won over to himself many Jews and many also of the Greek (nation). He was the Christ. And when, on the indictment of the principal men among us, Pilate had sentenced him to the cross, those who had loved (or perhaps rather " been content with ") him at the first did not cease ; for he appeared to them on the third day alive again, the divine prophets having (fore)told these and ten thousand other wonderful things concerning him. And even now the tribe (or " race "—ϕῦλον) of Christians, named after him, is not extinct.'

It is difficult to imagine what sort of Christian could have deemed it worth his while to interpolate this cool, objective,

[1] *Ann.*, xv. 44. Auctor nominis eius Christus Tiberio imperitante per procuratorem Pontium Pilatum supplicio adfectus erat.

[2] *Josephus the Man and the Historian*, 136 f.

patronising, and faintly contemptuous paragraph into the text of Josephus. On the other hand, it is quite likely that the passage as it now stands is not what Josephus wrote : that, in fact, the original was even cooler and more contemptuous than the existing text, and that the features most objectionable to early Christian piety have been toned down or removed. The question has been carefully discussed by Thackeray, and I will mention two points only. First there is the crucial sentence : ὁ Χριστὸς οὗτος ἦν. It seems to me that the statements of Origen [1] that Josephus ' did not admit our Jesus to be the Christ ' or ' disbelieved in Jesus as Christ ' together with Jeromes' variant reading *credebatur* [2] point in the one direction, namely that Josephus wrote ἐνομίζετο and that some pious Christian made what appeared to him the obvious and necessary correction. If so, Josephus testified that Jesus was considered (by his followers) to be the Messiah. The second is a conjectural emendation, but a very attractive one, attributed to Heinichen and regarded with considerable favour by Thackeray. It involves reading ΤΑΑΗΘΗ in place of ΤΑΛΗΘΗ, with the result that Jesus becomes ' a teacher of men who receive the abnormal with pleasure '. I should regard these two restorations as probable, and the former as practically certain.

Josephus then becomes a witness to the fact that Jesus existed, that he was regarded as a wonder-worker, that he was a teacher with unusual views, that he had a following who regarded him as Messiah, that he was crucified by Pilate on information laid by the Jewish authorities, that his followers had experiences which convinced them that he was still alive and active, and that (regrettably perhaps) the Church was still in existence when Josephus wrote.

This Jewish account of the matter can be paralleled in the small collection of evidence which Klausner extracted from the mass of Rabbinic material. The greater part of this material

[1] *Comm. in Matt.*, x. 17 (ed. Klostermann) τὸν Ἰησοῦν ἡμῶν οὐ καταδεξάμενος εἶναι Χριστόν.

c. *Cels.*, i. 47 (ed. P. Koetschau), ὁ δ' αὐτός, καίτοι γε ἀπιστῶν τῷ Ἰησοῦ ὡς Χριστῷ, ζητῶν τὴν αἰτίαν τῆς τῶν Ἱεροσολύμων πτώσεως κτλ.

[2] *De uir. ill.*, xiii. (Migne, *P.L.* xxiii., col. 663).

is quite worthless for the purposes of history ; but Klausner did succeed in distilling out enough to make a short narrative paragraph.   It runs as follows : [1]

> ' There are reliable statements to the effect that his name was Yeshua' (Yeshu) of Nazareth ; that he " practised sorcery " (i.e. performed miracles, as was usual in those days) and beguiled and led Israel astray ; that he mocked at the words of the wise ; that he expounded Scripture in the same manner as the Pharisees ; that he had five disciples ; that he said that he was not come to take aught away from the Law or to add to it ; that he was hanged (crucified) as a false teacher and beguiler on the eve of the Passover which happened on a Sabbath ; and that his disciples healed the sick in his name.'

If we set these two Jewish accounts side by side, we find that they agree on certain essential points. Both present Jesus as a wonder-working teacher, some of whose doctrine did not square with scribal orthodoxy : [2] both agree that he was crucified. On the second of these two points Tacitus gives explicit confirmation ; and it can be argued that his description of Christianity as a ' mischievous superstition ' [3] implies that Jesus had been a religious teacher. The common element in all three representatives of the non-Christian tradition about Christ may thus be represented by the formula ($\psi\epsilon\nu\delta o$)$\delta\iota\delta\acute{a}\sigma\kappa a\lambda os$ $\dot{\epsilon}\sigma\tau a\nu\rho\omega\mu\acute{\epsilon}\nu os$ [4]—a crucified (false) teacher.

If now we turn from these external testimonies to the earliest ascertainable form of the canonical tradition about the ministry of Jesus, we find that this same formula will cover the basic elements discovered by Synoptic source-analysis. For what source-criticism gives us is two types of document : the narrative and the didactic. The classical representatives of the two types are Mark and Q. Now it has often been observed that in Mark a very large proportion of the available space is given to the Passion narrative,[5] that the Passion narrative is the climax of the story and the nerve of the argument, and

---

[1] J. Klausner, *Jesus of Nazareth*, p. 46.

[2] The agreement about unorthodoxy in the teaching depends on accepting Heinichen's emendation of Josephus mentioned above.

[3] *Ann.*, xv. 44: repressaque in praesens exitiabilis superstitio rursum erumpebat, non modo per Iudaeam, originem eius mali, sed per urbem etiam, quo cuncta undique atrocia aut pudenda confluunt celebranturque.

[4] St. Paul, I Cor. i. 23 ; ii. 2 ; Gal. iii. 1. $X\rho\iota\sigma\tau\grave{o}s$ $\dot{\epsilon}\sigma\tau a\nu\rho\omega\mu\acute{\epsilon}\nu os$.

[5] I think that the amount is sometimes exaggerated.

that it is the part of the Gospel which offers the most stubborn
resistance to disintegration by form-critical analysis. It is
natural to make the inference that in all probability the first
section of the Gospel narrative to take definite and permanent
shape was the story of the Passion. Q is the earliest known
manual giving a systematic account of the teaching of Jesus.[1]

These two primitive types of document answer to the conditions in the primitive Church. The Passion story which is
the core of Mark's Gospel is likewise the core of the missionary
preaching of the earliest days : ' We preach a crucified Messiah ' ;
' I determined to know nothing among you but Jesus the
Messiah and a crucified Messiah at that ' ; ' Galatians . . .
before whose eyes Jesus the Messiah was placarded crucified '.[2]
The preaching of the Cross was the means by which converts
were to be made. The manual containing the record of the
teaching of Jesus was necessary for the instruction of the converted in the manners and customs of the new order into which
they were incorporated.

Something similar may be observed in other books of the
New Testament. The ground-plan of the Epistle to the
Romans gives an elaborate exposition of the Cross (with an
appendix on the Jewish problem) followed by instruction in
the duties of the Christian : the death of Christ for men and
the life of men in Christ. The same thing may be seen elsewhere
in the Pauline corpus, e.g. in Ephesians and Colossians, and
also—though somewhat obscured by the exigencies of polemics
—in Galatians and Philippians.

The formula ' Crucified Teacher ' thus covers the earliest
statements about Jesus whether pagan, Jewish, or Christian.
The differentia of the Christian statements is the assertion that
the Crucified Teacher is the Messiah. It is this differentia
that is, as St. Paul puts it in the fifties of the first century, ' to
the Jews a stumbling-block, to the Gentiles foolishness '.[3]

[1] I have discussed the tradition of the teaching of Jesus and attempted a
reconstruction and exposition of Q in *The Mission and Message of Jesus*, pp.
301-440.

[2] I Cor. i. 23 ; ii. 2 ; Gal. iii. 1.

[3] I Cor. i. 23. Foolishness ($\mu\omega\rho\iota\alpha$) as opposed to $\sigma o\phi\iota\alpha$. Paul's answer
to the criticism of the Hellenistic world is that the crucified Messiah is not

Why a stumbling-block to the Jews? Because a crucified Messiah was a flat contradiction of Jewish convictions and hopes. The Messiah was to be the glorious vindicator of Israel and the Israelite ideal against the wicked cruelty and godlessness of the world-empires. A crucified Messiah was a Messiah defeated by the heathen empire, and that was a contradiction in terms. Why foolishness to the Gentiles? Because a crucified Messiah meant to them merely a dangerous agitator very properly dealt with by the Imperial authorities. A justly convicted criminal of this kind could not even be thought of as a potential 'saviour' or 'benefactor' of mankind.[1]

These considerations determine the nature of the earliest Christian apologetic. To the Jewish critic it must be said that the crucified Messiah is the fulfilment of all the highest hopes of Hebrew religion. This involves an appeal to the Old Testament and the gradual accumulation of proof-texts (*testimonia*), a process whose earliest stages can be clearly discerned in the New Testament. This appeal to the Old Testament for the explanation of the Messianic cross goes back, in my opinion, to Jesus himself.[2] It is taken up in the oldest parts of the New Testament.[3] It reaches its fullest development in the New Testament in the Gospel of Matthew, which more than any other appears to be concerned to commend the Christian faith to the Jewish people.

To the Gentile world it must be said that the Cross was a miscarriage of justice; and this is precisely the point that is underlined in the Gospel of Luke, where the Passion is a martyrdom and Jesus a crucified benefactor of mankind. This appears most clearly in those parts of Luke that are peculiar to this gospel, and particularly in the 'Proto-Lukan' story of

foolishness but the very wisdom of God (I. Cor. i. 24). Surely Paul in this verse is not using δύναμις and σοφία as mere abstract nouns: surely he means that Christ on the Cross *is* the power of God in action—one might almost say God's ' mighty act '—and the wisdom of God, God's wise purpose in the very moment of its fulfilment.

[1] Cf. H. Preisker, *Neutestamentliche Zeitgeschichte*, pp. 189-208, and literature there cited.   [2] Lk. xxii. 37. Cf. *Mission and Message of Jesus*, 633 f.

[3] E.g. I Cor. xv. 3; Mk. xiv. 49 (Mk. xv. 28 must be rejected on textual grounds). On the Christian appeal to the O.T. in general see G. Schrenk in Kittel's *Theol. Wb. zum N.T.*, i. 755-761.

the trial of Jesus, in which Pilate, well aware of the innocence of the accused and anxious to acquit him, is overborne by the violent clamour of the mob.

This means that Matthew and Luke are essentially apologetic works, the one making its appeal to Jews, the other to Gentiles.[1] At this point it may be urged that to admit that two of the Synoptic Gospels have a controversial axe to grind is most damaging to their reputation as sober historical documents. And with that we are brought face to face with the fundamental issue raised by Form-criticism.[2] The matter can be put in this way. The Gospels show clear signs of propagandist intention. Source-criticism takes us back to earlier collections of sayings and doings of Jesus : and study of these collections seems to reveal motives at work. The collections were made with a purpose, and it can be plausibly argued that the purpose was governed by the immediate practical needs of the Christian community in preaching to the outsider, instructing the convert, defending the Gospel against its Jewish or Gentile critics. Then the vital question is : did the motives which produced these collections *create* the units of which they are made up or only *select* them from a larger mass of available material ? Again, supposing that the units were selected rather than created, have they been transmitted in their original state or have they been modified in the process ? And, supposing that they have been modified, were the forces that modified them foreign to the original impulse, or were they continuations of it ? Do the modifications work in the direction of bringing out more clearly the original intention of Jesus or do they obscure and distort his meaning ? These are questions of the highest importance which can be answered only by painstaking

[1] That the early Church had different ways of approach to Jews and Gentiles is clearly to be seen in the later apologetic literature, e.g. Justin Martyr's two *Apologies* and the *Dialogue with Trypho* ; Tertullian's four works addressed to Gentiles (*Ad Nationes, Apologeticum, De testimonio animae, Ad Scapulam*) and one to Jews (*Aduersus Judaeos*).

[2] Strictly speaking it is not a Form-critical issue, but one of historical judgement on documents as wholes. For Form-criticism, when it attends to business, is occupied with single units of narrative or discourse studied from one special point of view ; and our earliest sources except for a few Agrapha and the *Pericope de Adultera*, are already *collections* of such units.

study of the documents as wholes and of the individual pericopæ. The final test is whether there emerges from the study a portrait of Jesus that will make sense of the whole mass of material, so that we can say : Jesus being like that, and his followers being what they were, this was bound to be the outcome. So far from Jesus being the product of the tradition, he is imperatively required to explain the fact that the tradition as we know it exists at all.

The service of Form-criticism is that it compels attention to four points : (a) *Sitz im Leben;* (b) the question of order —real, topical, or merely mnemonic ; (c) the Marcan framework ; (d) the historical value of individual pericopæ. On each of these matters something must be said.

(a) The question of the *Sitz im Leben,* the concrete historical situation to which a Gospel story or saying really belongs, is of the highest importance. As it is usually posed the question requires us to decide between a *Sitz im Leben Jesu* and a *Sitz im Leben der alten Kirche.* In most cases it would be relevant to add a third possibility, a *Sitz im Leben des jüdischen Volkes.* The question is not one that can be answered *a priori,* but only after very careful examination of each case. In particular it is necessary to be on guard against the tacit assumption, all too easily made, that the possible historical contexts of a story or saying are mutually exclusive : that if it can be shown that a saying is the *mot juste* for some Church situation in the fifties of the first century, it cannot also be the actual spoken word of Jesus in some situation in the Ministry. The truth is that the history of the Church and the story of the Ministry overlap. The Church was in existence almost as soon as the Ministry began. The Church in the New Testament means Peter and James and John and the rest ; but we do not have to wait until after the Resurrection for that group to be formed. Further, while it is doubtless true that the first Good Friday and the first Easter introduced many new factors into the life and thought of the Church, and set many old ones in a new perspective, nevertheless there were issues that remained substantially unchanged, and many issues which became explicit in the Apostolic Age were implicit in the Ministry. Finally, before we too hastily assume that one of the main creative tasks of the Primitive Church was the putting back of its own ideas and beliefs into the mouth of Jesus, there is one fact worth pondering. We have a considerable collection of the written works of one of the most productive minds of the Apostolic Age, St. Paul. All his letters were probably written before any of the Gospels. They abound in striking sayings, brilliant ideas, and definite expressions of belief—a magnificent quarry for any evangelist. Yet how many Pauline sayings have been put into the mouth of Jesus?

(b) We have to take account of the fact that there were certainly no journalists in attendance on our Lord during the Ministry and no stenographers taking down accurate reports of all that was said. We are, in fact, dependent on what people remembered of the things seen and heard. Now people remember a long series of things mostly in one or other of two ways ; either by getting them into some sort of logical sequence or by means of catchwords. Both methods were in common use in the Rabbinical schools, and both may be seen in the Gospel material. The structure of the Mishnah is an example of the logical arrangement of a great mass of material under topical headings ; and the Talmud is full of examples of catchword connexions where a word or idea occurring at the end of one section suggests the topic that will occupy the next. Similarly, in the Gospels, we have only to compare Matthew's sermon on the Mount with the parallel discourse in Luke, to see how the various topics attract to themselves other logically relevant matter ; and this holds of all the great discourses in Matthew. The sayings that make up these discourses are there not because they were all spoken by Jesus on a single occasion and in the order in which they now appear, but because someone was interested in having an anthology of the sayings of Jesus on this or that topic. Similarly with catchwords. The stock example, Mk. ix. 48-50, is as good as any : v. 48 is linked to v. 49 by the word ' fire ' ; v. 49 is linked to v. 50a, and that to the independent saying in v. 50b by the word ' salt '. These connexions are purely verbal : the real connotation of ' salt ' is different in all three cases, and the arrangement of the sayings is a pure mnemonic device.

While this arrangement of material by topics or by sound associations is obviously most appropriate in making collections of sayings, the possibility cannot be excluded that it may affect the order of narrative also. We are all acquainted with the conversational formula : ' Speaking of *x* reminds me of an interesting experience . . . '. This leads on to some anecdote which has no real connexion with the previous story except the mnemonic link. Or again for the purposes of character-drawing we may select incidents from widely separate periods of a man's life in order to show that his attitude to this or that changed or did not change as he grew older. We can easily imagine that similar processes may lie behind the Gospel records. For example in Mk. ii. 1-iii. 6 we have a series of disputes between Jesus and the religious authorities : did they occur in precisely that order at that time, or did someone, before Mark began to write his Gospel, make a collection of anecdotes of this sort which the Evangelist later incorporated into his work ?

(c) Questions of the kind just raised bring us face to face with one of the really vital problems, that of the reliability of the Marcan framework. Any attempt at a full discussion of that problem would require a good deal of time and must be left to another occasion. For the present it must suffice to state conclusions. These are : (i) that it is no longer possible to regard the Marcan framework, in all its details, as a rigid and un-alterable scaffolding, into which everything must somehow be fitted ; (ii) that, while many concessions may have to be made to the disruptive criticism of Mark, it is nevertheless the case that a good deal of structure remains. When the lath and plaster is removed, it appears that there is some solid masonry underneath. The *main* outline is an outline of what really happened. Here we may take in Q, our other main source. Q, I believe, gives a topical order which, again in its main features, reflects the real order. Roughly speaking Mark as a whole leads up to the Cross and Resurrection : Q as a whole presupposes these events. Mark gives the realities of Christian-ity : Q its ideals. Mark gives the foundation on which Christian life is to be built : Q gives the plan for building on that founda-tion. That the two documents supplement one another, interpret one another, and reflect one another in the way they do is evidence not only of their general reliability but also of the fact that there is the most intimate and real connexion between the life and the teaching of Jesus.

(d) On the historical value of the individual pericope Form-criticism, like other kinds of criticism, can make suggestions. But it is only one of the criteria to be employed. Within its limits it is a useful test ; but it is not the only one, nor is it an infallible touchstone.

The importance of these considerations in any attempt to write the ' life ' of Jesus is obvious. The Church preaches—and has always preached from the beginning—Christ crucified and risen. That is, the Gospel is the proclamation of a supreme act of God (a *kerygma*), not the memoir of a distinguished prophet lately deceased. It is a gross error to suppose that the primitive preachers of Christianity came into the world with the story of Jesus, saying to men : ' Look at this and do your best '. The primitive *kerygma* is not good advice or good example but good news.

The *kerygma* stresses the following points :

(a) The Davidic descent of Jesus.

(b) The Ministry (in the most general terms, without details).

(c) The Cross.

(d) The Resurrection and Exaltation.

(e) The Second Coming.

These five points are enclosed in a dogmatic framework, which itself makes two further points :

(i) All this is part and parcel of God's plan announced beforehand by the Prophets.

(ii) The way of salvation is to accept and submit to the will of God now fully revealed in Christ.

In all this the Ministry has a bare mention ; but detailed account of the sayings and doings that made it up there is none.

Nevertheless, before the end of the first century we have gospels which offer a narrative of the Ministry. We have what Luke calls in his Preface a *diegesis* of the things that had happened, a detailed narrative that links the Ministry with the Passion. How was the transition from *kerygma* to *diegesis* made ? There lies one of the most fascinating as it is one of the most vital of Gospel problems.

D

THE FOUNDATION OF THE SYNOPTIC
TRADITION : THE GOSPEL OF MARK.
(1944)

THE first lecture in this series dealt with the materials for a Life of Jesus outside the New Testament. We saw that the reliable extra-canonical evidence, though very small in amount, corroborates some essential points in the primitive Christian *kerygma*. We found that both Christian and non-Christian statements agree in presenting the figure of a crucified teacher, with this difference that whereas the non-Christian sources, both Jewish and pagan, regard him as a false teacher who fully deserved the fate that overtook him, the Christian sources make the amazing claim that the crucified teacher is the promised Messiah, the hope of Israel and the world. To rebut Jewish and pagan criticisms and to establish Christian claims, it was necessary to produce the teaching of Jesus, necessary to describe the ministry. It was not sufficient to do this in general terms, merely asserting that Jesus taught as one having authority, or that he went about doing good : it was imperative to produce specimens of those oracles which had made so tremendous an impression, and of those mighty acts and gracious deeds of service which had drawn men and women to him and fastened their hopes upon him. To convince or convert the outsider detailed evidence in support of Christian claims was urgently required.

Nor was there any lack of interest in the words and deeds on the part of those who were already members of the Christian community. If the teaching and example of Jesus were to be authoritative for Christians, there was every reason why detailed knowledge of the Lord's Ministry should be made available in the Church. And indeed we have striking evidence that this was the case. In the fifties of the first century we find Paul dealing with the moral problems of the Corinthian community, and discriminating carefully between matters on which he can quote a ruling from the Lord and those on which he can offer only his own opinion.[1] Again, in dealing with the disorders of Corinthian Eucharistic worship, he appeals direct to the traditional account of what Jesus did at the institution of the Supper, evidently taking it for granted that that should be the norm for all Christians.[2] The inference has been drawn, rightly I think, that even at this early date there were available some more or less systematic collections of the Lord's teachings. It is possible, even probable, that such collections of teaching, and of narrative too, were more numerous than we commonly suppose, and that much of the material contained in them has been lost beyond recovery. Some of the fragments in Resch's great collection of *Agrapha* may well be the wreckage of early compilations of sayings. Again, Synoptic criticism and Form-criticism alike converge on the conclusion that between the unorganised mass of isolated *pericopæ* and isolated *logia* on the one side, and the completed Gospels on the other, there were blocks, groups, or aggregations of sayings or narratives, some of which in whole or part went to the construction of our existing Gospels. In Mark, for example, besides the Passion narrative, there are other groups which resist the attempt to break them up into their constituent elements. Thus the section, Mk. iv. 35—v. 43, to which we shall return later, is recognised by Dibelius and K. L. Schmidt as probably a unity before Mark wrote. This is a group of miracle stories, including the stilling of the storm, the cure of the Gerasene demoniac, the cure of the woman with the issue of blood, and the raising of Jairus' daughter. Similar aggregations are Mk. i. 23-38 (incidents placed on one day in Capernaum), ii. 15—iii. 6 and xii. 13-27 (disputes with opponents : possibly the two groups are really parts of a single collection broken up by the Evangelist) ; and, if Professor Dodd's hypothesis is right, Mk. i. 14-15, 21-22, 39 ; ii. 13 ; iii. 7b-19 ; vi. 7, 12-13, 30

[1] Cf. I Cor. vii. 10 f. ; ix. 14 ; Moffatt's Commentary on I Cor. p. 80 ; A. M. Hunter, *Paul and his Predecessors*, pp. 52-61.   [2] I Cor. xi. 23 ff.

(an outline of the Galilean ministry, broken up to accommodate other detailed materials).[1]   The Evangelist's task may well have been to select, simplify, and reduce, in order to bring what seemed to him an unwieldy mass of material within the compass of his papyrus roll.   It is clear from the treatment of Mark by Matthew and Luke that they were not afraid of editing, or even sub-editing ;   and what has happened in the case that we can check has doubtless happened in many another case that we cannot check.   We know what Matthew and Luke did to Mark : we can only guess what Mark did to the pre-Markan sources, and what Matthew and Luke did to sources other than Mark.

With these preliminary remarks we may turn to the earliest of our canonical Gospels, that of Mark.   This is the document upon which, more than any other, any critical attempt to write the life of Jesus must depend.   What does it offer ?   It presents an outline of the Ministry, starting from the activity of John the Baptist and ending with the discovery of the empty tomb.   It is generally acknowledged that the true text of Mark ends at xvi. 8 with the words ἐφοβοῦντο γάρ—' for they were afraid '.   There has been much debate on the question whether a sentence may end with γάρ, and enough evidence has been accumulated to show that the thing is possible ;   but it has been forcibly argued [2] that, while ἐφοβοῦντο γάρ may conceivably be the end of a sentence, it cannot well be the end of a Gospel, or even of a paragraph.   We must suppose that the end of the Gospel is lost, and that the additional verses which appear in our manuscripts are attempts to repair the damage.

How much of the original has been lost ?   To this question a firm answer is not possible ;   but, as we shall see, there is some reason for thinking that the amount is not great.   For the moment we leave the end of the Gospel and turn to the beginning.

The opening of Mark has long been as difficult a problem to commentators as its close, in some ways even more difficult. Verse 1 offers a subject with no predicate ;   verses 2 and 3 a subordinate clause with no main clause ;   and verse 4 gives a

---

[1] See Dodd's article ' The Framework of the Gospel Narrative ', in *Expos. Times*, xliii. pp. 396-400.

[2] By W. L. Knox, in *Harvard Theol. Rev.* xxxv. pp. 13-23.

statement of fact about John the Baptist, which seems to have
some links in thought with what has gone before, but no obvious
grammatical connexion. Various solutions of the problem have
been proposed. One of them—that defended by C. H. Turner[1]—
would, if it could be accepted, allow us to believe that the opening
of the Gospel has come down to us intact. It consists in taking
verse 1 as subject and verse 4 as predicate of a single sentence,
with verses 2 and 3 as a long parenthesis. The sense then is
(in Turner's words) : ' the beginning of the Good News of
Jesus . . . was John the Baptist's preaching of a baptism of repentance '. It is true that this interpretation has support from
the Greek Fathers, but even so it is more ingenious than convincing. If we reject it, as I think we must, the most obvious
alternative is to put (with Hort and von Soden) a full stop at the
end of verse 1, which is then to be regarded as a kind of title or
superscription to the whole book. Here again, if we may
regard the verse as genuine, it will be evidence that the beginning
of the Gospel has not been lost.

But now we are confronted by a difficulty raised forty years
ago by Spitta,[2] who argued that if verse 1 is a title, and the story
proper begins with verse 2, then we have to account for the
strange fact that an Old Testament text is cited as a proof-text
before any event has been mentioned which could be regarded
as the fulfilment of the prophecy in question. The normal
order is that first the fact is stated, and then the relevant text is
cited with the formula καθὼς γέγραπται or the like.

That this difficulty is a real one is shown by the fact that
both Matthew and Luke have rearranged the order, presumably
independently of one another. Both begin with a note of time
(Mt. : ἐν δὲ ταῖς ἡμέραις ἐκείναις. Lk. : ἐν ἔτει δὲ πεντεκαιδεκάτῳ
. . . Ἄννα καὶ Καϊάφα), followed by a description of the
appearance of John and his preaching of repentance. Then
comes the proof-text from Isaiah.

So far as Mark is concerned Spitta's solution is that the
Gospel lacks both beginning and end. The text offered by the
best MSS. is already patched up by the addition of verse 1. But

---

[1] *A New Commentary on Holy Scripture*, Part III, p. 50.
[2] *Z.N.W.*, V (1904), pp. 305-308.

once the patch is removed, it becomes clear that the genuine
beginning has been lost.

There are other, and even more drastic methods of dealing
with the opening verses. Some commentators have taken verse 1
as the title of the book and rejected verses 2 and 3. Others would
reject verses 1-3 altogether, and regard the story as beginning
with verse 4. These methods get rid of some of the difficulties ;
but they leave us with a very abrupt opening in verse 4, so abrupt
that if we suppose the authentic text of Mark to begin there, the
corollary would almost inevitably be that the true beginning of
the Gospel has been lost, and that verses 1-3 are patchwork of
the same order as the various ' endings '.

The conclusion to be drawn is, I think, that Mark as we know
it is defective both at the beginning and the end. It is at this
point that a new factor comes into the discussion, the fact that
the use of the codex rather than the roll is being pushed farther
and farther back in the history of early Christian book-production.
If the common ancestor of all our defective MSS. was written
in codex form we should have at once a simple and satisfying
explanation of the loss at the beginning and the end of the Gospel.
For that is what would happen if the outside leaves of the book
were lost, and it is just the outside leaves that are most liable to
loss or damage. If the Gospel was written in codex form it
would make a relatively small volume. Sir Frederic Kenyon has
estimated that it probably occupied some thirty pages of the very
ancient papyrus codex P45. If we suppose a much smaller size
of page we might double the number of pages, and even so we
should have only about fifteen sheets of papyrus in the codex.
(The Chester Beatty Isaiah, when complete, consisted of a single
quire of 112 leaves, and the codex of the Pauline Epistles (P46)
was a quire of 104 leaves.[1] Supposing that this is the right
explanation of the phenomena, it is reasonable to suppose that
the loss at the beginning and end of Mark is relatively small in
extent, since it is probable that only the outside pair of leaves
would be likely to be lost through fair wear and tear. But
though small in extent it must also be very early in date, for
neither at the beginning of the Gospel nor at the end is there

[1] Cf. F. G. Kenyon, *The Chester Beatty Biblical Papyri*, Fasc. I, pp. 9 ff. ;
Fasc. III Supplement, p. viii ; Fasc. VI, pp. v f.

any convincing indication that Matthew and Luke were any better off than we are.

I turn now to the much-discussed testimony of the Elder John quoted by Papias and from Papias by Eusebius :—[1]

' This also the elder used to say. Mark, indeed, having been the interpreter of Peter, wrote accurately, howbeit not in order, all that he recalled of what was either said or done by the Lord. For he neither heard the Lord, nor was he a follower of His, but, at a later date (as I said), of Peter ; who used to adapt his instructions to the needs [of the moment], but not with a view to putting together the Dominical oracles in orderly fashion : so that Mark did no wrong in thus writing some things as he recalled them. For he kept a single aim in view : not to omit anything of what he heard, nor to state anything therein falsely.'

This passage may be taken to represent the tradition about Markan origins as Papias held it early in the second century.[2] The Elder John, from whom he derived it, takes us a little farther back, perhaps into the closing years of the first century, that is, within some thirty years of the writing of Mark, on the commonly accepted date. Let us see what the testimony of the Elder comes to.

First of all it claims that at least one of the sources from which Mark derived his material was the teaching of Peter. As no other source is mentioned, we may assume that the Elder believed that the teaching of Peter was the only, or at least the principal, one. We, too, may well believe that it was the principal, though not necessarily the only, source. Secondly, it is made clear that Mark himself had no first-hand knowledge of the sayings and doings of the Lord : like Luke he was dependent for his materials on those who had been eye-witnesses and ministers of the word.[3] Thirdly, the information which he

---

[1] *H.E.* iii. 39. 15, Lawlor and Oulton's translation.

[2] The late Dr. Vernon Bartlet argued strongly for a date about 110 for Papias' *Expositions*. See *Amicitiæ Corolla*, pp. 15-44.

[3] The absoluteness of this statement *may* be modified if one possible interpretation of the fragmentary first line of the Muratorian Canon be accepted. In that case Mark will have been an eye-witness of some incidents of the Ministry. See Zahn, *Geschichte des ntlichen Kanons*, iii, pp. 18 ff.

derived from Peter had been picked up in the course of his employment as *hermeneutes*, interpreter, to the Apostle. (I have suggested elsewhere[1] that this office may have included the duties of a private secretary and an *aide-de-camp*.) Further, it was not an organised body of teaching—a course of lectures by Peter which were later published by Mark.[2] It was a loose collection of the sayings and stories which the Apostle had brought out from time to time to meet the needs of the moment. The way in which this kind of thing happened can be illustrated from Paul's First Epistle to the Corinthians, to which reference has already been made. Here we see the teaching or practice of the Lord adduced as authoritative for the settlement of the day-to-day problems of the Corinthian community. These quotations are very precious ; but they are not very numerous ; and we may imagine that Mark might have been a long time with Peter and still not have got anything like a complete and comprehensive account of the Ministry.

When Mark decided to write a connected account of the Ministry, he had these unorganised sayings and anecdotes which he had heard during his attendance on Peter. The Elder clearly implies that there was no longer any possibility of going to Peter and asking to have these pieces arranged in order. It must be assumed that the connexion between the Apostle and the Evangelist had come to an end, either by the death of Peter or for some other reason.[3] Mark thus had to do the best he could with his reminiscences of Peter's teaching and such other material as he possessed. That other material was at his disposal there is no good reason to doubt. We need not suppose that he came to Peter with his mind a *tabula rasa*. On the contrary, if he is the John Mark of the early chapters of Acts, he must have known

[1] *Teaching of Jesus*, p. 23, n. 1.

[2] As, for example, Adamson's lectures on the history of modern philosophy were posthumously published from his students' notebooks, and at once became a standard work on the subject.

[3] This consideration settles the translation of γενόμενος in the opening sentence of the Papias statement. We must render ' having been ' with Lawlor and Oulton rather than ' having become ' with Lightfoot (*Apostolic Fathers*, p. 529). In all probability we have here an example of the use of γενόμενος as we use ' ex- ' to indicate the holder of an office now given up. See Moulton and Milligan, *Vocabulary*, p. 126.

a great deal of the tradition about Jesus before he became Peter's assistant. Let us look at what we know about John Mark and his opportunities for becoming acquainted with facts about Jesus before he attached himself to Peter.

The earliest piece of evidence about Mark—if it can be accepted as such—is a bit of autobiography embodied in his Gospel. In Mk. xiv. 51 f. we read that

' A certain young man followed with him, having a linen cloth wrapped round him over his naked body : and they lay hold of him ; but he left the linen cloth and fled naked '.

It has been pointed out that :

(*a*) This bit of narrative is peculiar to Mark.

(*b*) It cannot well be derived from any of the disciples, since they had already run away ; and the description does not suggest that the young man himself was one of the Twelve.

(*c*) It can hardly come from Jesus, who apparently had no further communication with his friends after the arrest.

The natural inference is that the story came from the young man himself : and it is in itself so insignificant a detail that there seems no good reason why Mark should have troubled to relate it unless he himself was the young man. From this it is an easy step to the conjecture that the reason why the young man came to be there was that he had followed the party from the house where the last supper was held—and that the house was his home. This again fits in quite well with what we subsequently learn from Acts about the place taken by Mark's home and family in the life of the early Jerusalem community.

There is, however, one difficulty in the way of accepting the theory. It is this. There is a discrepancy between the Synoptics and John with regard to the date of the last supper. The details are too complex to be discussed here, but the upshot of the matter is that the Johannine tradition, supported indirectly by Paul and the *Didache*,[1] makes the last supper fall on the evening twenty-four hours before the Jewish Passover meal, while Mark, followed by Matthew, identifies the last supper with the Passover meal. The opinion of scholars is still divided on this problem.

---

[1] I do not think it is possible to bring in ' Proto-Luke ' or Luke's special source as a witness on this side.

There are some who hold that on this point John is right as against the Synoptics. Others, including Dalman[1] and J. Jeremias,[2] hold to the view that the last supper *was* a Passover meal. There is a third solution proposed by Billerbeck,[3] who holds that in the year of the Crucifixion, owing to a dispute between Pharisees and Sadducees about the calendar, the Passover was celebrated twice, the Pharisees observing it on Thursday evening, the Sadducees on Friday evening. Jesus and his disciples fell in with the Pharisaic arrangement. John records the Sadducean date. This is very ingenious; but the evidence on which Billerbeck relies is too scanty to warrant any real confidence in his theory.

Now if we leave Billerbeck on one side we must choose between Mark and John; and it seems to me that the balance of probability is decidedly in favour of John. But if we accept John's date for the last supper, it seems fatal to the identification of the young man who fled naked with Mark. For if that young man was from the house where the last supper was held, he *must* have known whether or not it was a Passover meal; if that young man wrote the Gospel he could not possibly—one would think—have forgotten what night it was when these things happened. It does not seem possible to maintain both the Johannine date for the last supper and the identification of the young man with Mark: and of the two I should be more ready to sacrifice the identification.

We are on firmer ground when we come to Acts. From the early chapters it appears that Mark's home and family played a prominent part in the life of the Early Church. His mother (at this time a widow) was a member of the Jerusalem community, and her house was a regular meeting place of the brethren. When Peter escaped from prison, it was the first place he made for (Ac. xii. 12), and there he found a prayer meeting on his behalf in progress. Mark was also in the movement: he was, in fact, what we call a Jewish Christian. He accompanied Paul and Barnabas on the first missionary journey in the capacity of ὑπηρέτης (Ac. xii. 25; xiii. 5)—assistant or general factotum.

[1] *Jesus-Jeschua*, pp. 80-166, E.T., *Jesus Jeshua*, pp. 86-184.
[2] *Die Abendmahlsworte Jesu.*   [3] *Kommentar*, ii., pp. 812-853.

He continued with them until they came to Perga, where, for some reason, he decided to return to Jerusalem (Ac. xiii. 13). The result of this was that when Paul and Barnabas planned the second journey, Paul would not have Mark again. Barnabas, who was related to Mark (first cousin or uncle), was equally determined to take him, with the result that Paul and Barnabas fell out, and Barnabas undertook a missionary trip of his own to Cyprus, taking Mark with him (Ac. xv. 36-41). These events may be placed in the late 'forties of the first century. There is an interval of about a dozen years before we hear of Mark again in Col. iv. 10 f. and Phm. 24, written from Rome during Paul's detention there. By this time Paul and Mark are completely reconciled. Mark is praised and commended to the Church at Colossæ. It is suggested that he may pay them a visit in the near future. Still later we have a note preserved in II Tim. iv. 11 where Timothy is commanded to bring Mark with him to Rome, ' for he is useful to me for ministering '.[1] Finally, he is referred to by the author of I Peter v. 13, as ' Mark, my son '.

The New Testament evidence goes to show that Mark had considerable opportunities of gathering knowledge of the kind that would later be useful in the composition of the Gospel. It is very far from being the case that Peter was the only one from whom he could learn facts about the Ministry.

The Patristic evidence from Papias onwards lays stress on the Petrine connexion. According to the anti-Marcionite prologue to the Gospel Mark was Peter's dragoman,[2] and the Gospel was composed in Italy after Peter's ' departure '. This information is also given by Irenæus. Ecclesiastical traditions preserved by Eusebius (H.E. ii. 16. 1 and ii. 24) declare that Mark was the first to evangelize Egypt, and the first to found churches in

---

[1] On this passage see P. N. Harrison, *The Problem of the Pastoral Epistles*, p. 123.

[2] ' Marcus adseruit, qui colobodactylus est nominatus, ideo quod ad ceteram corporis proceritatem digitos minores habuisset. iste interpres fuit Petri. post excessionem ipsius Petri descripsit idem hoc in partibus Italiae euangelium.' (See De Bruyne, *Rev. Biblique*, 1928, pp. 193-214 ; Harnack, *SBA*, 1928, pp. 322-341 ; Howard, *Exp. Ti.*, xlvii. (1936), pp. 534-538). Harnack assigns the prologue to the period A.D. 160-180, and regards the testimony of Irenæus (iii. i, 1, Harvey, ii. 4 ff.) as derived from it.

Alexandria; and that in the eighth year of Nero's reign he was succeeded in the Ministry (λειτουργία) of the community at Alexandria by Annianus.[1] If this implies the death of Mark, then Mark died in 63. But the death of Mark is not explicitly stated by Eusebius in ii. 24, and the tradition transmitted by Irenæus puts the composition of the Gospel in the period after the ἔξοδος of Peter and Paul, which, if it means their death, implies probably a date after 64. It is not necessary to suppose that Mark's activities in Alexandria were terminated by death : a founder-missionary might well move on to other fields when he had got a Church established.

The evidence of Clement of Alexandria [2] places the composition of the Gospel in Rome at the request of those who heard the preaching of Peter and wished for a permanent record. The views of Peter on this proceeding are not stated in the *Adumbrationes* passage ; in Eus. *H.E.* vi. 14. 6, he is represented as non-committal ; while in *H.E.* ii. 15 he is said to have authorised the book for reading in the churches.

We have thus evidence from three centres of Early Christianity : Asia, represented by Papias quoting the Elder ; Alexandria represented by Clement ; and Rome (with Gaul) represented by the anti-Marcionite prologue (followed by Irenæus). The tradition from these three centres is second century. It is of one voice as to the connexion of the Gospel with the preaching of Peter. Clement locates the composition in Rome ; the anti-Marcionite prologue says *in partibus Italiæ ;* Papias gives no indication. Clement places the writing in the lifetime of Peter, the prologue places it after his ' departure ' (*excessio*) ; Papias implies that the Gospel was written when Mark was no longer associated with Peter, but leaves open the question whether the contact had been terminated by Peter's death or in some other way.

Looking at this tradition as a whole, one begins to wonder

---

[1] For the Alexandrian Episcopal succession, see Harnack, *Chron.*, i. 96 f., 138 ff., 202 ff.

[2] Clement is cited by Eusebius, *H.E.* ii. 15 and vi. 14. 6 : the two passages do not entirely agree. There is a further passage in the *Adumbrationes*, on I Pet. v. 13 (ed. Stählin, iii. p. 206).

whether we have not gone a little too fast in taking Papias and interpreting him in the light of Irenæus (having settled that ἔξοδος in Irenæus must mean Peter's death). There are considerations which suggest that the Alexandrian tradition of Clement should not be dismissed without being carefully weighed. First of all there is the fact that ecclesiastical tradition connects Mark himself with the Alexandrian church. Even if this means no more than that the Alexandrian community was a daughter-community of Rome,[1] it does imply a close connexion between Rome, the place of origin of the Gospel, and Alexandria. Secondly while the office of *hermeneutes*, discharged by Mark for Peter, may doubtless be understood in the wide sense already suggested, it would be a mistake to leave out of account the primary significance of the word—'interpreter'. But if Mark was Peter's interpreter during such time as the Apostle was touring the Gentile world, including Rome, that very fact suggests that the tour cannot have been prolonged. If Peter had spent many years in Rome or elsewhere in the Hellenistic world, he would surely have picked up enough Greek to dispense with the services of an interpreter. In that case we should expect that any of his hearers who wished for a permanent record of his teaching could have made one with little or no difficulty. The traditions regarding the origin of Mark's Gospel are not favourable to the theory of a prolonged activity of Peter in the Gentile Christian field. Nor does the New Testament evidence suggest anything of the sort. For the period down to about A.D. 50 all the indications are that Peter's base is Jerusalem, and that his sphere of work is Palestine and Syria. Later, in the middle 'fifties there are traces in Paul's Corinthian correspondence which *may* mean that Peter's following in Corinth was the result of a personal visit to the city.[2] If he visited Corinth, he may also have gone on to Rome ; but there is no trace of his presence there in the closing chapters of Acts or in those letters of Paul which probably

---

[1] Lietzmann, *Geschichte der Alten Kirche*, ii. pp. 57 f.

[2] See Lietzmann, *Geschichte der Alten Kirche*, i. pp. 109 f. That Peter had visited Corinth was certainly the opinion of Dionysius, Bishop of Corinth, in the second half of the second century. Whether this opinion (stated in a letter to Rome quoted by Eusebius, *H.E.* ii. 25. 8) was an inference from the Corinthian letters or rested on local tradition we cannot say.

belong to the Roman captivity. Yet those very letters, which show no trace of Peter's presence, contain greetings from Mark.[1] If Peter had paid a visit to Rome some time between 55 and 60 ; if Mark had been his interpreter then ; if after Peter's departure from the city Mark had taken in hand—at the request of the Roman hearers—a written record of what Peter had said ; then the essential points in the evidence would all be satisfied.

A record of what Peter had said on a visit of his kind would not necessarily be a Gospel such as that of Mark now is ; but it might well have formed the nucleus of such a work. Further, if Mark had acted as Peter's interpreter in other places besides Rome, he would have a fairly extensive body of Petrine reminiscences at his disposal, when in Rome he undertook the task of writing.[2] But Petrine material would not be all that he had.

The upshot of all this is that Mark, from the early days of the Jerusalem community, was in touch with the Christian tradition, and had ample opportunity of learning facts about the Ministry quite apart from his association with Peter. There does not seem to be any reason why he should not have used this information in the composition of his Gospel, along with that derived from Peter, especially since, as we have already seen, the Petrine information was not a dictated continuous story, but only separate pieces or small groups gathered probably over a considerable period and recalled at a later date. We should, *prima facie*, expect to find in the Gospel matter that can be called without hesitation ' Petrine ' ; other material which *may* be Petrine ; and, again, other which there is no good reason to assign to Peter at all. That expectation is borne out when we examine the text.

In his valuable and stimulating commentary on Mark,[3] C. H. Turner drew attention to a frequently recurring phenomenon in the Gospel. He describes it thus (p. 48) :

---

[1] Col. iv. 10 ; Phm. 24.

[2] If there is anything in this, it suggests that the date of Mark may be a few years earlier than is usually thought likely. A date before 60 would be quite possible.

[3] In *A New Commentary on Holy Scripture*, Pt. III, pp. 42-124.

In strong contrast to Matthew and Luke, Mark's Gospel
may be called autobiographical. They write Lives of
Christ, he records the experience of an eye-witness and companion. It is crucial in this respect to note the predominant
use of the plural in the narrative of Mark. Time after time
a sentence commences with the plural, for it is an experience
which is being related, and passes into the singular, for the
experience is that of discipleship to a Master. So in i. 21
'they enter Capernaum ; and at once he taught on the
sabbath in the synagogue '; v. 38, 'they come to Jairus's
house ; and he sees the tumult . . .'; ix. 33, 'and they came
to Capernaum : and when he was in the house he asked
them . . .'; x. 32, 'and they were on the road going up to
Jerusalem, and Jesus was going on ahead of them . . .';
xi. 12, 'and on the morrow, when they had left Bethany, he
hungered'; xi. 27, 'and they came again to Jerusalem : and
as he was walking in the temple . . .'; xiv. 32, 'and they
came to . . . Gethsemane : and he saith to his disciples . . .'.
In none of these cases do either Matthew or Luke retain
the plural. . . .

If the reader will now take one step further and put
back Mark's third person plural into the first person plural
of the narrative, he will receive a vivid impression of the
testimony that lies behind the Gospel : thus in i. 29, 'we
came into our house with James and John : and my wife's
mother was ill in bed with a fever, and at once we tell him
about her '.

In his note on Mk. i. 21 (p. 54) Turner gives a list of passages
in which ' Mark's third person plural may be reasonably understood as representing a first person plural of Peter's discourses '.
The list is as follows : i. 21, 29 ; v. 1, 38 ; vi. 53, 54 ; viii. 22 ;
ix. 14, 30, 33 ; x. 32, 46 ; xi. 1, 12, 15, 20, 27 ; xiv. 18, 22, 26,
32. In what follows I shall refer to the phenomenon appearing
in these passages as ' Turner's mark '.

Now if we take the passages that have Turner's mark and
examine them in their context, it becomes clear that in some
cases the adjoining passages belong naturally to the passages
with the mark. For example, in the first chapter, verses 21-28,

the account of the visit of Jesus and his disciples to the Capernaum Synagogue has the Turner mark; and it presupposes verses 16-20 which do not have the mark, but which describe the call of the first four Apostles. Further, in verses 29-31, the cure of Peter's mother-in-law, Turner's mark is present; and again verses 32-39 are the sequel. Now it is admitted by K. L. Schmidt that verses 23-38 form a pre-Markan unity. Similarly, iv. 35-41, which has not the Turner mark, is bound up with v. 1-20 and 21-43, two passages which have the mark; and again the whole section, iv. 35—v. 43, is recognised as a pre-Markan unity by Dibelius and Schmidt. Pursuing this line of inquiry, it becomes possible to draw up a tentative list of Petrine paragraphs in Mark, consisting of those paragraphs which have the Turner mark along with other paragraphs which seem to attach themselves. The extent of the Petrine matter is as follows: i. 16-39; ii. 1-14; iii. 13-19; iv. 35—v. 43; vi. 7-13, 30-56; viii. 14—ix. 48; x. 32-52; xi. 1-33; xiii. 3-4, 32-37; xiv. 17-50, 53-54, 66-72.

The matter dealt with in these sections are the call of the first disciples, the Synagogue service, the cure of Peter's mother-in-law, travel-preaching in Galilee, the cure of the paralytic at Capernaum, the appointment of the Twelve, the storm on the lake, the cure of the Gerasene demoniac, the Hæmorrhousa and the raising of Jairus' daughter, the Mission of the Twelve, their return and the feeding of the 5000, the walking on the sea and the return to Gennesaret, the warning against the leaven of the Pharisees and of Herod, the healing of the blind man at Bethsaida, Peter's confession and the first prediction of the Passion, the Transfiguration, and healing of the epileptic boy, the second prediction of the Passion, the rebuke to jealousy and self-seeking among the disciples. All these events are set on the Galilean background, with Capernaum as the principal centre.

A second group begins with the third prediction of the Passion, on the road going up to Jerusalem, the request of the sons of Zebedee, the cure of Bartimaeus, the triumphal entry, the story of the barren fig-tree and the cleansing of the Temple, the question about Jesus' authority, the question about the time of the end, the last supper, the events in Gethsemane, the arrest of Jesus and removal to the High Priest's house, Peter's denials.

Of the material that falls outside this collection it is not possible here to make a detailed examination. For the present it must suffice to notice a few well-defined blocks. Mark i. 1-15 covers the period prior to the call of Peter ; and, at the other end of the story, xiv. 55-65 and xv. 1—xvi. 8 describe incidents at which Peter was not present. (Mk. xiv-xvi is regarded as a pre-Markan unity by K. L. Schmidt.)

The account of the death of the Baptist (vi. 17-29) has its peculiar problems. At the same time, it has all the appearance of being a piece of Palestinian (originally Aramaic) tradition. The most attractive solution is perhaps that proposed by J. Thomas,[1] that the Evangelist has here made use of a written document embodying the tradition of the followers of John, what might be called the *Passio Iohannis* as it circulated in the Johannite[2] sect.

The so-called ' Little Apocalypse ', which appears in the non-Petrine collection, is thought by many to have circulated in the Early Church as a separate document ; and it is at least possible that the specimen parables, given with comment in iv. 1-34, were extracted from a collection of parables. The passage x. 1-12 is regarded by Dibelius[3] as a pre-Markan unity.

Specially interesting are the two groups of polemical passages in chapters ii-iii and xii. These have been the subject of an illuminating discussion by B. S. Easton.[4] He observes that the former block *ends* at Mk. iii. 6 with the statement that the Pharisees and Herodians plotted to kill Jesus : the latter *begins* at xii. 13 with the statement that the Pharisees and Herodians sent representatives to entrap him in his talk. Apart from a parallel in Mt. xxii. 16 to Mk. xii. 13, these are the only instances of ' Herodian ' in the New Testament. The difficulty about the word, according to Easton, is that while in Galilee ' Herodian '

---

[1] *Le Mouvement Baptiste en Palestine et Syrie*, pp. 110 f.

[2] Following a suggestion made by Thomas, I use Johannite as a convenient means of distinguishing persons and things connected with the Baptist from those connected with the John (or Johns) of the Early Church.

[3] *Formgeschichte des Evangeliums*,[2] p. 223.

[4] *Studies in Early Christianity*, ed. S. J. Case, pp. 85 ff.

E

could mean any official of Herod, it could hardly mean that in Jerusalem where Herod's writ did not run. Hence it must be explained in Jerusalem as being the name for those in Jerusalem who supported Herodian rule, and, since that was not in force in the capital, supported the Roman rule as the next best thing.[1] But it is awkward to have to give two interpretations of the same term. Easton further noted that the plot mentioned in iii. 6 leads to nothing, and indeed comes too early in the story. In xii. 13 however, he argues, the appearance of the Herodians is natural. They were the one class of Jews who favoured the payment of tribute to Rome.

Easton also notes that the matters discussed in these polemical passages would not have any very lively interest for Gentile converts. From that it would presumably follow—though Easton does not argue the case in this way—that they would not be likely to form part of Peter's preaching to the Gentiles.

Easton's solution is that ii. 13—iii. 6 and xii. 13-27 originally formed a single continuous whole ; that ' this account was formed in pre-Markan times and belonged to the tradition of the Palestinian Christian community '.[2] Why did Mark split it up ? Having begun to incorporate it where he does he had to ' break off at iii. 5, for tribute to Rome, the theme of the next paragraph was paid only in Judæa, while the Sadducees of xii. 18-27 were scarcely to be found in Galilee. But as iii. 5 was too abrupt a conclusion for the first part, Mark wrote iii. 6, forming it out of the next sentence in the tradition (xii. 13), without noticing (or caring) that he had made Galilean characters of the Herodians. The remainder of the tradition he was obliged to postpone until his narrative could treat of Jerusalem events.'[3]

All this seems to be quite possible. The only reservation that needs to be made is in favour of ii. 13-14, the call of Levi.[4] This paragraph seems to me to hang together with the preceding matter.

With this somewhat hasty survey of a large subject the

[1] For a full discussion of the name ' Herodian ', see H. H. Rowley's article, ' The Herodians in the Gospels ', *J.T.S.* xli. (1940), pp. 14-27.

[2] *Op. cit.* p. 92.   [3] *Ibid.*

[4] I very much doubt whether ii. 15-17 has anything at all to do with ii. 13-14. They could—so far as Mark goes—be treated perfectly well as separate paragraphs.

present discussion must close. It is obvious that there are—and probably always will be—many loose ends. But a few things seem to emerge fairly clearly. First and foremost is the conclusion, suggested by converging lines of argument, that the basis of the Markan story is a good deal broader than we sometimes think. Petrine reminiscence is part of the foundation, perhaps the main part ; but other sources have made their contribution. And we need not suppose that 'non-Petrine' necessarily means inferior in historical worth. The further we go back the larger the number of available first-hand witnesses becomes. If the identification of the Evangelist with John Mark of Jerusalem is sound, he was from the beginning in touch with many such witnesses. And, secondly, if our interpretation of the traditions about Peter, Mark and the Gospel is anywhere near the truth, the composition of the Gospel may be put several years earlier than the date commonly accepted.

4.

THE WORK OF ST. LUKE.
(1944)

I HAVE put down Luke's work for this lecture because, on the whole, I think that in the true chronological order of the Gospels Luke should follow Mark and precede Matthew and John. Both Matthew and Luke make use of the early collection of sayings of Jesus known as Q[1]: in the course of prolonged and detailed study of this source as preserved in Matthew and Luke, I have come to the conclusion that Luke used a more primitive rendering of the original Aramaic than Matthew. Similarly, both Matthew and Luke use Mark, but with a difference. Matthew produces a new, enlarged, and enriched edition of Mark, while Luke uses Mark as a quarry from which to extract such materials as he chooses to incorporate in a new work of his own. This suggests that by the time that Matthew wrote, the Gospel of Mark had attained a prestige (through its association with the name of Peter) which ruled out the possibility of cutting it about as Luke had done.

For the purposes of this lecture I shall assume as a working hypothesis that Luke and Acts are the work of the same writer, who is to be identified with one of the companions of St. Paul, covered by the 'We' in the 'We-passages' of Acts, and in all probability with the Luke who is referred to in Col. iv. 14;

---

[1] I think it probable that Q was put together in Aramaic about the middle of the first century as a manual of instruction for Christian converts. The original order is best preserved in Luke. The following portions of Luke should probably be assigned to the source Q (brackets indicate doubt) : Lk. iii. 7-9, 16, 17 ; iv. 1-13 ; vi. 20-49 ; vii. (1-6a), 6b-9 (10), 18-35 ; ix. 57-62 ; x. 2, 3, 8-16, 21-24 ; xi. 9-26, (27-28), 29-36, (37-41), 42-52 ; xii. (1), 2-12, 22-34, (35-38), 39-46, (47-50), 51-59 ; xiii. 18-30, 34, 35 ; xiv. 15-24, 26, 27, (34, 35) ; xvi. 13, 16-18 ; xvii. 1-6, 22-37. For an attempted reconstruction of Q with a commentary, see *The Mission and Message of Jesus*, pp. 331-440.

Phm. *v.* 24; II Tim. iv. 11; and possibly (in the form Λούκιος) in Rom. xvi. 21.[1]

I begin with a short consideration of the early Church tradition regarding the work of Luke. Most of it is available in very convenient form for English readers in a contribution by H. J. Cadbury to the *Beginnings of Christianity*, ii. 209-264. The first thing that strikes one about this material is the absence of any considerable body of very early testimony of the sort that cannot be explained as inference from statements in the New Testament itself. This is in marked contrast to what we found in the case of Mark; and it calls for explanation. The facts are as follows :

There is nothing from Papias. Eusebius gives us traditions preserved by the Bishop of Hierapolis concerning Mark, and (as Papias supposed) Matthew. But there is no word about Luke; and it is reasonable to suppose that Eusebius would have reported it, had it been available.

The Muratorian Canon, which may be taken to give the views current in Rome in the second century, and may perhaps be the work of Hippolytus, says :[2]

' The third book of the Gospel, according to Luke, Luke that physician, who after the ascension of Christ, when Paul had taken him with him as companion of his journey, composed in his own name on the basis of report. However, he did not himself see the Lord in the flesh and therefore as he could " trace the course of events " he set them down. So also he began his story with the birth of John.'

There is nothing here that could not be inferred from the New Testament (Luke, Acts, and Pauline Epistles) by an intelligent student of the text. This conclusion holds good in the case of Irenaeus, our other second century witness in Europe,[3] who not only gives his conclusions but sets out the arguments by which they are derived from the New Testament.

The African and Egyptian Fathers add little or nothing.

---

[1] On the identification of the Λουκᾶς of Col., Phm., and II Tim. with the Λούκιος of Rom., and of both with the author of the ' We '-passages, see Deissmann, *Licht vom Osten*,[4] pp. 372-377 ; H. J. Cadbury in *Beginnings of Christianity*, v. 489-492.

[2] Trans. Cadbury, *Beginnings*, ii. 211.

[3] Cadbury, *ibid.*, ii. 212-221.

Tertullian lays great stress on the fact that Luke was one of Paul's followers. Clement of Alexandria mentions the theory that Luke translated the Epistle to the Hebrews into Greek. Origen tells us that Luke ' made for converts from the Gentiles the gospel praised by Paul '.[1] This last statement is again an inference, and probably an illegitimate one, from the passage in II Cor. viii. 18 where Paul speaks to the Corinthian community of sending to them ' the brother whose praise in the Gospel is through all the churches '. The brother is not named and there have been many guesses at his identity ; but they remain mere guesses. The description given is quite ambiguous. What it means is that the brother in question has a great and widespread reputation as an Evangelist ; but whether ' Evangelist ' means a preacher of the Gospel or the composer of a gospel, we have no means of determining.[2] It seems that Origen was the first to interpret II Cor. viii. 18 of Luke and his Gospel : he has had many followers in ancient and modern times—Chrysostom, Ephrem Syrus, Eusebius, Jerome, Ambrose ; and in more recent days Rendall, Plummer, Bachmann, and others. But the identification remains no more than a guess.[3]

The only early document to give particulars apparently independent of the New Testament is the anti-Marcionite Prologue to the Gospel. The credit for showing the date and importance of the anti-Marcionite prologues belongs to Dom D. de Bruyne, whose conclusions were published in the *Revue Bénédictine* for July 1928 (pp. 193-214), and accepted by Harnack in a paper published in the same year.[4] Three Prologues are extant, to Mark, Luke, and John. All three are in Latin ; but for Luke the Greek original has also survived. They belong to the second century and most probably to the time before Irenaeus. The Greek prologue to Luke runs as follows :[5]

[1] Cadbury, *ibid.*, ii. 227.

[2] For an excellent discussion of the problems raised by II. Cor. viii. 18, see E. B. Allo, *Seconde Épître aux Corinthiens* (*Études Bibliques*), pp. 224 ff.

[3] It may be remarked in passing that Origen here gives the four gospels in the order Matthew, Mark, Luke, John, which he evidently regards as the chronological order of composition.

[4] *SPAW*, Phil. Hist. Kl., 1928, XXIV, pp. 322-341.

[5] I translate De Bruyne's text as given by Harnack.

' Luke was a Syrian of Antioch, a physician by profession. A former disciple of the Apostles who afterwards accompanied Paul until his (Paul's) martyrdom, who served the Lord continually, unmarried, childless, he fell asleep at the age of eighty-four in Boeotia, full of the Holy Spirit.

' This man, when there were already Gospels in existence —that " according to Matthew ", written down in Judaea, and that " according to Mark ", in Italy—impelled by the Holy Spirit, composed this whole Gospel in Achaea, making clear by his Preface this very fact that before him other (Gospels) had been written, and also that it was necessary to set forth an accurate account of the (Christian) dispensation for the believers of Gentile origin, so that they should neither be disturbed by Jewish tales, nor, through the deceitful influence of heretical and empty imaginings, miss the truth. Accordingly at the very outset (of the Gospel) we have transmitted to us as being most essential (the account of) the birth of John, who is " the beginning of the Gospel ". who was the forerunner of the Lord and shared in the preparation of the Gospel, in the baptismal instruction, and in the fellowship of the Spirit.[1] Of this dispensation a prophet, one of " The Twelve ",[2] makes mention.

' And then at a later date this same Luke wrote the Acts of the Apostles, and afterwards John the Apostle, one of the Twelve, wrote the Apocalypse in the island of Patmos and after that the Gospel.' [3]

The strong anti-Marcionite polemic of this Prologue is evident at every turn. Against Marcion's reduction of the whole

[1] ' Shared . . . spirit.' The Greek text is κοινωνὸς ἔν τε τῷ καταρτισμῷ τοῦ εὐαγγελίου καὶ τῇ τοῦ βαπτίσματος διαγωγῇ καὶ τῇ τοῦ πνεύματος κοινωνίᾳ. The old Latin version has : et fuit socius ad perfectionem populi, item inductionem baptismi atque passionis socius. This implies τοῦ λαοῦ in place of τοῦ εὐαγγελίου, εἰσαγωγῇ for διαγωγῇ, and παθήματος for πνεύματος. Harnack follows the Latin in all three points, thus obtaining an easier text, which could be translated, ' shared in the preparation of the people, in the introduction of baptism, and in the fellowship of suffering '.

[2] Malachi. The Latin version says ' Malachiel propheta, unus de duodecim.

[3] The Latin adds ' in Asia '.

Bible to a mutilated edition of Luke and the Pauline Epistles, we have Luke himself brought in to testify to the existence of other Gospels. We have a strong insistence on the *complete* Gospel of Luke with all the things, the story of John the Baptist for example, that Marcion had deleted. We have the insistence on the Old Testament prophecy of the Forerunner. All this points to a time when the Marcionite dispute was a living issue, that is the second half of the second century.

Along with this obviously polemical matter we have a number of details about St. Luke, which do not serve in any way to grind the anti-Marcionite axe. We learn (1) that Luke was first a disciple of the Apostles; (2) that subsequently he became a companion of St. Paul and remained with him till his martyrdom; (3) that he wrote the Gospel in Achaea; (4) that he was unmarried and childless; (5) that he reached the age of 84; and (6) that he died in Boeotia. These details were not invented to help the case against Marcion. But equally they were not, for the most part, the product of arm-chair detective work on the text of the New Testament. The first two items might conceivably be guesses based on Luke's Preface, the narrative of Acts, and the references to Luke in the Pauline Epistles. The remainder could hardly have come in that way. Indeed anyone who made inferences from the New Testament would have had good reason to choose Macedonia or Caesarea or Rome as the place of writing of the Gospel and of the death of Luke, rather than Achaea or Boeotia. The fact that we have Achaea and Boeotia suggests that we have to do either with genuine tradition or pure invention. The same holds of the remaining details. The information that Luke was unmarried and childless could not possibly help the case against Marcion, who repudiated marriage and the procreation of children with horror and disgust.[1] Nor could these points have been deduced from Scripture. They are here either because they were invented by the author of the Prologue—and what purpose could the invention serve ?—or because they were believed to be true statements. Similarly, there was no point in giving Luke's age when he died unless there was some ground for believing that that was in fact his age. We

---

[1] Harnack, *Marcion*, p. 97.

may conclude that there is at least a *prima facie* case for accepting the tradition as generally reliable.

As to its origin and date, De Bruyne has shown good reason for placing the composition of the Prologues in the second half of the second century and making their home at Rome. Harnack puts forward as alternative suggestions for the place of origin Achaea and Asia ; but he admits that Rome is more probable than these. I venture to propose a compromise solution to the problem. Accepting De Bruyne's arguments in favour of Rome as the place of origin of the Prologues, we may ask whence the personalia regarding Luke were obtained. And to that question the most obvious answer is Achaea. If details of this kind were to be preserved at all, it would most probably be in the place to which they were native. Moreover the information could easily have been transmitted to Rome. To name only one possible way, we know that the episcopate of Dionysius of Corinth over-lapped that of Soter of Rome (c. 166-174), that Dionysius was a strong anti-Marcionite, and that he wrote at least one letter to Rome.[1] I suggest, therefore, that the Prologue to Luke was composed in Rome in the latter half of the second century on the basis of information supplied from Achaea.

The tradition makes Luke a Syrian of Antioch. We are bound to consider the relation of this statement to the well-known variant reading in the text of Acts xi. 28. In the R.V. Acts xi. 27 f. reads as follows :—

> 'Now in those days there came down prophets from Jerusalem unto Antioch. And there stood up one of them named Agabus, and signified by the Spirit that there should be a great famine over all the world : which came to pass in the days of Claudius.'

After 'Antioch' the Codex Bezae, with support from Latin MSS. and ecclesiastical writers, has :—

> 'And there was much rejoicing, and when we had been in conversation together, one of them named Agabus spoke signifying by the Spirit . . .'

[1] Eusebius *HE*, iv. 23.

If this reading is genuine, it is the first of the ' We-passages '
in Acts, and the inference is that the author of these passages
(whom I regard as the author of the whole book) was associated
with the community at Antioch at the time of this incident
(c. A.D. 45). Naturally there has been considerable discussion
of the relation between the variant in Acts and the tradition
connecting Luke with Antioch. This mostly takes the form of
asking whether the reading is derived from the tradition or the
tradition from the reading. The former view was apparently
held by J. H. Ropes ;[1] the latter is regarded as more likely by
Cadbury [2] and accepted by A. C. Clark.[3] There is, of course,
a third possibility, which seems to me to be more credible than
either of the other two. That is that the tradition and the reading
are independent of one another, that the reading is genuine and
the tradition true, and that both depend on the fact that Luke
was an Antiochene Christian who was a member of the church
in that city at the time in question. If Luke was an early member
of the Antiochene community, he would naturally come under
the influence of the leaders of the Palestinian Church before
attaching himself to Paul.

The result of our examination of the early tradition is that
what there is seems to originate in one locality—Achaea. Along
with this result goes the fact that while the other Gospels seem
to be fairly firmly attached to leading centres of early Church
life—Mark to Rome, Matthew to Antioch, John to Asia and
Ephesus—Luke's Gospel has no such traditional connexion. It
seems to me that both facts may be explained in the same way,
that Luke's work in its final form was not done at the request of
any particular Christian community for lectionary use in its
worship, but that it was done on his own initiative for publication
to the outside world. That this was the case seems to be clearly
implied in the author's own preface to the Gospel, where he tells
Theophilus—and through him all the other readers of the work—
how he came to the decision [4] to add one more to the existing

---

[1] See his note ad. loc. (Beginnings of Christianity, iii. 108).

[2] Beginnings, ii. 248.

[3] The Acts of the Apostles, p. 348.

[4] ἔδοξε κἀμοί : ' I also decided '. It is made quite plain that the job was
not undertaken at the request of a Church or Christian group. There is nothing

accounts of the beginnings of Christianity. The statement of the Preface is corroborated (or interpreted) by the *Muratorian Canon*, which tells us that Luke ' composed ' (the Gospel) ' in his own name on the basis of report ' ;[2] and by the anti-Marcionite Prologue, which says that he wrote ' impelled by the Holy Spirit '.[3] That is to say Luke's work was regarded by himself and by later Christians as a personal undertaking for which he took personal responsibility. Doubtless Luke himself, and certainly the author of the anti-Marcionite Prologue, believed that in taking this decision and carrying it out the Evangelist was guided by the Holy Spirit.

The upshot of the preceding discussion is that we should recognize in Luke-Acts the first conscious and deliberate attempt to write a History of Christianity, an attempt made by an individual on his own initiative, using materials collected by himself, intended for publication to the world outside the Church under the name and on the responsibility of the author. These conclusions are, in part at least, supported by the analysis of the documents themselves.

We may begin with the familiar and widely-accepted conclusions of synoptic criticism. First, that the Gospel of Luke incorporates a little over half of Mark ; from which it at once follows that Luke, *in its present form*, is later than Mark. Second, that when the Marcan matter is removed from Luke, we are left with a body of teaching and narrative, some of which corresponds to and is often in close verbal agreement with non-Marcan sections in Matthew. This non-Marcan matter common to Matthew and Luke is assigned to a hypothetical source Q. It is clear that we can confidently claim acquaintance with Q only at those points where Matthew and Luke coincide in their borrow-

to suggest that the Gospel and Acts were put together as a kind of brief for the defence of Paul in his trial at Rome. All that the preface says is that Luke, for reasons that seemed good to him, made up his mind to tell the world what he knew about the ministry of Jesus and the early years of the Church. Later in this lecture I suggest a possible reason why Luke made this decision.

    [2] *nomine suo ex opinione conscripsit*. The translation is Cadbury's. (*Beginnings*, ii. 211.)

    [3] προτραπεὶς ὑπὸ πνεύματος ἁγίου : Lat. *sancto instigatus spiritu.*

ings from it. Either may also have borrowed passages which the other has left untouched. In these cases we may suspect that a passage in Matthew or Luke is from Q ; but we cannot be sure. Again there may well have been sections of Q which neither Matthew nor Luke chose to incorporate. Here our ignorance is total. There may have been such passages. If there were, we know nothing about them ; and we do not even know whether such passages existed or not. My own attempts to reconstruct Q have led to the conclusion that there are in Luke some 222 verses, which I should assign confidently to that source, and another 24 which *may* have come from it.

If we remove the Q material as well as the Marcan, the remaining matter in Luke is peculiar to this gospel. It includes the stories of the birth of John the Baptist and Jesus, an account of an incident in the Temple when Jesus was twelve years old, a genealogy of Jesus different from that given in Matthew, and large body of stories and teachings from the Ministry and the Passion. The late Dr. Streeter formed a hypothesis to cover the data presented by the analysis of Luke into its components. He suggested that the first draft of the Gospel consisted of matter from Q and matter peculiar to Luke, without the Marcan extracts and without the Birth and Infancy narratives. This first draft, which Streeter called Proto-Luke, opened with the elaborate time-reference at the beginning of chapter iii. It consisted of narrative and teaching and made a document about the same size as Mark. It seems to me that Streeter was right in his main contention that the document Proto-Luke was a definite stage in the composition of our Luke and that the next step was the incorporation of extracts from Mark into Proto-Luke rather than the expansion of Mark by the insertion of Proto-Lukan material.

A question of some importance still remains. Granted that Proto-Luke had a separate existence, what was the manner of its existence ? Was it a heap of notes ; or a properly written account of the Ministry based on all the materials then available (viz. Q and L) ; or a definite first edition of the Gospel, not only written down but put into circulation ? The question was raised by Dr. Headlam,[1] who, rejecting the idea of two editions, suggested that ' St. Luke had probably collected much material and planned his work before he came in contact with St. Mark's Gospel, which he would not do until he reached Rome '. Streeter, in reply to this,[2] said :

> ' All I am concerned to argue is that Proto-Luke was, and was originally intended as, a complete Gospel ; but it is quite likely that it was only meant for what in modern phrase would be called " private circulation ".'

In considering this problem it is necessary to be clear about terms like ' edition ', ' circulation ', ' publication '. As I see it there were two kinds of Gospel-writing in the early Church. One sort of Gospel was produced primarily to meet the needs of the existing Christian community in a particular centre. It was composed for them and read to them or by them. If it later came to the knowledge of other Christian communities, that was something extra, which need not even have been foreseen when the work was done originally. I think that Q, Mark, Matthew (probably), and John (probably) were works of this sort. The second kind of Gospel, represented by Luke along with its continuation in Acts, was prepared for publication in our sense of the word, to instruct the outsider even more than to edify the Church member, though the latter aim is not excluded. As will appear later, I think that Luke-Acts was written and published by Luke to meet a particular emergency. But it is not necessary to suppose that Proto-Luke was either published in this sense (I don't believe it was) or even written with publication in this sense in view. It seems to me much more likely that Proto-Luke was written with the needs of the Christian communities in mind, though I do not think that it was written at the request of any particular congregation. The following hypothetical recon-struction of the history of Luke-Acts covers (I think) the data and contains (I hope) nothing incredible.

Credible tradition connects Luke with Antioch. It is prob-able, in my judgement, that the document Q and the earliest

---

[1] *Life and Teaching of Jesus Christ*, p. 20, n. 1.
[2] *The Four Gospels*, p. 221.

rendering of it into Greek also belong to Antioch.[1] Luke may well have possessed one of the earliest copies of Q in Greek. Now Q was essentially a manual of instruction for Church members ; and it seems to me that the process which produced Proto-Luke was first and foremost the effort of the working missionary Luke, the assistant of Paul, to make Q a still more comprehensive and effective manual of instruction. There were doubtless many opportunities for adding to Q, the greatest of all being the long stay in Caesarea when Paul was a prisoner there and Luke was in attendance on him. Later came the journey to Rome and a knowledge of the Roman Gospel of Mark. Mark had matter that was new to the author of Proto-Luke ; but it was not immediately necessary to appropriate any of it in a work of edification seeing that it was already available for that purpose in the Church. The advisability of adding Marcan material to Proto-Luke would only become apparent when the decision was taken by Luke to present to the non-Christian world a full-dress account of the Life of Jesus and the Beginnings of the Church. I think that the most obvious occasion for such a public defence of Christianity comes with the savage attack on the Church made by Nero in A.D. 64 and the Jewish war of A.D. 66-70. The publication of Luke-Acts could be placed at any time in this period of crisis (64-70) or in the years immediately following. Thus the process which begins with the possession of a copy of Q and ends with the publication of Luke-Acts may have occupied anything from fifteen to twenty-five years of Luke's life.

The fact that Luke borrowed rather more than half of Mark for his published Gospel provides us with an excellent test of his reliability as a transmitter of material which he collected. We can compare Mark with Mark-according-to-Luke, note, classify, and count up the editorial alterations,[2] and so reach conclusions which will be of help when we are dealing with other parts of the Gospel where the sources used have not survived in their original form. On the whole it may be said that the

---

[1] On Q see *The Mission and Message of Jesus*, pp. 307-312.
[2] This work has been admirably done by H. J. Cadbury, *The Style and Literary Method of Luke*, Pt. II, *The Treatment of Sources in the Gospel*.

examination tends to strengthen our confidence in Luke's faithfulness to his sources.[1]

Again the method by which he combines materials from different sources is helpful to the student. For he does not, as a rule, conflate different accounts of the same incident or saying. His way is to follow one source at a time ; and the result is that his Gospel is in the form of successive layers of material drawn from the different sources. In some places, the Passion Narrative for example, the layers are thinner and more closely packed than elsewhere ; but, generally speaking, the structure is the same throughout, and it is not difficult to split the layers apart. This means that we have, as Streeter saw, a reasonable probability that Luke preserves his sources in something like their original order. My own dealings with Q-according-to-Luke tend to raise that probability for me to something like certainty.

So much can be gathered about the Evangelist's method of work from the study of his Gospel. Something can also be learned about his motives and purposes.

In the first place we have adequate reason for holding to the tradition that the author of the Gospel and Acts was Luke the companion and assistant of Paul. That being so, we may expect that the missionary motive will be strong. Nobody in whom the missionary motive was not strong was likely to remain long in Paul's entourage. And it is the case that nowhere in the New Testament outside the Pauline Epistles, is the missionary interest so strong and obvious as it is in Luke and Acts. Mark depicts as objectively as possible the Messianic Ministry, letting the facts speak for themselves. Matthew shows us the Messiah as Founder of the Church, who by his life and teaching lays down the Rule of Faith and the Rule of Life for the community. The Gospel of John is written ' that ye may believe that Jesus is the Christ,

[1] See F. C. Burkitt in *Beginnings*, ii. 106-120 ; W. L. Knox, *Some Hellenistic Elements in Primitive Christianity*, p. 9 : ' In general . . . he shows a remarkable fidelity to his sources . . . (It) seems . . . that Luke was often content to copy out his sources faithfully and was a very slovenly corrector. . . . On the other hand, from time to time we find alterations in which Luke betrays himself by a use of Greek which shines like a good deed in a naughty world both in the Gospel and in the Acts.' My own impression is that Luke's alterations are largely attempts to improve the language and style of his sources, and that this revising activity is least in evidence where the words of Jesus are concerned.

the Son of God; and that believing ye may have life in his name': [1] its object is to lead Christians to a right theological interpretation of the fact of Jesus Christ. On Luke-Acts I think the just word was spoken by C. H. Turner: [2]

> 'The Gospel and Acts form two halves of a simple and connected scheme, and . . . in order to understand it we have only to attach to the two books some such labels as these: Λόγος α΄, "How Jesus the Christ preached the Good News to the Jews, and how after His Death and Resurrection He commissioned His Apostles to preach it to the Gentiles ": Λόγος β΄, "How they brought the Good News from Jerusalem to Rome ".'

This intense missionary interest is reflected in some of the characteristic features of the Gospel particularly in its universalism and its interest in the despised and outcast. Sayings, parables, and incidents are reported showing that the Gospel is for all and that it is offered first where the need is greatest. True, universalism and interest in the outcast and needy are not missing in the other gospels. Indeed, we have excellent reason for believing that they are an integral part of the Gospel in the mind of Jesus himself. But nowhere else are the points stressed and the examples multiplied as they are in Luke's work.

It is in Luke that the genealogy of Jesus is carried back beyond Abraham the father of Israel to Adam the father of mankind. It is in Luke that the infant Jesus is hailed as 'a light to lighten the Gentiles'. It is in Luke that the first recorded sermon of the Galilean Ministry speaks of divine blessings conferred on a Sidonian widow and a Syrian soldier. The disciples are the light of the world: [3] it is Luke who sees the function of the light as that of guiding people outside into the house, whereas Matthew sees it as that of giving illumination to those who are already in. In Luke's account of the Resurrection appearances of Jesus, a Christian mission to all nations starting from Jerusalem is declared to be part and parcel of the Divine purpose foreshadowed

---

[1] John, xx. 31.
[2] *The Study of the New Testament 1883 and 1920*, p. 30.
[3] Luke xi. 33, compared with Matt. v. 15.

in the Scriptures and brought to fulfilment in the Ministry of
Jesus and his followers.[1]

Again it is Luke who embodies in his Gospel a whole series of
teachings, parables, and stories, which I have called ' The Gospel
of the Outcast '. I venture to repeat here part of what I wrote
about it in *The Mission and Message of Jesus* (p. 574) :

' The L material in chapters xv-xix might be called in a
special sense the Gospel of the Outcast. There is in this section
a great concentration of teaching, chiefly in the form of parables,
whose purpose is primarily to demonstrate God's care for those
whom men despise and condemn. This appears very clearly
in the three parables which together make up chap. xv, in the
parables of the Poor Widow (xviii. 1-8) and the Pharisee and the
Publican (xviii. 9-14), and in the story of Zacchaeus (xix. 1-10).
This divine love for the unloved and unlovable is, indirectly,
the condemnation of the harsh and censorious attitude taken
towards these unfortunates by more righteous folk. That the
righteous fail from lack of kindness and human sympathy, and
spoil themselves by pride, is one of the lessons of such passages
as Luke xvi. 1-8, 14 f., 19-31 ; xviii. 9-14. Again it is taught
that even from the most unpromising people there can be a
genuine response to kindness and understanding (xvii. 11-19 ;
xix. 1-10). In Luke's arrangement this mass of material leads
up to the account of Passion Week : it is as though the whole
of Luke from chap. xv. onwards were written to illustrate the
Pauline text, " God commendeth his own love toward us, in that,
while we were yet sinners, Christ died for us ".'

A third point which deserves to be noticed is the extent to
which Luke's editorial activities serve the purpose of ' putting the
Gospel across ' to the Graeco-Roman world. In a most interesting and instructive study [2] recently published Canon W. L.
Knox makes a great deal of the missionary motive as a factor in
the Hellenization of the Gospel. ' The Gospel must be preached
to all the world ; it had therefore to be translated into the
Greek language and accommodated to the general theological

---

[1] Lk. xxiv. 47.

[2] *Some Hellenistic Elements in Primitive Christianity*—the Schweich Lectures
for 1942.

F

conceptions of the hellenistic world, and worked out into a coherent scheme of thought '.[1]

Alongside the missionary motive and equal to it in importance is the apologetic interest. Luke-Acts is the first publication in defence of Christianity against suspicion, misunderstanding, and misrepresentation. The defence makes two principal points.

The first is that the Christian community is not to be associated with the contemporary Jewish community. All the Gospels have something to say about the incompatibility between Jesus and his people, between his Messianic hope and theirs. The opposition was a fact and Jesus himself was well aware of it and spoke of it. But none of the Evangelists gives it the prominence that Luke gives it : none produces so many instances of Jewish neglect, ingratitude, and hostility. It is Luke who, in his version of the parable of the servants left in charge of their master's property, provides the additional detail that the master was claiming a throne and that his prospective subjects rejected his claim.[2] It is Luke who records the bitter saying that Jerusalem must not be deprived of her rights in the matter of murdering prophets.[3] It is Luke who records the enigmatic conversation about the swords,[4] which, whatever else it means, certainly presupposes bitter hostility between the Disciples and their fellow-countrymen. It is Luke who shows us Jesus weeping over a Jersualem that would make no effective response to his appeals.[5] It is Luke who records the healing of ten lepers of whom only one, and he a Samaritan, returned to say Thank you.[6] In the story of the Passion it is Luke who tells us of the contemptuous dismissal of Jesus by Herod Antipas,[7] and takes great pains to show that the condemnation by Pilate was forced from him by the violence and clamour of the Jewish mob.[8] On the other side, it is Luke who gives us the picture of Jewish mourners as Jesus goes on the way to execution ;[9] but even here it is only the women who show sympathy. The story of hostility is continued in Acts in a long series of incidents both in Palestine and

---

[1] *Op. cit.*, p. 1.
[2] Lk. xix. 12-15a, 27 (L).
[3] Lk. xiii. 31-33 (L), 34f. (Q).
[4] Lk. xxii. 35-38 (L).
[5] Lk. xix. 41-44 (L).
[6] Lk. xvii. 11-19 (L).
[7] Lk. xxiii. 6-12 (L).
[8] Lk. xxiii. 18-23 (L).
[9] Lk. xxiii. 27-31 (L).

in the synagogues of the Disperson. From beginning to end Luke-Acts is out to show the width and depth of the breach between Jesus and his Jewish contemporaries, between the Synagogue and the Church.

There are two things to be said about this. The first is that it is reported because it was fact, and a very important fact in the story of the Ministry of Jesus and the Early Church. The second point is that we must ask ourselves why Luke not only reports the fact but underlines it, continually reminding the reader that the Church has nothing to do with contemporary Judaism for the simple and conclusive reason that contemporary Judaism will have nothing to do with the Church, rejecting the Gospel of Jesus the Messiah just as it had rejected Jesus the Messiah himself and compassed his death at the hands of Pilate. And it is to be noted that Luke is no Marcionite before Marcion. He sets forth Jesus as the fulfilment of all the Divine promises in the Old Testament. The breach is not between the Old Covenant and the New but between Jesus and his Church on the one side and first-century Judaism and the Jewish Community on the other. This breach was a fact. At what time or times was it important to impress the fact upon the Imperial Government and the Graeco-Roman public ? To put this question in this way is to get a clue to the date of Luke-Acts.

The matter can be put in this way. In the early days of the Church there were strong inducements to maintain a connexion with official Judaism and indeed to incorporate all converts into the Jewish nation. For the Jewish nation occupied a privileged position in the Roman Empire so far as religion was concerned ; and the privilege enjoyed by the nation as a whole could be claimed by any local Jewish community.[1] It is probable that the strong desire of a large section of the Early Church to hold on to their Jewish affiliation was not unconnected with the wish to have the status of a *religio licita*. At the same time there is a certain amount of evidence that some members of the early Church cherished the hope of the return of Jesus in glory in a form that differed little if at all from current Jewish Messianic hopes. It is likely enough that the two groups coincided or overlapped,

[1] See Juster, *Les Juifs dans l'Empire Romain*, i. 246, 422, n. 8 ; Tertullian *Apol.*, xxi. 1.

that a desire to remain affiliated to Judaism and a cherishing of the hope of the Parousia in Jewish Messianic form went together. The position was never easy to maintain : it was assailed from both sides—by the orthodox Judaism of the Synagogue and the radical Christianity of Paul. But it seems to have survived until the Jewish War of A.D. 66-70 killed it.

I venture to think that it was that disastrous revolt against the Empire that made it important to say to the Roman Government and people : ' Not only have we no share in this enterprise ; we are not a part of the Jewish community at all. Long ago the Jews rejected Jesus, and the synagogue has been doing its best ever since to be rid of his followers. Our Founder was accused of seditious activities against the Empire ; but the Procurator declared the charge to be unfounded.[1] Our leading missionaries have been examined by Roman magistrates and whenever the hearing has been before a man of courage and independence of mind, it has been made clear that the Christians harbour no designs against the peace and security of the Empire. It is true that we speak of a ' kingdom of God ' and a Messiah, just as the Jews do ; but our Messiah is no rebel against Rome, and the kingdom of God that we preach is a spiritual kingdom. So far as the Empire is concerned, Christianity is politically innocuous.' Something like that Luke-Acts is trying to say.

In the seventies of the first century it might well have seemed an urgent task to clear the Church of any suspicion of being mixed up with the rebellious Jews. I doubt whether a like urgency would be felt again before the later years of Domitian's reign in the nineties. But by that time the collection of the Pauline letters was going ahead, as we can see from *I Clement* ; and there is nothing in Acts to incline us to the belief that its author had access to those documents, all or any of them. I venture to think that this practically certain ignorance of the Pauline epistles is a stronger argument against the later date than a problematical acquaintance with the *Antiquities* of Josephus can be for it.[2]

[1] Lk. xxiii. 2-5.
[2] This paragraph and part of that which follows are taken from my Presidential Address to the Oxford Society for Historical Theology. The Address is printed in the *Proceedings* of the Society for 1941-42, and I am grateful for permission to make use of these paragraphs here.

Suppose then that Luke, in the seventies of the first century, sits down to write a history of the Christian movement. Suppose that the tradition is true and that the work is being done somewhere in the province of Achaea. What helps are available for the work and what hindrances stand in the way at this *early* date? For his account of the life and teaching of Jesus he has his own copy of Q enriched by all the additional material collected during a quarter of a century of Christian work. He has the Roman Gospel of Mark, which, if my dating is correct, was already in existence when Luke came to Rome with Paul. He has some other pieces of narrative dealing with the birth of John the Baptist and Jesus and the childhood of the latter, and a genealogy of Jesus. The materials are not very abundant, and, because of the way in which they were collected, there is no guarantee that they are in chronological order.

That brings us to a great handicap under which Luke had to labour. Not only were his materials scanty: it was also very difficult—indeed almost impossible—even at this relatively early date, to supplement them or to obtain clarification where the data were confused or inconsistent with one another. For example, Mark gave an account of the conversation between Jesus and the Jewish lawyer about the greatest commandment in the Law.[1] Here Jesus himself gives the answer to the question. But Luke's note-book contained an independent account [2] of a conversation on this subject, only in this case the answer is supplied by the lawyer. What is the evangelist to do? Treat them as separate incidents and record both? Or take them as variant accounts of one and the same incident and then decide which is the more accurate? But in that case how is the decision to be made? The witnesses who might settle the point are no longer available. Some of the original Disciples are dead. Jerusalem is destroyed and the remnants of the Mother-Church of Primitive Christendom are beyond Jordan at Pella in the Decapolis. The only kind of research that could be of any use to the Evangelist would involve long journeys for himself or his messengers and inevitable delay in the completion of the work; and I think we have good reason to suppose that Luke thought his task urgent.

[1] Mk. xii. 28-34.   [2] Lk. x. 25-28.

In the particular case we are considering he preferred the version of the Great Commandment conversation which he had in his own note-book to that offered by Mark. We don't know on what grounds : we may suppose that he just relied on his own judgement. In some such way Luke's Gospel and the Acts got written, the author doing his best with the materials at his disposal. And—this is the point—even as early as the seventies it is doubtful whether anything much better could have been done.

It seems to me that somewhere about A.D. 65 there is a dividing line. Before that date it was comparatively easy to pick up first-hand information about the Ministry of Jesus and the early history of the Church, particularly if the enquirer could go to Palestine and conduct his researches on the spot. Afterwards the difficulties increased very rapidly, and after A.D. 70 they were almost insuperable.

There are two matters bearing on the date of Luke's work that ought to be considered before we leave the subject. They are the abrupt ending of Acts and the alleged dependence of Luke on the *Antiquities* of Josephus. If the latter point were established it would compel us to put the composition of Acts in the last years of the first century. The essential facts are stated clearly and fairly in *The Beginnings of Christianity*, ii. 355-358. The strongest statement of the case for Luke's dependence on Josephus is that of F. C. Burkitt in his book *The Gospel History and its Transmission*, pp. 105-110. On the other side Eduard Meyer [1] found the arguments completely unconvincing. The verdict of the editors of *The Beginnings of Christianity* and Professor Cadbury is that 'the case (for dependence) will always rest on three passages, and it is safe to say that they can never be completely explained away, yet will never convince every one'.[2] I must confess that they do not convince me.[3]

---

[1] *Ursprung und Anfänge des Christentums*, i. 47 ff. ; ii. 404 f. ; iii. 11.

[2] *Beginnings*, ii. 356.

[3] I give my reasons in barest outline. (1) Of the three cases of alleged dependence, only the first need be taken seriously. This is Acts v. 36 f., where Gamaliel is made to refer to the Jewish uprisings led by Theudas (during the procuratorship of Fadus, c. A.D. 44-46) and Judas the Galilean (in the days of the census under Quirinius, c. A.D. 6) in this order. (2) It is clear that, at the time

The ending of Acts has given rise to much debate. The
essence of the matter is simply this, that the whole course of the
narrative of Acts from the moment when Paul sets out on the last
journey to Jerusalem seems to be leading up to the grand climax
of the trial of Paul in the Imperial Court at Rome. The reader
is prepared by full accounts of the proceedings in the courts
below for the final scene in which Paul will give his testimony
before the supreme tribunal of the Empire and achieve either a
triumphant acquittal or a glorious martyrdom. But the climax
never comes. We are left with a picture of Paul waiting for his

when Gamaliel is supposed to have spoken, the revolt of Theudas was still in the
future ; I should say more than ten years in the future. It follows that this is a
case where Luke has put into the mouth of the speaker sentiments which he
considered suitable. He is therefore presenting cases of fruitless rebellion of
which he had heard. (3) His first example, Theudas, is introduced by the words
πρὸ γὰρ τούτων τῶν ἡμερῶν. This expression occurs again in xxi. 38, where
it evidently refers to an event in the very recent past. It is arguable that that
should be the meaning here, that Luke knew that the Theudas revolt had taken
place somewhere in the period covered by Acts i.-xii, and mistakenly thought it
came before the date of Gamaliel's ' speech ' rather than afterwards. We should
then take πρὸ τούτων τῶν ἡμερῶν to mean ' in the recent past '. That involves
a reconsideration of the μετὰ τοῦτον which introduces Judas the Galilean. If the
argument so far is sound μετὰ cannot here mean ' after ', for Luke must have
known that the Judas who raised a revolt in the days of the census could not be
' after ' the Theudas who revolted recently. But μετὰ c. acc. pers. can mean
' besides ', ' in addition to ' (Moulton and Milligan, Vocab. s.v.). I suggest that
the μετὰ here means to say, ' my next example is . . . '.   (4) But even if this be
rejected, there are insuperable difficulties in supposing that Luke constructed
Acts, v. 36 f. out of the data supplied by Josephus in Ant. xx. For (a) Josephus
says that the revolt of Theudas took place when Fadus was procurator. (b) Josephus
does not say that the revolt of Judas took place after that of Theudas ; but that
the execution of two sons of Judas occurred during the procuratorship of Tiberius
Alexander the successor of Fadus. (c) Both Josephus and Luke state explicitly
that the revolt of Judas took place at the time of the census. By that Josephus
means the census of c. A.D. 6, made during the procuratorship of Coponius the
first procurator of Judaea. Luke evidently thinks—rightly or wrongly—of an
earlier census taken while Herod the Great was still on the throne. In either case
there was no procurator before the procurator of the census of A.D. 6. And in
either case it is incredible that Luke should have supposed that the Theudas
revolt in the procuratorship of Fadus took place before the census, that is, before
there was any procurator of Judaea at all. (d) In a word, the theory requires us
to suppose that Acts v. 36 f., is based on Josephus : I cannot see how any intelligent person could possibly produce Acts, v. 36 f., as it is usually interpreted,
out of the passage in Josephus. If that is so, we are driven back to the alternative
suggested in (3).

case to be called, carrying on missionary work in Rome while he waits ; and the story just peters out. Various explanations have been proposed : an excellent summary of them is given at the end of Lake and Cadbury's commentary on Acts.[1] In many ways the most attractive solution is that defended by Lake [2] and Ramsay,[3] that the trial itself petered out because no one appeared from Jerusalem to prosecute within the period—whatever it was : two years or eighteen months—during which an appearance could be put in. If this is the right answer, it explains why there is no triumphant acquittal or glorious martyrdom for Paul. It just did not happen in that way.

But if we accept this solution, certain consequences follow. The first is the release of Paul ; and the question at once arises, what did Paul do next ? To this question varied answers are supplied directly or indirectly by the Pastoral Epistles, the apocryphal *Acts of Paul*, the *Muratorian Canon*, the Vercelli *Acts of Peter*, and *I Clement*. The Pastorals imply activity in various parts of the Mediterranean area, the *Acta Pauli* [4] seem to describe what might be called the ' Fourth Missionary Journey ' covering the ground from Damascus to Rome and ending in martyrdom. The *Muratorian Canon* and the Vercelli *Acts of Peter* both send Paul off to Spain in fulfilment of the plan mentioned in Rom. xv. 22-29, and *I Clement* also is widely believed to imply the journey to Spain.[5] This is not the place to enter into a discussion of the value of these different stories ; and indeed, competent scholars differ widely in their estimates. The main point is that while the stories differ as to how the Apostle spent his time after the two years in Rome, with which Acts closes, they all assume that he had some time to spend. That is to say,

[1] *Beginnings*, iv. 349 f. This should be supplemented by the further discussion by Cadbury, *Beginnings*, v. 326-338.

[2] *Theologisch Tijdschrift*, xlvii. (1913), pp. 356 ff, repeated with additional matter in *Beginnings*, v. 326-338.

[3] *Expositor*, March 1913, pp. 264-284 ; *Teaching of Paul in Terms of the Present Day*, 346-382.

[4] I cannot think that the *Acta Pauli* are meant to describe anything but the period between the end of Acts and the death of Paul.

[5] The case against this interpretation of the τέρμα τῆς δύσεως in *I Clem.* v. is most strongly argued by P. N. Harrison, *The Problem of the Pastoral Epistles*, 107 f.

there was, by the end of the first century or early in the second a fairly widespread tradition that the Roman captivity of Acts did not end with an execution.

Luke is silent about all this, and we may make conjectures about the cause of the silence. They will be no more than guesses. I am not prepared to engage in conjecture on any large scale ; but I will venture the surmise that Luke tells no more because he knew no more. It may be the case that at some time during the two years in Rome, or at the end of it, Luke was sent back to Greece and so lost sight of any subsequent activities of Paul. This would not be at all surprising when we consider how little Luke has to say about Paul's doings when they were separated at earlier times in the missionary career of the Apostle. If Paul was released and set out on new adventures, and Luke was where tradition says he was, in Achaea, it is quite possible that he did not hear what Paul was doing or where he went. And Luke does not use his imagination to fill up gaps in his information. There is, however, one event that would probably not have escaped the notice of Luke, wherever he might be : that is the martyrdom of Paul. The fact that Luke has nothing to say about it, supposing that it occurred anywhere near the dates usually given for it, is very difficult to explain ; so difficult as to call for a reconsideration of the traditions which are held to testify to it. But this is not the place to begin that enquiry.

To conclude, the internal and external data seem to me to be satisfied if Luke-Acts was the work of Luke, the companion of Paul, written in Achaea round about A.D. 70 as a public defence of the Christian Church against the suspicion of being mixed up with the rebellious Jews, and a public assurance that the Christian Gospel was no seditious propaganda but a message of universal peace and goodwill.

5.

THE GOSPEL ACCORDING TO ST. MATTHEW.
(1946)

THE Gospels of Matthew and John present the most formidable difficulties to the student of early Christian literary history. The present paper will attempt to deal with some of the problems concerning the origin and dissemination of the Gospel according to Matthew.* It may be salutary to begin by surveying the difficulties that have to be met. First is the fact that some sources of early information, which were available for the study of Lukan origins, are not at our disposal for Mt. The *Muratorian Canon* undoubtedly had something to say about this Gospel; but the relevant part of the document has unfortunately been lost. Again the *Anti-Marcionite Prologues* to the Gospels fail us for Mt. Our earliest information comes from Papias, Irenaeus, Clement of Alexandria and Tertullian. Our second difficulty arises from the existence, in the Eastern part of the early Christian world, of a Gospel or Gospels in ' Hebrew ', appearing under a variety of designations and used by a variety of people, and related in some way to Mt. The surviving fragments are more astonishing than edifying; and patristic statements about the Semitic Gospel or Gospels are extremely confused and bewildering. The third difficulty arises out of the other two. It is that our earliest traditions about Mt. speak of a composition by Matthew in ' Hebrew '; the Fathers tend to identify this ' Hebrew ' original of Mt. with one or other of the ' Hebrew ' Gospels circulating in the East;

---

* Hereinafter Mt. = the Gospel, Matthew = the Evangelist. Both names are used as labels, without prejudice to the question whether they are, in fact, the right labels.

and yet our Gospel according to Matthew is quite clearly a Greek document, made up from Greek sources, of which our Greek Mk. is one. These are the problems we have to face : we may begin by marshalling the scanty evidence from early patristic sources.

I. Traditions Regarding Mt.

Here pride of place belongs to Papias, who has already appeared as the transmitter of earlier tradition regarding the work of Mark. He has a single brief statement about the activities of Matthew. It is as follows :—

Ματθαῖος μὲν οὖν Ἑβραΐδι διαλέκτῳ τὰ λόγια συνετάξατο, ἡρμήνευσεν δ' αὐτὰ ὡς ἦν δυνατὸς ἕκαστος.[1]

' So then, Matthew compiled the oracles in the Hebrew language ; but everyone interpreted them as he was able .'

This sentence has been as widely discussed as almost any in the literature of the early Church. The main points are : (1) whether it merely represents the views of Papias himself or is an earlier tradition handed on by him ; (2) whether it refers to Mt. (as we know it and also in an earlier Semitic form), or, as many scholars from Schleiermacher to Eduard Meyer have held, to the Synoptic source Q, or to some other document. As these points are of vital importance I propose to examine some recent discussions of them.

The works with which I am particularly concerned are *Studies in Matthew* by the late Prof. Bacon, and a pamphlet entitled *The Logia in Ancient and Recent Literature*, by the late Fr. John Donovan. These two writers are agreed on one point—though they differ on almost every other—namely that τὰ λόγια in the Papias fragment meant the Gospel of Matthew and nothing else. Bacon, however, regards the fragment as the composition of Papias himself ; Donovan thinks (p. 33) that it came to him from John the Elder. Bacon regards the fragment as worthless : Donovan regards it as early and valuable evidence. Bacon tries to explain the choice of the odd

[1] Papias *ap.* Eus. *HE.* iii. 39. 16.

name τὰ λόγια for the Gospel by saying that it is a description
of the Gospel in terms of what were for Papias its most important
contents, i.e. the five great discourses incorporated in it.
Donovan on the other hand maintains that Papias or rather his
source called the Gospel τὰ λόγια because that was what τὰ λόγια
meant. Bacon—on his view of the matter—has to furnish some
explanation of the way in which Papias arrived at the curious
conclusions embodied in the fragment : Donovan is not under
that necessity.

It will be obvious that the point on which everything turns
is that of the meaning of the words τὰ λόγια ; but before attempting to deal with that question, I may indicate the points
on which I am inclined to agree with the adversary. I should
think it probable that Papias himself, at the time when he wrote
the words, understood them to refer to the Gospel. Further
I should agree with Donovan against Bacon that the fragment
on Mt. is tradition derived by Papias from the Elder John—
or some similar source.

It has been argued that there is nothing in Eusebius to
indicate that the Mt. fragment is traditional material : and it
is true that Eusebius does not expressly describe it as such.
But there is a certain amount of indirect evidence. There is
first the evidence of Papias himself, quoted by Eusebius in
HE. iii. 39. 3 f., that he set great store by what was handed down
from earlier times and took great pains to acquire such traditional
material wherever he could. Second, and even more important,
is Eusebius' own estimate of Papias given in this same chapter
(§ 13) : ' For he evidently was a man of exceedingly small intelligence, as one might say judging from his discourses ' (Lawlor
and Oulton's translation). Is it likely that Eusebius would have
troubled to quote the private opinion of a man, whom he rated
as low as this, on a point of such importance ? It seems to me
that the probabilities are against it and that we are justified in
supposing that Eusebius regarded this fragment as a piece of
earlier tradition preserved by Papias. He may have been mis-
taken about that, but that is another question.

If this inference is correct, it cuts at the roots of Bacon's
view that Papias' account is Papias' own composition made up

from what he could infer from having in his hands a copy of
Matthew's Gospel with the superscribed name of the supposed
author. But we must nevertheless examine the process by which
Papias is supposed to have reached his conclusion about the
Gospel a little more closely.

'Matthew compiled the oracles.' The Gospel purports to
be by Matthew. True it contains much more than oracles ;
but then 'the oracles ' is not the title of the book but a description
of it in terms of its contents, and not the whole contents, but
only those things in which Papias was specially interested—the
five great discourses compiled out of separate oracles of the
Lord.

'In the Hebrew tongue' is a simple inference. Papias
knew that Jesus and the Apostles spoke not Greek but Aramaic
(= Hebrew). Hence the Greek Gospel must first of all have
been written in the native language of the Apostle.

'Every one translated as he was able.' We know that in
bilingual countries the practice obtained in public worship of
reading Scripture in the original and then giving a rendering
in the vernacular. Papias probably knew this too and used the
fact to account for the appearance of Mt. in a Greek dress.
But if this is so, we should have expected the imperfect instead
of the aorist, to describe what was a regular practice in bilingual
churches. The statement of Papias does not read like an attempt
to explain how Greek Mt. arose out of a process of casual tar-
guming, but like an attempt on somebody's part to explain
the existence of differing Greek versions of an original Aramaic
document.

The upshot is that the testimony of Papias to Matthew's
Gospel is pure guesswork and—on Bacon's view—his guesses
are all wrong. The only thing that can be safely inferred is—
I suppose—that at the time when Papias wrote, the superscription
κατὰ Ματθαῖον was already part of the text of Mt.

At this point the question arises again : suppose that Papias
is not freely composing, but reporting something from older
tradition. What then ? *Must* we accept an interpretation of
the tradition—even so ingenious an interpretation as Bacon's—
when all that it does is to make nonsense of our earliest bit of

external evidence ? Would it not be worth while to look again
and see whether the tradition does not fit the document Q,
seeing that it will not fit the Gospel of Matthew. Suppose that
what happened was not that Papias made a faulty analysis of
the contents of Mt. and then wrote a misleading label and stuck
it on the bottle, but that he found a label from another bottle
and stuck it on to the Matthew bottle.

This seems to be the reasonable thing to do ; but just at
this point Donovan enters his protest. For the thesis of his
pamphlet is that the words of Papias must refer to the Gospel
of Matthew and nothing else *because that is what* τὰ λόγια *means.*
He proposes to show that from the time of the LXX translation
to the days of Papias and long after τὰ λόγια does not mean what
we should naturally suppose it to mean, but something else.
' The oracles ' is not the right translation. What the right
translation is varies from place to place, and here in Papias it
means ' the Gospel '. It is necessary, therefore, to dispose of
this point before we can proceed further.

The task is complicated by the fact that while we are no longer
allowed to translate τὰ λόγια by ' the oracles ', it is not made
clear what we are to say instead in the numerous places where
τὰ λόγια occurs. Thus (p. 10) Donovan says, ' After perusal
of the various passages where λόγια τοῦ θεοῦ or λόγια τοῦ κυρίου
occurs in the O.T., it may be definitely stated that this expression conveys the idea which to us is familiar under the name
of " Inspired Word " or " Divine Revelation " '. ' In Philo, as
in Josephus, λόγια τοῦ θεοῦ is the virtual equivalent of our
" Scripture ".' In Rom. iii. 2, ἐπιστεύθησαν τὰ λόγια τοῦ θεοῦ,
' the Apostle is merely proclaiming the historical fact that the
Jews held the custody of the Old Testament ' (p. 11). In Acts
vii. 38 (Stephen's speech) ' λόγια ζῶντα is manifestly used to
signify the revelation made directly to Moses. It is here, as
elsewhere equivalently " the Inspired Word " and inferentially
the Scripture, in which that revelation is recorded ' (p. 13).

There are two remarks to be made at once on this new interpretation : (i) It is surely very odd that the word λόγια, which
proclaims in every letter that it is concerned with the verb

meaning ' to speak ', should come to mean primarily that which is written, especially when there is such a word as γραφή lying ready to hand.

(ii) It is noteworthy that in order to carry out this interpretation the meaning of τὰ λόγια has to be generalised into something like ' Scripture '. How we are to get back again to a particular book of Scripture, which is what is required for the Papias passage, is not so clear. But these are merely general objections ; and it is in the examination of the particular bits of evidence that this theory reveals its insufficiency. I therefore go on at once to state the results of an independent examination of the evidence.[1]

(1) LXX and other Greek versions of the O.T.

Here it is possible to distinguish four meanings of the word λόγιον or the plural λόγια :—

(a) Direct oracular communications of God to man or prophetic oracles (6 cases).

(b) Divine commands or precepts (13 cases).

(c) Divine promises (16 cases).

(d) Human utterance in worship (1 case).

In 7 cases the text is corrupt and nothing definite can be determined. In no case is it possible to get away from the idea of utterance. With the single exception—Ps. xviii. (xix). 14, where the meaning is human speech in worship as distinguished from meditation in the heart—all the cases considered, where the text is reliable, clearly indicate that it is God's utterance that is meant, either directly to a prophet (once to a patriarch) or through such a medium to his people in commands and promises. That these utterances of Jehovah may be written down is not disputed, but that is nothing to do with the case. What is meant by the word is not Scripture but some things which are contained, along with other things, in Scripture, the things, namely, that God has said for the guidance or encouragement of Israel.

(2) Donovan asserts (p. 10) that ' In Philo, as in Josephus, λόγια τοῦ θεοῦ is the virtual equivalent of our " Scripture ". For them it is θεία γραφή, nothing less than the Sacred Written

---

[1] The evidence is set out in the Appendix at the end of this article.

Word. It is unnecessary to quote examples, as the deduction drawn cannot be contested.' One wonders how one ought to translate such a passage as this from the *Contemplative Life* (ed. Conybeare, p. 61), νόμους καὶ λόγια θεσπισθέντα διὰ προφ- ήτων καὶ ὕμνους. Further, according to Schlatter (*Die Theologie des Judentums*, p. 66). λόγιον is the regular word in Josephus for a prophetic utterance foretelling something.

(3) Really detailed discussion of texts by Donovan begins with the four passages in the N.T. where the word occurs. In each of these a better and more natural interpretation is obtained by sticking to the sense or senses of λόγια found in the LXX than by following Donovan. When ' Scripture ' or an equivocal term like ' Revelation ' is substituted the passages do not become clearer but more obscure. I take a single example. In Rom. iii. 2, Paul is trying to answer the question what advantage the Jew has over other people, and he begins thus : πρῶτον μὲν ὅτι ἐπιστεύθησαν τὰ λόγια τοῦ θεοῦ. Donovan (p. 11) says : ' Here the Apostle is merely proclaiming the historical fact that the Jews had held the custody of the Old Testament. To them had been confided the Revelation of the Old Law, with guardian- ship of the Sacred Books.' Here the second sentence with its ambiguous word ' Revelation ' rather fogs the clear impression produced by the first sentence. But if we take the meaning to be that the Jews had held the custody of the Sacred Books, how are we to interpret what Paul goes on immediately to ask ? ' Even supposing some of them have proved untrustworthy is their faithlessness to cancel the faithfulness of God ? ' (Moffatt). What meaning can we assign to faithlessness in the custody of the O.T. ? They had not lost or sold or otherwise made away with the Sacred Books.

We can find a perfectly good and satisfying meaning if we take τὰ λόγια τοῦ θεοῦ in the sense that is given in the LXX. There the primary meaning is oracles of God given to prophets ; and these oracles can be subdivided into commandments and promises. Then the faithlessness of the Jews is their disobedience to God's commands ; and the faithfulness of God is the fact that he will not go back on his promises. These commands and promises together make up the terms of the Covenant between

God and Israel : and Paul's point is that though Israel has broken the Covenant God still upholds it.

(4) When we turn from the New Testament to the Apostolic Fathers we find that the interpretation of λόγια established for the LXX and found to fit the N.T. passages answers equally well in the four passages in *I. Clem.*, one in *II Clem.*, and one in Polycarp. The same applies to the three examples in Justin Martyr. It would be wearisome to go through them all in detail : the conclusion which I should draw from my observations in these passages is somewhat as follows.

Λόγιον means in the first instance a divine revelation by way of a spoken word—normally the recipient of the λόγιον is a prophet and the process of revelation is audition in contrast to vision. The plural τὰ λόγια indicates a collection of such utterances. It does not mean Scripture as a whole or even a book of Scripture. It means a group of quite definite recognisable things which may be found in certain parts of Scripture. When Philo speaks of τὸ τελευταῖον τῶν δέκα λογίων, he does not mean by τῶν δέκα λογίων 10 Bibles or 10 Biblical books but 10 sentences known to us as the Ten Commandments. The passage already quoted from the *Contemplative Life* makes it clear where the λόγια are chiefly to be found in the O.T.—in the prophetic books. The usage of the LXX shows that the content of the λόγια can be summed up under two heads—commandments and promises of God. And it can fairly be claimed that this definition of λόγια in terms of form and content gives a perfectly good sense when applied to the passages in the N.T. and earliest Christian literature, where the word is used. When, therefore, Papias or his informant says that Matthew compiled τὰ λόγια, the simplest and most natural meaning to be given to the words is that Matthew made a collection of oracles, i.e. sayings analogous to those of the old prophets, uttered by divine inspiration and containing the commandments and promises of God for the new Israel, the Church of Christ.

' Matthew compiled τὰ λόγια in the Hebrew tongue and every man translated them as he was able.' This brief sentence makes four separate assertions :—

G

(a) That a book of λόγια was composed.

(b) That it was composed in the Hebrew tongue (i.e. probably in the spoken language of the Palestinian Jews—at that time = Aramaic. Parallels to this use of ' Hebrew ' where ' Aramaic ' is meant in Dalman, *Gramm.*, § 1.)

(c) That the composer of this work was named Matthew— presumably the Apostle.

(d) That various people translated it as best they could— doubtless into Greek.

If we try applying these propositions to the Gospel of Matthew we find that they do not fit. As applied to Mt. (a) and (d) are, I think, demonstrably false. One of the really assured results of Synoptic criticism seems to be the priority of Mk. : and, if that is so, Mt. becomes a Greek document from the first and not an Aramaic composition subsequently translated into Greek. It is true that Prof. Torrey in his book, *The Four Gospels*, maintains the view that Mt. is a translation from Aramaic ; but even he has to make allowance for the results of synoptic study by the hypothesis that ' each of the translators, Mt. and Lk., adopts the Greek wording of his predecessor, *wherever a faithful use of his source permits him to do so* ' (p. 275). This would imply that the translator of Mt. had before him, not only the Aramaic original of this Gospel but also the Greek version of Mk. ; while Luke, who on Torrey's reconstruction both composed and translated his Gospel, had his own Aramaic original, the Greek version of Mk. and the Greek version of Mt. This seems rather too elaborate to be plausible. Further it is worth noting that among the evidences of translation from Aramaic which Torrey finds in Mt., the most convincing in Marcan contexts are already to be found in Mk. That is to say they are not really evidence for an Aramaic original of Mt. in those sections at all. More than that : where Matthew does not reproduce Mk.'s supposed mis-rendering of a Semitic original, what he does give looks very like a conjectural improvement on Mark's Greek rather than a correction of it from the Aramaic original. A good example of this is Mk. xiv. 72 = Mt. xxvi. 75. Mk. has καὶ ἐπιβαλὼν ἔκλαιεν. ἐπιβαλών has always been a problem. Torrey says it is a literal but unidiomatic rendering of an

Aramaic original which meant ' as he thought upon it '—i.e. his denial of the Lord. But Mt. has neither ἐπιβαλών nor anything representing the supposed Aramaic behind ' as he thought upon it '. He has ἐξελθών.

In general it may be said that the notes to Torrey's translation do not prove Aramaic originals for Mt. and Lk. At most they make a case for Aramaic sources behind those Gospels and possibly behind Mk. and Jn. also. Mt. remains a Greek work compiled most probably from Greek sources—of which Mk. in Greek was one. These sources may quite well go back to more primitive Aramaic documents of which they are translations. That the Gospel of Mt. ever existed *as a whole* in Aramaic I do not believe.

That Mt. consists of λόγια is not correct if we take λόγια in the plain and natural sense. It contains λόγια : indeed, it contains five considerable collections of λόγια ; but it is not itself τὰ λόγια. It is a book made up partly of collections of λόγια and partly of narrative.

Finally the statement that Mt. as we know it was the work of Matthew the Apostle is, to say the least, improbable.

Suppose then, seeing that the identification of τὰ λόγια with Mt. breaks down, we try again with the other way and see whether the four statements of Papias will fit Q.

(a) There was a compilation of the Oracles. This as applied to Q is absolutely correct. Q is a compilation of oracles—sayings of Jesus and nothing else, except a few similar oracles of John the Baptist, and a line or two of narrative in the Temptation story. But it may be objected that Q did contain narrative : that the story of the Centurion's servant stood in the document, and that some at least of the Q sayings have narrative settings. The answer is that there is no evidence that the story of the Centurion's servant stood in Q at all. What did stand there was the account of a conversation between Jesus and a Centurion, the point of which was the saying of Jesus, ' I have not found such faith—no, not in Israel '. Nor is there any evidence that the narrative settings of Q sayings belonged to Q. For, after all, what is the ground for believing that anything is derived from Q? It is verbal agreement between Mt. and Lk. And the narrative settings of Q sayings and conversations is just the place where we do not get this agreement, but wide divergence. In the Centurion passage agreement between Mt. and Lk. begins where the conversation begins and ends where it ends. There is simply nothing to show that Q contained anything except sayings and conversations.

(b) and (c) This document was composed in Aramaic and everyone translated it as best he could. These two statements can be taken together : and the conditions are met if we can show a probability that (1) Q was written in Aramaic and (2) that Mt. and Lk. represent two versions of this Aramaic original. There are several lines of argument tending towards such a conclusion.

(i) The probabilities of the case. The sayings of Jesus were certainly uttered in Aramaic—perhaps some of them in scholastic Hebrew. If a collection of them were made, it would be most probable that it should be by one of his own circle and naturally in the original language. Jesus was regarded as 'the prophet of Nazareth' and it was in accordance with custom that the oracles of a prophet should be preserved by his disciples.

(ii) The analogy of the O.T. points to the possibility, at least, of several translations of such a document into Greek. There were at least four Greek versions of the O.T. made at various times and for various reasons.

(iii) We can compare the versions of Mt. and Lk. with parallel cases in O.T. For example the book of Daniel possesses two complete Greek versions, the old LXX and the translation of Theodotion. We select a passage at random and compare the two. The Aramaic passage Dan. vii. 9-14 is turned by LXX into 166 Greek words by θ' into 157. There is complete agreement in 105 of these and partial agreement in 12. The differences amount to about 27 per cent. of the total. We take a passage of about the same extent from Q—the testimony of Jesus to John the Baptist. Mt. gives it in 158 words, Lk. in 170. There is complete agreement about 115 words, partial agreement about 20 and the difference comes to about 19 per cent. of the total. Mt. and Lk. stand rather closer to one another than LXX and θ' ; but the general resemblance is very striking.

(iv) The most cogent evidence of translation is mistranslation. And such evidence is not wanting. The most notable instance is in the well-known Q passage about the cleansing of the inside and outside of the dish. Mt. correctly gives ' cleanse the inside of the dish ' while Lk. has the absurd text ' give alms of the inside '. Wellhausen showed that Luke's ' give alms ' is a mistranslation of the Aramaic verb rightly rendered by Mt. A similar misrendering may underlie ' Wisdom is justified of her children (works) ' and ' He who does not take up his cross . . . is not worthy of me' ⎱
      cannot be my disciple'⎰

Fortunately such cases are rare enough to permit us to keep our confidence in the ability of the translators of Q.

(v) There is still another sign of translation in those cases where Mt. and Lk. have different words or phrases either of which is a legitimate rendering of a single Aramaic original. These are more numerous : and I have made a collection of them. All that is required is Hatch and Redpath's concordance to the LXX, Field's *Hexapla*, and unlimited patience. You start with a Q passage in which Mt. and Lk. are agreeing fairly closely. Then there comes a difference : Mt. uses one word, Lk. another. It may be that these are just different ways of rendering the same Semitic original. The matter can be tested. There are four Greek versions of the O.T. Unhappily three of them survive only in fragments, which are collected in Field's *Hexapla* and indexed in Hatch and Redpath. We can soon see whether the same divergence occurs in the Greek versions of the O.T. Now the interesting thing is that it does. In quite a number of cases we have exact parallels for the differences of wording in Mt. and Lk. in Greek texts which are undoubtedly translations of the same Hebrew original.

For example : He who does not take up his cross and follow me is not worthy of me (or cannot be my disciple). Mt. x. 38 = Lk. xiv. 27.

Mt. has the verb $\lambda\alpha\mu\beta\acute{\alpha}\nu\epsilon\iota$ (R.V. ' take up '). Lk. has $\beta\alpha\sigma\tau\acute{\alpha}\zeta\epsilon\iota$ (R.V. ' bear '). Now in Numbers xiv. 33 f. the verb נשׂא occurs twice. In the first case it is translated by βαστάζειν in σ' and in the second by λαμβάνειν in ο'. Here then we have in Mt. and Lk. possible alternative renderings of the same Semitic original ; and we know that they are possible because they actually occur in the Greek versions of the Hebrew O.T.

In Lk. vi. 37 : Judge not and ye shall not be judged.

Mt. vii. 1 : Judge not that ye be not judged.

Ex. xxx. 20 ο' : ' and they shall not die ') rendering identical
21 ο' :   ' that they die not ' } Hebrew.

Similarly in I Reg. xxix. 7 : ο' καὶ οὐ μή. σ' ἵνα μή.

Lk. x. 6 and Mt. x. 13 : And if a son of peace be there your peace shall rest upon him : but if not, it shall turn to you again (ἀνακάμψει) ;

Mt. : let your peace return to you (ἐπιστραφήτω).

The same thing occurs in Ps. lviii (lix) twice, vv. 7 and 15 : ο' επιστρ. σ' ανακαμπ., and in Ezekiel viii. 17 : θ' επιστρ. σ' ανακαμπ. In all cases translating the same Hebrew verb (שׁוּב).

Lk. x. 3 : Behold I send you forth as lambs (ἄρνασ) in the midst of wolves.

Mt. x. 16 : Behold I send you forth as sheep (πρόβατα) in the midst of wolves.

Lev. iii. 7 : ο' ἄρνα. σ' πρόβατον (Heb. כֶּשֶׂב).

II Regn. vi. 13 : ο' ἄρνα. σ' πρόβατον (Heb. מְרִיא).

I have reserved to the last what seems to me the most interesting and instructive case of all. The Golden Rule is given by Mt. and Lk. in almost identical words. The main difference is in the few words at the beginning. Mt. (vii. 12) has πάντα οὖν ὅσα ἐὰν θέλητε ; Lk. (vi. 31) καὶ καθὼς θέλετε. In Gen. xliv. 1 ὅσα ἐάν translates the Heb. כאשר (Tg. ד כמא) : in Gen. viii. 21 ; xviii. 5 ; xli. 13 καθώς translates כאשר (Tg. ד כמא). It is thus possible to make the equation ὅσα ἐάν (Mt.) = καθώς (Lk.). The πάντα in Mt. is then left in the air. This, however, is easily explained. In eleven passages where Mt. is parallel to and presumably dependent on Mk. we have in Mt. some form of the word πᾶς to which nothing corresponds in the

Markan original. For example in relating the feeding of the four thousand Mk. says (viii. 8): ' and they ate and were satisfied ' ; Mt. (xv. 37) : ' and they all ate and were satisfied '. That is to say one of the literary habits of the author of the First Gospel is to heighten his effects by using the word ' all ' from time to time. It is easy to suppose that this is what has happened here. The question remains : which of the two renderings ὅσα ἐάν and καθώς comes nearer to the mind of Jesus. Both are legitimate renderings of what may be supposed to be the underlying Aramaic : yet there is a subtle difference. ὅσα ἐάν suggests individual acts—things to be done and things not to be done. It could easily become the foundation of a New Law-code. καθώς on the other hand suggests a manner of behaviour, a motive and spirit that should govern action. I add to this consideration the fact that the use of the pronoun rather than the adverb is in line with Jewish formulations of the Rule.

Hillel (b. *Sabb.* 31a) : דעלך סני לחברך לא תעביד

Tob. iv. 15 : ὃ μισεῖς μηδενὶ ποιήσῃς.

Philo. (*ap.* Eus. *Praep.* viii. 7) : ἃ τις παθεῖν ἐχθαίρει, μὴ ποιεῖν αὐτόν.

We may also note that in the two versions of the Lord's Prayer, Mt.'s introductory πάτερ ἡμῶν ὁ ἐν τοῖς οὐρανοῖς is a regular Jewish formula, while Luke's πάτερ agrees with our Lord's own practice (Mk. xiv. 36) and with the earliest church usage (Gal. iv. 6 ; Rom. viii. 15).

This discussion of the Golden Rule seems to me to show how it is possible to do something in detail towards a fairly reliable restoration of Q. Where Mt. and Lk. part company in a Q context there are at least two ways of seeking an explanation of the divergence. One is by applying the knowledge we can get about their editorial methods from comparison between them and Mk. where they are dependent on Mk. This method is illustrated by the πάντα in Mt.'s version of the Golden Rule. The other way is by reference to a possible underlying Aramaic original. In that case we may think that there has been mistranslation in one or other of the versions offered. Or we may conclude, as in the present case, that both versions are legitimate renderings of the original, but that one is better than the other.

I do not maintain that the facts which we have been considering *prove* that Q is the Aramaic document called the λόγια in the Papias fragment. But I do maintain that the phenomena presented by Mt. and Lk., in the passages where we may suppose them to have used Q, are consistent with that hypothesis. Three out of the four propositions contained in the Papias testimony fit Q like a glove.

(*d*) There remains the fourth—that the author of this document was Matthew—presumably Matthew the Apostle. This, of course, cannot be tested in the same way as the others. There is, however, this much to be said for it :

(i) On the supposition that the Papias tradition does refer to Q, we can see that three of its four statements are reliable. There is therefore a presumption that the fourth will also hold good.

(ii) If the Papias statements really refer to Q then they must be much older than the time of Papias. That is, the tradition is thrown back to the end of the first century or the very beginning of the second. It is thus brought very close to the events which it reports.

(iii) An Aramaic original of Q implies a Palestinian authorship and that means a Palestinian Christian. Nobody else in Jewish circles would have the inclination to compile such a record and of those who would be inclined, those would be best qualified for the task who had been—in Lk.'s words—eyewitnesses and ministers of the word from the beginning. There was a Matthew among those who were in close contact with Jesus during his ministry. And there we are. The bits of the puzzle fit in satisfactorily enough. The whole thing is consistent on the supposition, not hard to make, that Papias had this older tradition about Q, and, misled by the mention of Matthew, supposed it to refer to the Gospel current in his day under Matthew's name.

Our conclusion is that the statement reported by Papias refers not to Mt., but to one of the sources of Mt., the document

Q. We now have to consider the other early *testimonia* in the light of this fact. We may well suppose that statements which speak of a Hebrew Gospel of Matthew prior in composition to all the others are either descended from the original mis-interpretation of the tradition in Papias, or else are similar misinterpretations of a parallel tradition.

Irenaeus, iii. 1. 2 *ap.* Eus. *H.E.* v. 8. 2 : ὁ μὲν δὴ Ματθαῖος ἐν τοῖς Ἑβραίοις τῇ ἰδίᾳ αὐτῶν διαλέκτῳ καὶ γραφὴν ἐξήνεγκεν εὐαγγελίου, τοῦ Πέτρου καὶ τοῦ Παύλου ἐν Ῥώμῃ εὐαγγελιζομένων καὶ θεμελιούντων τὴν ἐκκλησίαν.

' Matthew published a Gospel in writing also, among the Hebrews in their own language, while Peter and Paul were preaching the Gospel and founding the church in Rome ' (Lawlor and Oulton's translation).

Fragment 27 in Harvey's edition of Irenaeus (ii. 493) tells us that Mt. was written πρὸς 'Ιουδαίους. The Jews desired a Messiah of Davidic descent, and Matthew set out to convince them that Christ was so descended.

Clement of Alexandria is reported by Eusebius (*H.E.* vi. 14. 5) to have inserted in his *Hypotyposeis* a tradition of the primitive elders (παράδοσιν τῶν ἀνέκαθεν πρεσβυτέρων) regarding the order of the Gospels. It begins : προγεγράφθαι ἔλεγεν τῶν εὐαγγελίων τὰ περιέχοντα τὰς γενεαλογίας. ' He said that those of the Gospels that contain genealogies (i.e. Mt. and Lk.) had been written first '. This tradition will not square with the conclusions of Synoptic study.

The principal statements of Origen, as it happens, belong to the period after his removal from Alexandria to Caesarea. They are the *Commentary on John*, t. vi. 32 (ed. Brooke, i. 148) ; a scholion on Lk. i. 1 f. (Zahn, *G.K.* ii. 626 f.) ; and a passage from the *Commentary on Matthew*, quoted by Eusebius (*H.E.* vi. 25. 4). In the first of these Origen gives it as a tradition concerning Matthew that he was the first of the evangelists and produced his Gospel for Hebrew converts from Judaism. In the second he insists that Mt. is not one of the documents referred to in Luke's preface, since Matthew did not ' take in hand ' to write a Gospel, but did so ' being moved by the Holy Spirit '.

The third again reports tradition to the effect that the first Gospel to be written was that of Matthew the ex-publican who became an Apostle of Jesus Christ and published it, a composition in the Hebrew language, for converts from Judaism. It may well be that this represents the tradition in Caesarea in the first half of the third century.

Tertullian (*adu. Marc.* iv. 2) maintains the apostolic origin of Mt. and Jn.

There are two points, in this small body of material, to which we should give our attention. The first is the date assigned by Irenaeus for the composition of Mt. It is a little difficult to dismiss this as the product of Irenaeus' imagination ; and I should not exclude the possibility that what he reports is in the main traditional and in its original form referred to Q. Its application to Mt. would then be a misinterpretation of the same kind as that in Papias.

The second point to be noticed is the stress laid on the purpose of the Gospel of Matthew. It is written in ' Hebrew ' for Hebrews. Its purpose is to gain and confirm converts from Judaism. There can be little doubt that this opinion was fortified by the fact that in Palestine, where it is most at home, there coexisted information about a document or documents actually existing in a Semitic tongue and bearing a more or less close resemblance to our Mt. We have statements about this literature from a considerable number of early Fathers from Irenaeus to Epiphanius and Jerome ; and we have a number of extracts translated into Greek or Latin.

We may begin with the statement of Irenaeus (*Haer.* I. xxii ; Harvey, i. 213) where, describing the Ebionites he says : solo autem eo quod est secundum Matthaeum Euangelio utuntur, et apostolum Paulum recusant, apostatam eum legis dicentes. Quae autem sunt prophetica, curiosius exponere nituntur ; et circumciduntur ac perseuerant in his consuetudinibus, quae sunt secundum legem, et Iudaico charactere uitae, uti et Hierosolymam adorent, quasi domus sit Dei. With this should be compared the account given by Eusebius (*H.E.* iii. 27), who seems to be dependent on Irenaeus, but, instead of ' the Gospel according to Matthew ', has ' the Gospel called " according to the

Hebrews " '. Irenaeus' description of the Ebionites as a sect using Mt. only, rejecting Paul as an apostate from the Law, interpreting the O.T. (Messianic) prophecies in their own way, maintaining the Jewish Law and the Jewish customs including that of turning towards Jerusalem in prayer, all this gives us a glimpse of people whom we may fairly regard as the lineal successors of the Jewish Christians whom we find in opposition to Paul in the New Testament. Their Gospel is referred to by Origen and Eusebius, and perhaps also by Clement of Alexandria, as τὸ καθ' Ἑβραίους εὐαγγέλιον ; and in Eusebius (H.E. iii. 25. 5) we are told that it is used by Ἑβραίων οἱ τὸν Χριστὸν παραδεξάμενοι. By Jerome the people who use the Gospel according to the Hebrews (variously described as ipsum Hebraicum, Euangelium iuxta Hebraeos, Eu. secundum Hebraeos, Eu. quod Hebraeo sermone conscriptum, Eu. . . . quod uocatur a plerisque Matthaei authentiam) are called Nazaraei or Nazaraeni. Most probably we should regard this name as the equivalent of the designation applied to the Hebrew Christians by the Synagogue [1] (הנוצרים). The names of the sect (Ebionites, Nazarenes) reflect the speech of Palestine and Syria ; the name of their Gospel (according to the Hebrews) reflects the terminology of the Gentile Christian communities.

This Gospel is sufficiently near to Mt. to be taken for the supposed ' Hebrew ' original. Eusebius (Theoph. iv. 12) can compare its version of the Parable of the Talents with the text of Mt. and from it obtain a suggestion for the interpretation of Mt. xxv. 29 f. Finally a number of manuscripts of the Gospels (von Soden's I^r group), which have some connexion with Jerusalem, give readings from τὸ Ἰουδαϊκόν as marginal notes to the text of Mt. There is a good deal of further evidence, all of which seems to point in the direction of the hypothesis that our Greek Mt. was translated into Hebrew or Aramaic at a very early date for the use of Jewish Christians in Palestine and Syria and that it did not escape modification, though not perhaps to a very great extent, with the passage of time.

[1] For a very clear statement of the matter regarding the terms Ναζαρηνός and Ναζωραῖος see G. F. Moore in Beginnings of Christianity, i. 426-432.

There are two bits of Rabbinic tradition which have their bearing on this. First there is the story told in *b. Sabb.* 116[ab] concerning Imma Shalom, Rabban Gamaliel (II), and a (Jewish Christian) philosopher. This incident would be dated about the end of the first century, and in the course of the story the ' philosopher ' refers to a written ' Gospel '. The point is that he refers to it by its *Greek* name εὐαγγέλιον ; and the inference is that any written Gospels that were current among Jewish Christians at this date were the literary work of Gentile rather than Jewish Christianity. The other bit of Rabbinic evidence, given in *b. Sanhedrin* 43[a] names five disciples of Jesus and heads the list with Matthew (מתאי). We may infer that the prominence of Matthew was not unconnected with the earliest traditions which make him the compiler of the oracles of the Lord, and the later ones which attributed our First Gospel and the Semitic version of it to him.[1]

The conclusion of the study of the external evidence is that it suggests that the document Q was the work of Matthew ; that he composed it in the vernacular of Palestine ; that it consisted for the most part of sayings and speeches of Jesus ; that various renderings of it (into Greek) were made ; and that one of these renderings furnished material for the First Evangelist. Further it would seem that the First Gospel, when made, was very early translated into the Palestinian vernacular for the use of Jewish Christians, and as an instrument of propaganda among Jews. The name of Matthew, which had been mistakenly transferred from Q to the First Gospel, stuck, and continued to stick, until scientific study of the relations between the Gospels made the hypothesis of an original' Hebrew Mt. untenable.

Scientific study of the Synoptic Gospels has established clearly enough what Mt. is : it is a revised and enlarged edition of Mk. It has also established fairly clearly that the reviser who produced Mt. betrays no acquaintance with the work of

[1] Of the Gospel used by the Ebionites described by Epiphanius in *Haer.* xxx, I do not think it necessary to say anything here. It is clear that if it began as a version of Mt. it had suffered drastic transformation before Epiphanius became acquainted with it. It does not seem likely that it can supply any light on the origins or early history of Mt.

Luke, nor does Lk. show any sign that its author had access
to Mt. As Lk. was written for publication, and Mt. rapidly
became very widely known and greatly valued in the Churches,
the most likely explanation of this mutual ignorance is that
Mt. and Lk. were produced about the same time. I have already
argued for a date round about A.D. 70 for the composition of
Lk.-Acts ; and it seems to me that a date in the decade following
the destruction of Jerusalem in A.D. 70 is as likely as any for
Mt.

Regarding the place of writing there is not much to be said
that is not already in the standard works on Introduction to the
New Testament. There are strong indications connecting the
Gospel with the neighbourhood of Antioch ; and if that were
the place of origin it would help to explain the rapid dissemination of Mt. in both East and West. In a way Mt. has some
resemblances to Josephus' account of the Jewish war. This
was written first in Aramaic soon after A.D. 70 to show the Eastern
Jews that such revolts were foredoomed to failure. Shortly
afterwards it was translated into Greek. One wonders if the
First Gospel was not written about the same time in Greek
and quickly translated into Aramaic to tell the same people for
whom Josephus wrote, where the true hope of their nation lay.

APPENDIX.

1. *ΛΟΓΙΑ in the Greek versions of O.T.*

Nu. xxiv. 3, 4. From a poetic utterance put in the mouth of Balaam. B. is
subject.

φησιν βαλααμ υιοσ Βεωρ,
φησιν ὁ ανθρωποσ ὁ αληθινωσ ὁρων,
φησιν ακουων λογια θεου,
ὁστισ ὁρασιν θεου ειδεν κτλ.   v.l. ισχυρου

M.T.
נאם בלעם בנו בער
ונאם הגבר שתם העין :
נאם שמע אמרי־אל
אשר מחזה שדי יחזה וגו'

Tg. O.   מימר מן קדם אל
Tg. J.   מימר מן קדם יי אלהא חייא

Here $\lambda o \gamma \iota a$ $\theta \epsilon o v$ (אמרי אל) stands in parallelism with $\delta \rho a \sigma \iota \nu$ $\begin{cases} \theta \epsilon o v \\ \iota \sigma \chi v \rho o v \end{cases}$

(מחזה שדי) : and the meaning is thereby determined : divine revelations received in the form of auditions as distinct from those received in the form of visions.

Nu. xxiv. 16. From another poetic utterance of Balaam.

$$a \kappa o v \omega \nu \, \dot{\lambda} o \gamma \iota a \, \theta \epsilon o v,$$
$$\epsilon \pi \iota \sigma \tau a \mu \epsilon \nu o \sigma \, \epsilon \pi \iota \sigma \tau \eta \mu \eta \nu \, \pi a \rho a \, \dot{v} \psi \iota \sigma \tau o v,$$
$$\kappa a \iota \, \delta \rho a \sigma \iota \nu \, \theta \epsilon o v \, \iota \delta \omega \nu \, \kappa \tau \lambda.$$

נאם שמע אמרי אל וידע דעת עליון
מחזה שדי יחזה וגו׳

Tg. O. as above.   Tg. J. מימר מן קדם אלהא

The meaning in this case is identical with that in xxiv. 4.

Dt. xxxiii. 9. From the ' Blessing of Moses ' to Levi.

$$\dot{o} \, \lambda \epsilon \gamma \omega \nu \, \tau \omega \, \pi a \tau \rho \iota \, \kappa a \iota \, \tau \eta \, \mu \eta \tau \rho \iota \, O v \chi \, \dot{\epsilon} o \rho a \kappa a \, \sigma \epsilon,$$
$$\kappa a \iota \, \tau o v \sigma \, a \delta \epsilon \lambda \phi o v \sigma \, a v \tau o v \, o v \kappa \, \epsilon \pi \epsilon \gamma \nu \omega,$$
$$\kappa a \iota \, \tau o v \sigma \, v \dot{\iota} o v \sigma \, a v \tau o v \, a \pi \epsilon \gamma \nu \omega \cdot$$
$$\epsilon \phi v \lambda a \xi \epsilon \nu \, \tau a \, \lambda o \gamma \iota a \, \sigma o v,$$
$$\kappa a \iota \, \tau \eta \nu \, \delta \iota a \theta \eta \kappa \eta \nu \, \sigma o v \, \delta \iota \epsilon \tau \eta \rho \eta \sigma \epsilon \nu.$$

M.T.   כי שמרו אמרתך
              ובריתך ינצרו :

Tg. O.   ארי נטרו מטרת מימרך וקימך לא אשניאו

Tg. J.   מטול דקיימין עשרין שנין במטרתהון במימרך
              וקיים פולחן קודשך נטרין :

Here τa $\lambda o \gamma \iota a$ $\sigma o v$ stands in parallelism with $\tau \eta \nu$ $\delta \iota a \theta \eta \kappa \eta \nu$ $\sigma o v$ and means the command(s) of Jehovah. Cf. Driver, ad loc.

R. Simeon b. Jochai (c. 150) explains $\epsilon \phi v \lambda a \xi \epsilon \nu$ τa $\lambda.$ $\tau o v.$ as abstinence from idolatry and $\tau.$ $\delta \iota a \theta.$ $\sigma o v$ $\delta \iota \epsilon \tau.$ of the observance of circumcision. SNu. ix. 5, §67 (17a). SB. II, 681. Cf. Ex. R. 19. SB. IV, 39.

Ps. xi (xii), 6 (7)

$$\tau a \, \lambda o \gamma \iota a \, K v \rho \iota o v \, \lambda o \gamma \iota a \, \dot{a} \gamma \nu a$$

M.T.   אמרות יהוה אמרות טהרות

Tg.   מילין דיהוה מילייא דכיין

Here the meaning appears to be that the promises of Jehovah—especially those favourable to his people—are reliable, notwithstanding appearances to the contrary.

Ps. xvii (xviii), 30 (31)

> ὁ θεοσ μου, αμωμοσ ἡ ὁδοσ αυτου,
> τα λογια Κυριου πεπυρωμενα
> ὑπερασπιστησ εστιν παντων των ελπιζοντων επ᾽ αυτον.

M.T.
האל תמים דרכו
אמרת יהוה צרופה
מגן הוא לכל החוסים בו :

Tg.
אוריתא דיהוה בחירא

In II Sam. xxii. 31, the LXX version is :

> ὁ ισχυροσ, αμωμοσ ἡ ὁδοσ αυτου,
> το ῥημα Κυριου κραταιον, πεπυρωμενον·
> ὑπερασπιστησ εστιν πασιν τοισ πεποιθοσιν επ᾽ αυτῳ.

> M.T. = that of ψ.
> Tg. II S. as above.

The sense seems to be much the same as in ψ xi (xii) above.

Ps. xviii (xix), 14 (15).

> και εσονται εισ ευδοκιαν τα λογια του στοματοσ μου
> και ἡ μελετη τησ καρδιασ μου ενωπιον σου δια παντοσ.

M.T
יהיו לרצון אמרי־פי והגיון לבי לפניך

Tg.
יהון לרעוא מימרי פומי וגו׳

Here λογια of *human* utterance. The parallelism shows that λ. = the actual utterance as distinguished from the inward thought.

Ps. civ (cv), 19.

> μεχρι του ελθειν τον λογον αυτου,
> το λογιον κυριου επυρωσεν αυτον.

M.T.
עד־עת בא־דברו אמרת יהוה צרפתהו

Tg.
עד עידן דאתא פתגמיה מימרא דיהוה סניך יתיה

An account of Joseph in Egypt. The reference of these lines is to Joseph's divinely inspired interpretation of Pharaoh's servants' dreams, Gen. xli, 13.

'Der Göttliche Ausspruch, die Traumdeutung, liess Joseph als echtes Metall erscheinen, als Besitzer des von Jahwe dem Samen Abrahams mitgegebenen Wortes.' (Duhm., *ad loc.*)

Ps. cvi (cvii), 11.

> ὁτι παρεπικραναν τα λογια του θεου,
> και την βουλην του ὑψιστου παρωξυναν·

M.T. כי־המרו אמרי־אל'
ועצת עליון נאצו :

Tg. ארום סריבו על מימריה דאלהא
ומלכת עילאה רחיקו :

Cf. Ps. xviii (xix), 14 above. The antithesis is the same. Here τα λογια
του θεου practically = the commandments of God and την βουλην his purpose. Kittel translates ' Geboten . . . Rat '.

Ps. cxviii (cxix), 11.

εν τη καρδια μου εκρυψα τα λογια σου,
όπωσ αν μη άμαρτω σοι.

M.T. בלבי צפנתי אמרתך
Tg. בליבי אשישית מימרך

Here the meaning is clearly God's commands.

Ib. 25.   ζησομαι κατα το λογιον σου

M.T. חיני כדברך   ζησομαι] ζησον με ART.
Tg. אסי יתי כדבריך   το λογιον א AᵃʼR] τον λογον A*T.

The word = the promises of Jehovah (Kittel, *ad loc.*). It is doubtful whether
το λογιον here is true text of LXX. Rahlfs follows the readings of AT : ζησον
με κατα τον λογον σου.

Ib. 38.   στησον τω δουλω σου το λογιον σου,
εισ τον φοβον σου.

M.T. הקם לעבדך אמרתך אשר ליראתך :
Tg. אקים לעבדך מימרך די לדחלתך :

' v. 38, bittet um den der Gottesfurcht verheissenen Lohn ' (Kittel). Hence
το λογ. σου = ' thy promise '.

Ib. 41.   και ελθοι επ' εμε το ελεοσ σου, Κυριε,
το σωτηριον σου κατα το λογιον σου.

M.T. . . . תשועתך כאמרתך :
Tg. . . . פורקנך היך מימרך :

Here = promise.

Ib. 50.   ότι το λογιον σου εζησεν με.

M.T. כי אמרתך חיתני :
Tg. ארום מימרך קיימת יתי

" Sein Trost ist Jahwes Verheissung 49 f." Kittel.
Hence = promise.

Ps. cxviii (cxix), 58.

ελεησον με κατα το λογιον σου

M.T. חנני כאמרתך
Tg. חוס עלי היך מימרך
= Promise.

Ib. 65. χρηστοτητα εποιησασ μετα του δουλου σου,
Κυριε κατα το λογιον σου. τον λογον אᶜˑᵃT.

M.T. ... כדברך
Tg. ... היך דבריך

In any case = promise. Here Rahlfs reads κατα τον λογον σου.

Ib. 67. ... το λογιον σου εφυλαξα.

M.T. ... אמרתך שמרתי :
Tg. ... מימרך נטרית :
= Command.

Ib. 76. γενηθητω δη το ελεοσ σου του παρακαλεσαι με
κατα το λογιον σου τω δουλω σου.

M.T. כאמרתך לעבדך :
Tg. היך מימרך לעבדך :

"Wie du deinem Knecht verheissen." Kittel.
= Promise.

Ib. 82. εξελιπον οι οφθαλμοι μου εισ το λογιον σου

M.T. כלו עיני לאמרתך
Tg. ספו עיני למימרך
= Promise.

Ib. 103. ωσ γλυκεα τω λαρυγγι μου τα λογια σου.

M.T. מה־נמלצו להכי אמרתך
Tg. מה חלין למוריגי מימריך

The context certainly suggests that the meaning here is 'commands

Ib. 107. Κυριε, ζησον με κατα το λογιον σου.

M.T. יהוה חיני כדברך
Tg. יהוה אסי יתי היך דבריך
Promise ?

Rahlfs reads κατα τον λογον σου.

H

Ps. cxviii (cxix), 116.

αντιλαβου κατα το λογιον σου, και ζησομαι,
και μη καταισχυνησ με απο τησ προσδοκιασ μου.

M.T.   סמכני כאמרתך ואחיה ואל־תבשני משברי :

Tg.   סמוך יתי במימרך ואחי . . .

Promise.

Ib. 123.   οἱ οφθαλμοι μου εξελιπον εισ το σωτηριον σου
και εισ το λογιον τησ δικαιοσυνησ σου.

M.T.   עיני כלו לישועתך ולאמרת צדקך :

Tg.   עיני סברו לפורקנך ולמימר צדקך :

"deiner gerechten Verheissung." Kittel.

Promise.

Ib. 124.   ποιησον μετα του δουλου σου κατα το λογιον σου
λογιον] ελεοσ א[c·a]RT.

M.T.   כחסדך   Tg.   היך חסדך

Rahlfs reads ελεοσ.

Ib. 133.   τα διαβηματα μου κατευθυνον κατα το λογιον σου,
και μη κατακυριευσατω μου πασα ανομια.

M.T.   פעמי הכן באמרתך

Tg.   אסתורי אתקין במימרך

The context shows that God's commands are meant.

Ib. 140.   πεπυρωμενον το λογιον σου σφοδρα

M.T.   צרופה אמרתך מאד

Tg.   סניגא מימרך לחדא

= Commandment, as appears from the context.

Ib. 148.   προεφθασαν οἱ οφθαλμοι μου προσ ορθρουν,
του μελεταν τα λογια σου.

M.T.   קדמו עיני אשמרות לשׂיח באמרתך :

Tg.   אקדימו עיני מטרתא דצפר ורמש למללא במימרך :

Commandments.

Ib. 149.   τησ φωνησ μου ακουσον, Κυριε, κατα το λογιον σου.
λογιον] ελεοσ אART.

M.T.   כחסדך   Tg.   היך חסדך

Rahlfs reads ελεοσ.

Ps. cxviii (cxix), 158.

ειδον ασυνθετουντασ και εξετηκομην,
ότι τα λογια σου ουκ εφυλαξαντο.

M.T.   . . . אשר אמרתך לא שמרו

Tg.   . . . די מימרך לא נטרו

Commands.

Ib. 162.   αγαλλιασομαι εγω επι τα λογια σου,
ώσ ό εύρισκων σκυλα πολλα.

M.T.   שש אנכי על אמרתך כמוצא שלל רב :

Tg.   חדי אנא על מימרך . . .

Commands, as appears from the context.

Ib. 169.   κατα το λογιον σου συνετισον με.

M.T.   כדברך   Tg.   היך פתגמך

Promise.

Ib. 170.   κατα το λογιον σου ρυσαι με.

M.T.   כאמרתך הצילני

Tg.   היך מימרך פצי יתי

Promise.

Ib. 172.   φθεγξαιτο ή γλωσσα μου το λογιον σου,
ότι πασαι αί εντολαι σου δικαιοσυνη εστιν.

M.T.   תען לשוני אמרתך כי כל-מצותיך צדק :

Tg.   מימרך

Commands.

Ps. cxxxvii (cxxxviii), 2 A'E'

M.T.   כי הגדלת על-כל-שמך אמרתך

ο' ότι εμεγαλυνασ επι παν το ονομα το άγιον σου
σ' εμεγαλυνασ γαρ ύπερ παντα τα ονοματα σου την ρησιν σου.
α'ε'   το λογιον σου.

Tg.   ארום אסגיתא על כל שמך מימרי תושבחתך

Commentators read על-כל שמך and regard אמרתך as a gloss.

On LXX text of this vs. see Hedley in *Harvard Theol. Rev.*, xxvi, p. 72. Rahlfs, following Grabe, adopts λογιον in his text (conj. emend.) against the αγιον of the MSS.

Ps. cxlvii. 4 (5).

> ὁ ἀποστελλων το λογιον αυτου τῃ γῃ,
> ἕωσ ταχουσ δραμειται ὁ λογοσ αυτου.

M.T.   השלח אמרתו ארץ עד־מהרה ירוץ דברו

Tg.   דמשדר מימריה לארעא . . .

Command.

WISDOM, xvi. 11.

> εισ γαρ ὑπομνησιν των λογιων σου ενεκεντριζοντο,
> και οξεωσ διεσωζοντο.   Syriac   ܡܠܬ̈

Siegfried trans.   Denn zur Einprägung deiner Gebote wurden sie gestochen usw.   Kautzsch, *Apok. u. Pseud.* i, 502.

ECCLUS. xxxvi. 19 (16).

> πλησον Ciων αρεταλογιασ σου,
> και απο τησ δοξησ σου τον λαον σου.
> αρεταλογιασ] αραι (αρε אA) τα λογια B^bא A^vid.

λαον] ναον is the true reading with Heb. and Syr.

Syr. (Lagarde, p. 37, line 2).

ܡܠܐ ܨܗܝܘܢ ܡܢ ܫܘܒܚܟ ܂ ܘܥܡܟ ܐܝܩܪ ܘܗܝܟܠܟ ܂

Heb.   מלא ציון את הודך ומכבודך את היכלך

See Hart, *ad loc.*

ISAIAH, v. 24.

> ου γαρ ἠθελησαν τον νομον Κυριου σαβαωθ,
> αλλα το λογιον του ἁγιου Ισραηλ παρωξυναν.

M.T.   כמאסו את תורת יהוה צבאות
        ואת אמרת קדוש־ישראל נאצו :

Tg.   ארי קצו באוריתא דיהוה צבאות
        וית מימר קדישא דישראל רחיקו :

το λογιον in synonymous parallelism with τον νομον. For the force of תורה, cf. Skinner on Is. i. 10 : religious direction, prophetic teaching. το λογιον = the command of God.

Ib. xxviii. 13.

> και εσται αυτοισ το λογιον Κυριου θλιψισ επι θλιψιν κτλ.

M.T.   והיה להם דבר יהוה
        צו לצו וגו '

Tg.

ודין יהי כס פורענותהון על דעברו על פיתגמא דיהוה על דאיתפקדו
למעבד אוריתא ומא דאיתפקדו לא צביאו למעבד בכין יתמסרון
לעממיא דלא ידעו אוריתא וגו '

Here το λογιον $\overline{Kυ}$ serves to introduce the following *oracle.*

ISAIAH xxx: 11.

και αφελετε αφ' ήμων το λογιον του Ισραηλ.

M.T.   השביתו מפנינו את־קדוש ישראל

Inner Greek corruption :   ΤΟΛΟΓΙΟΝ
                             ΤΟΝΑΓΙΟΝ.

Tg.   ארחיקו מן קדמנא ית מימר קדישא דישראל

Pesh.   ܘܐܪܚܩ ܡܢ ܠܩܘܒܠܢ ܠܩܕܝܫܐ ܐܝܠ

σ' παυσατε εκ προσωπου ήμων τον άγιον του Ισραηλ.

Tg. appears to combine the readings of LXX and M.T. מימר = το λογιον,
קדישא = τον άγιον. But this may be deceptive and perhaps Tg. may be regarded
as paraphrase = mention of the Holy One of Israel. In that case Tg. would
appear to give the sense of the protest in M.T. = say no more about the Holy
One of Israel !

Ib. xxx. 27.

Ιδου το ονομα κυριου ερχεται δια χρονου, καιομενοσ θυμοσ ·
μετα δοξησ το λογιον των χειλεων αυτου, το λογιον οργησ πληρεσ,
και ή οργη του θυμου ώσ πυρ εδεται.

M.T.   הנה שם־יהוה בא ממרחק
               בער אפו וכבד משאה
               שפתיו מלאו זעם
               ולשונו כאש אכלת :

Pesh.

το λογιον 1° corresponds to משאה ; but the LXX is corrupt at this point.

Ib. xxxii. 9 A'.

נשים שאננות קמנה שמענה קולי
בנות בטחות האזנה אמרתי :

ο' λογουσ μου.   α' λογιον μου.   σ' τασ ῥησεισ μου.
             θ' τα ρηματα μου.

Introducing a prophetic oracle.

JEREMIAH viii, 9 A'.

הנה בדבר־יהוה מאסו

o' ὅτι τον λογον Κυριου απεδοκιμασαν
σ' τον γαρ λογον
α' ιδου το λογιον—not really α'.

See Lütkemann and Rahlfs, *Mitteilungen des Septuaginta-Unternehmens*, Heft 6, pp. 240 ff.

A' übersetzt nach festes Praxis אָמַר oder אָמַר durch λόγοσ und das längere hebräische Wort אמרה durch das längere griechische λόγιον, dagegen דבר durch ῥῆμα. (Lütkemann-Rahlfs, *op. cit.*, p. 240).

Summary.

(a) λογιον or λογια used of direct oracular communications of God to man or of prophetic oracles : Nu. 24⁴,¹⁶ ; Ps. 104 (105)¹⁹ ; Isa. 28¹³, 32⁹ᵃ' ; Jer. 8⁹ᵃ' wrongly ascribed.

(b) λογιον or λογια = divine commands : Dt. 33⁹ ; Ps. 106 (107)¹¹, 118 (119)¹¹, ⁶⁷, ¹⁰³, ¹³³, ¹⁴⁰, ¹⁴⁸, ¹⁵⁸, ¹⁶², ¹⁷², 147⁴(⁵) ; Isa. 5²⁴.

(c) = divine promises : Ps. 11 (12)⁶, 17 (18)³⁰, 118 (119)[²⁵], ³⁸, ⁴¹, ⁵⁰, ⁵⁸, [⁶⁵], ⁷⁶, ⁸², [¹⁰⁷?], ¹¹⁶, ¹²³, ¹⁶⁹, ¹⁷⁰ ; Wisd. 16¹¹. Square brackets indicate that the LXX reading is uncertain.

(d) = human utterance (in worship) : Ps. 18 (19)¹⁴.

Text corrupt : Ps. 118 (119)¹²⁴, ¹⁴⁹ ; 137 (138) 2ᵃ'ᵉ' ; Ecclus. 39, ¹⁹ (¹⁶) ; Isa. 30¹¹, ²⁷.

Conclusion.—In no case is it possible to get away from the idea of utterance. With a single exception—Ps. 18 (19), 14, where the meaning is human speech in worship as distinguished from meditation in the heart—all the cases considered, where the text is reliable, clearly indicate that it is God's utterance that is meant either directly to a prophet (once a patriarch) or through such a medium to his people in commands and promises. That these utterances of Jehovah may be written down is not disputed but it is nothing to do with the case. What is meant by the word is not Scripture but some things which are contained, along with other things in Scripture, the things namely, that God has said for the guidance or encouragement of Israel.

2. ΛΟΓΙΑ in N.T.

Ac. vii. 38.

οὑτοσ εστιν ὁ γενομενοσ εν τῃ εκκλησιᾳ εν τῃ ερημῳ . . .
. . . ὁσ εδεξατο λογια ζωντα δουναι ἡμιν . . .

Subject of εδεξατο is Moses.

d. qui accipit eloquia uiuentium dare nobis.

Iren. iv. 15, 1 (26, 1): accepit praecepta dei uiui dare nobis.

Pesh. ܘܡܕܟ ܩܕܠ ܣܬܐ؛ ܝܟܝ ܝܐܠܟ

Vulg. qui accepit uerba uitae dare nobis.

[Date of Iren. Lat. iii or iv A.D., probably the former. Harnack, *A.C.L. Chron.*, II, 320.]

Donovan, p. 13: ' In this passage λογια ζωντα is manifestly used to signify the revelation made directly to Moses. It is here, as elsewhere, equivalently " the Inspired Word ", and inferentially the Scripture, in which that revelation is recorded.'

The first sentence of this is quite correct. Thus far and no farther D. is entitled to take us. When he goes on to make it equivalently this and inferentially that, he is no longer telling us what the phrase means in its context, but what he would like it to mean for the purposes of his argument. It is worth noticing that the author of the Latin version of Irenaeus (? 3rd cent. A.D.) was apparently still unaware of the ' equivalent ' and ' inferential ' meanings of λογια ζωντα in this passage ; and contented himself with the rendering *praecepta*, in support of which he could have quoted—on my reckoning—thirteen passages from the LXX.

Ro. iii. 2. WH.

πρωτον μεν [γαρ] ὁτι επιστευθησαν τα λογια του θεου.

πρωτον] πρωτοι Orig. Eus.   μεν (om. γαρ) BD*G *al* £$(vg)𝕰(boh) Chr. Orig. ½ *al*. :

μεν γαρ ℵAΩ$ (hl.) : γαρ (*sine* μεν) Orig. ½ Eus.

Moffatt : ' the Scriptures of God '.

Lietzmann (*HBNT.* (1910), *ad loc.*) : ' Dass mit λόγια " die Verheissungen " (9⁶) gemeint sind, lehrt das folgende '.

Jülicher (*SNT³*) : ' Gottes Offenbarungs-Worte '. In the exposition further defined thus : ' . . . Gott ihnen seine Offenbarungen (das A.T.) anvertraut hat. P mag besonders an. die Verheissungen gedacht haben ; deutlich hat er solche Beschränkung aber nicht vollzogen.'

Pesh. ܡܠܟܘܗܝ ؛ܐܠܗܐ| Vulg. eloquia Dei.

Lipsius (Holtzmann's Hand-Commentar (1891), *ad loc.*) : Vorerst dass sie mit den Verheissungssprüchen Gottes betraut worden sind.

For discussion of this passage see the text of the lecture.

HEB. v. 12.

και γαρ οφειλοντεσ ειναι διδασκαλοι δια τον χρονον, παλιν χρειαν εχετε του διδασκειν ὑμασ τινα τα στοιχεια τησ αρχησ των λογιων του θεου, και γεγονατε χρειαν εχοντεσ γαλακτοσ, ου στερεασ τροφησ.

Windisch (*HBNT*. (1913), *ad loc.*) : τα λογια του θεου . . . sind die Worte Gottes, die den Inhalt der zusammenhängenden israelitisch-christlichen Offenbarungsgeschichte und Offenbarungsverkündigung ausmachen.

Hollmann (*SNT*[3], *ad loc.*) : Sie haben immer noch mit den Anfangsgründen der von Gott in Christus gesprochenen Worte (1, 2 : 2, 3, ; 6, 1) zu tun, während sie Lehrer sein und Andere unterrichten müssten. Welche Aufangsgründe der Verfasser meint, sagt 6, 1 f.

Moffatt (*ICC, ad loc.*) : ' the rudimentary principles of the divine revelation '.

Donovan (p. 13), winding up a detailed discussion as to the meaning of this passage, says : ' The conclusion as to the meaning of λόγια is obvious '—so obvious that he does not say what it is, but continues : ' At any rate, it remains indisputably true that in these two instances of the use of λόγια occurring in the Pauline Epistles, the word appears as synonymous either with Revelation or Holy Writ '. That it is synonymous with Revelation we need not trouble to deny. The question is whether the terms Revelation and Holy Writ are so readily interchangeable as D. seems to think. Taking this passage on its merits and in its context it is clear enough that τα στοιχεια τησ αρχησ των λογιων του θεου means much the same thing as τον τησ αρχησ του χριστου λογον. And Hollmann is no doubt right in bringing i. 1 f. and ii. 3 into account. God, who in former times had given λογια to the Prophets and through them to Israel, has in these times given them in his son. The new λογια are the demands and promises of God revealed in Christ. The elementary portions of these λογια are further specified in vi. 1 f. : repentance, faith, baptisms, laying on of hands, resurrection and, judgement. But the writer contends that there is more in the λογια than that : in other words, there is a deeper meaning in the revelation that God has given in Christ. He is certainly not talking here about O.T. and/or N.T. but about the significance of Christ considered as an oracle of God, newer and better than the oracles given to the prophets and, like the old oracles, requiring understanding.

I PET. iv. 11.

ει τισ λαλει, ὡσ λογια θεου·
ει τισ διακονει, ὡσ εξ ισχυοσ ἡσ χορηγει ὁ θεοσ.

Bigg, *ICC* : ' λογια means Scripture ', ' " as Scripture speaks ", with sincerity and gravity '.

Windisch, *HBNT* : ' wenn einer redet (betrachte er seine Worte) als Worte Gottes '. ' Herausgehoben werden die Lehrer und die Diener der Gemeinde ; beiden Gruppen wird gesagt (nicht dass sie ihre gottgegebenen Fähigkeiten auch gebrauchen sondern), dass sie die Kraft, die sie haben und verwenden, als gottgegeben anerkennen, damit in allen Regungen der Gemeinde die Allwirksamkeit Gottes zum Bewusstsein komme 2[12].

Gunkel, *SNT* : ' Redet Jemand, so rede er als ein Sprecher Gottes'.

' Wer eine Gabe des Redens hat, soll sich nicht eitel selbst zur Schau stellen und nichts Eigenes einmischen wollen, sondern bedenken, dass er Gottes Sprecher, Herold ist, dass es " Gottes Sprüche ", d.h. seine Orakel, seine Offenbarungen sind, die er verkündet.'

Either interpretation—Windisch's or Gunkel's—is preferable to Donovan's —and Bigg's—that ' the Church speaker is bidden to mould his discourse on *the divine model ;* his speech is to be as *the Inspired Word*, the Oracular Word of God ' (p. 13). D. says that it is not necessary to answer the question whether it is the Old revelation or the New that is referred to here. This is a pity, for it would certainly have been useful to preachers to know whether they should mould their discourses after the style of O.T. or N.T. As it seems to me, the real force of the injunction is excellently brought out in Dean Selwyn's new commentary on I Peter : ' the speaker in the congregation should reckon himself to be charged not with his own opinions but the utterances of God '.

Conclusion.

In every one of the four N.T. instances a better and more natural sense is obtained by sticking to the original sense of λογια as found in LXX. When ' Scripture ' or some equivocal term like ' Revelation ' is substituted the passages do not become clearer but rather more obscure. In every case D.'s argument fails to convince.

3. *ΛΟΓΙΑ in the Apostolic Fathers.*

I Clem. xiii. 4 ; cit. of Is. lxvi. 2.

Clem.   επι τινα επιβλεψω, αλλ' η επι τον πραυν και ἡσυχιον
           και τρεμοντα μου τα λογια.

LXX B.   πραυν] ταπεινον | μου τα λογια] τουσ λογουσ μου.

M.T.   ואל־זה אביט אל־עני ונכה־רוח וחרד על־דברי

Orig. Hex.   עני   ο' τον ταπεινον   α' πραυν   σ' πτωχον   θ' συντετριμμενον.

Skinner, *Camb. Bib.* : ' The " word " of the Lord is that spoken by the prophets, and the " trembling " of these devout hearers expresses their scrupulous anxiety to conform with its requirements.'

Duhm., *ad loc.* : ' die . . . um das Gesetz eifrig bemühte Gemeinde des Zionstempels '.

Marti., *ad loc.* : ' heilige Ehrfurcht vor meinem Gesetze haben und ihm gehorsam sind '.

Two points are clear. (1) τα λογια is Clem.'s equivalent for τουσ λογουσ of LXX. (2) τουσ λογουσ of LXX = the commandments of God. That Clem. also takes τα λογια in the same sense is strongly suggested by the immediately following words (xiv. 1) : ' Therefore it is right and holy, my brethren, for us to obey God rather than to follow those who in pride and unruliness are the instigators of an abominable jealousy ' (Lake's trans.).

Further, it should be noted that the immediately preceding xii. 2 is filled with ethical precepts of Jesus, sayings which illustrate exactly what we should naturally take τα λογια to mean.

There is no support in this passage for any interpretation that would make τα λογια the equivalent of ' Holy Writ '.

The Latin version of Clem. (ed. Morin : *Anecd. Maredsol*, Vol. II) has Super quem respiciam nisi super humilem et mansuetum et trementem uerba mea.

I. CLEM. xix. 1.

τουσ τε καταδεξαμενουσ τα λογια αυτου (God) εν φοβῳ και αληθειᾳ.

Lake.　' who received his oracles in fear and truth '.

Ltft.　' that received his oracles in fear and truth '.

O.L.　qui perceperunt eloquia eius cum timore et ueritate.

Syr.　ܠܘܬܗ ܘܡܩܒܠ ܩܠܘܗܝ ܕܐܠܗܐ ܕܒܚܝܠܬܐ ܘܒܫܪܪܐ

Donovan.　who received *God's Oracular Word* in fear and in truth.

D. 16f.

' This passage must be taken as affording an instance where λογια primarily refers to Revelation yet with implied connotation of Holy Writ. . . . In this, as in the other passages, the allusion is to Revelation collectively, and not to any individual component parts or excerpts, much less to sources.'

On this it is sufficient to remark that D. achieves his desired result by first of all paraphrasing the text instead of translating it, and then interpreting his paraphrase in the sense which favours the thesis which he is defending. I am content to accept the rendering given by the ancient versions and by Lightfoot and Lake—as also Harnack ' seine Aussprüche '—and to understand the oracles of God to mean what they mean in LXX : the commands and promises of God, with special reference to the former. This fits in well with the whole course of the argument of the epistle in the preceding chapters with its praise of the humble submissiveness of the Old Testament worthies before God.

I. CLEM. liii. 1.

επιστασθε γαρ και καλωσ επιστασθε τασ ιερασ γραφασ, αγαπητοι και εγκεκυφατε εισ τα λογια του θεου.

O.L. (ed. Morin).

Scitis enim et bene didicistis sanctas scripturas, dilectissimi et introiuistis in eloquia Dei.

introiuistis] scripsi, non sine scrupulo.　Codex perperam : "intonuistis".

Syr.　ܡܝܕܥ ܐܢܬܘܢ ܓܝܪ ܐܢܬܘܢ ܘܝܕܥܝܢ ܐܢܬܘܢ ܡܝܕܥ
ܐܢܬܘܢ ܠܟܬܒܐ ܩܕܝܫܐ ܚܒܝܒܝ. ܘܥܠܬܘܢ ܒܡܠܐ
ܕܐܠܗܐ.

Ltft.

For ye know, and know well, the sacred scriptures, dearly beloved, and ye have searched into the oracles of God.

Lake.

For you have understanding, you have a good understanding of the sacred Scriptures, beloved, and you have studied the oracles of God.

Donovan, rightly I think, holds (p. 18) that Clement in this passage 'must have had the Old Testament in mind'. That by τασ ἱερασ γραφασ he means the O.T. may be freely admitted. Whether, as D. maintains, 'τα λογια του θεου becomes for practical purposes synonymous with γραφη' is quite another question. Here again it may fairly be claimed that what is meant by τα λογια του θεου is something which diligent students of the O.T. will find therein. Clement is not saying, 'you know and know well the sacred scriptures and you have searched into the Bible'; but rather, 'you know your Bible well, and in it you have studied closely those utterances of God which are the direct revelation of his will and purpose.'

I. CLEM. lxii. 3.

σαφωσ ηδειμεν γραφειν ημασ ανδρασιν πιστοισ και ελλογιμωτατοισ και εγκεκυφοσιν εισ τα λογια τησ παιδειασ του θεου.

O.L.

pro certo sciebamus scribere uobis uiris fidelibus et probatis et oboedientibus eloquiis doctrinae Dei.

Syr.

ܪܘܡ ܗܘܐ ܡܢ ܠܡܣ ܘܒܚܕܐ ܠܚܝܕܐܬ ܡܩܡܚܠܝ ܘܬܠܡܕܐ ܘܐܪܡܘ ܠܐܬ ܩܩܠ ܗܐ ܘܡܚܘܪ ܘ ܐܬܐܐ

Ltft.

we knew well that we were writing to men who are faithful and highly accounted and have diligently searched into the oracles of the teaching of God.

Lake.

we knew quite well that we were writing to men who were faithful and distinguished and had studied the oracles of the teaching of God.

D. p. 18.

. . . 'persons also, who have been students of God's instructive Oracles'. 'It is here Revelation, viewed in its moral and educational effects' (ib.).

On this passage it is to be remarked that where Clement elsewhere uses παιδεια it has quite definitely the sense of discipline—moral training by precept, example, or chastisement. It is therefore natural to take τα λογια τησ παιδειασ του θεου here as having the same shade of meaning. The oracles in question are God's disciplinary oracles, i.e. his commandments. The O.L. translator seems to have felt this when he rendered εγκεκυφοσιν by oboedientibus. That being so we ought not to regard the phrase as meaning 'Revelation viewed in its moral and educational effects' but rather as meaning 'such divine oracles as bear directly on the moral training of God's people'.

II. CLEM. xiii. 3.

τα εθνη γαρ, ακουοντα εκ του στοματοσ ημων τα λογια του θεου, ωσ καλα και μεγαλα θαυμαζει· επειτα, καταμαθοντα τα εργα ημων ότι ουκ εστιν αξια των ρηματων ών λεγομεν, ενθεν εισ βλασφημιαν τρεπονται, λεγοντεσ ειναι μυθον τινα και πλανην.

Syr. ܥܡ̈ܡܐ ܓܝܪ ܟܕ ܫܡܥܝܢ ܡܢ ܦܘܡܢ ܡ̈ܠܐ
ܕܐܠܗܐ ܐܝܟ ܕܫ̈ܦܝܪܬܐ ܘܪ̈ܘܪܒܬܐ ܡܬܕܡܪܝܢ
ܒܗܘܢ. ܒܬܪܟܢ ܕܝܢ ܟܕ ܝܠܦܘܢ ܥܒ̈ܕܝܢ ܕܫܘܝܢ
ܕܠܐ ܐܝܟܘܬܗܘܢ ܕܗܘܝܢ ܠܡ̈ܠܝܢ ܕܐܡܪܝܢ ܡܢ
ܗܦܟܝܢ ܠܓܘܕܦܐ ܡܬܗܦܟܝܢ ܟܕ ܐܡܪܝܢ ܕܡ̈ܠܐ
ܡܕܡ ܕܒܛܠ ܐܝܬܝܗܝܢ ܘܛܥܝܘܬܐ.

Ltft.

'For the Gentiles, when they hear from our mouth the oracles of God, marvel at them for their beauty and greatness; then, when they discover that our works are not worthy of the words which we speak, forthwith they betake themselves to blasphemy, saying that it is an idle story and a delusion.'

Ltft. takes *τα λ. τ. θεου* here to be 'a synonyme for the Scriptures'. D. says (p. 27), 'The writer is a Christian teacher addressing a Christian community. Christian practice must be in keeping, he insinuates, with Christian teaching. This Christian teaching pagans learn indirectly from the *λογια του θεου*—i.e. the Scriptures, including the Gospel.'

The context does not support either Ltft. or D. The writer is dealing with the text, Is. lii. 5, *δια παντοσ το ονομα μου βλασφημειται εν πασιν τοισ εθνεσιν*. He asks How? and the answer of God is *εν τῳ μη ποιειν ὑμασ ἁ βουλομαι*. Then in further explanation of this follows our passage. The Gentiles hear the *λογια* and see how splendid they are. Then they observe that Christians do not themselves obey these excellent *λογια*, and blaspheme. The phenomenon is as well known in our own day as in the day of II Clem. And the sense in which *λογια* is meant here is crystal clear. It is the oracles as revealing God's will concerning man's behaviour. And this is shown still more clearly by the example given immediately afterwards. The oracle concerning love to enemies becomes an occasion of blasphemy among the Gentiles because Christians not only do not obey it but also add to their disobedience failure to love even their friends.

Ep. Polycarpi. vii. 1.

και ὁσ αν μεθοδευῃ τα λογια του Κυριου προσ τασ ιδιασ επιθυμιασ, και λεγει μητε αναστασιν μητε κρισιν, οὑτοσ πρωτοτοκοσ εστι του Σατανα.

Ltft.

And whosoever shall pervert the oracles of the Lord to his own lusts and say that there is neither resurrection nor judgement, that man is the first-born of Satan.

According to D. (p. 20) '*το μεθοδευειν τα λογια του κυριου* . . . is obviously "distortion of Holy Writ"'. This 'could signify either distortion of meaning, or mutilation and interpolation of the sacred books received by the Church' (p. 21). 'As he uses *τα λογια του κυριου* rather than the more generic *τα λογια του θεου*, he very probably has in mind the evangelical Scriptures' (p. 20).

But here again we have to take account of the phrase *προσ τασ ιδιασ επιθυμιασ*. This indicates clearly enough what is meant by the *λογια*. Also the accompanying denial of the resurrection and judgement points in the same direction. The writer has in mind two directions in which religious perversity can manifest itself. The first is false doctrine about Christ. This is dealt with in the opening clauses of the section. From that he passes to what so often accompanied false doctrine —moral laxity. Twisting the Lord's oracles to their own lusts and denying the one thing which at that time was the supreme sanction of morality ; the belief that all must appear before the judgement seat of Christ to give account of the deeds done in the flesh. λογια bears the same meaning that we have found elsewhere. It may well be that του κυριου means that it is the oracles of Christ that are thought of ; and the oracles, in that case, will be such things as are found in what is called his ethical teaching.

4. ΛΟΓΙΑ in the Apologists.

Justin Martyr.

APOL. I. 32 (end).

και Ιεσσαι προπατωρ μεν κατα το λογιον γεγενηται, κτἑ.

The λογιον here referred to is the prophetic oracle cited just before και Ησαιασ . . . ούτωσ ειπεν· Ανατελει αστρον εξ Ιακωβ, και ανθοσ αναβησεται απο τησ ριζησ Ιεσσαι· και επι τον βραχιονα αυτου εθνη ελπιουσιν. This λογιον Justin declares has been fulfilled in Christ. There is no doubt what the word means here. It is the promise of God.

DIAL· xviii· I (Otto I, ii. 64).

επειδη γαρ ανεγνωσ, ω Τρυφων, ώσ αυτοσ ὁμολογησασ εφησ, τα ὑπ' εκεινου του σωτηροσ ἡμων διδαχθεντα, ουκ ατοπον νομιζω πεποιηκεναι και βραχεα των εκεινου λογια προσ τοισ προφητικοισ επιμνησθεισ.

D. (pp. 29 f.) : ' there emerges a fully literal yet correct translation, " Brief oracles from among *His Oracles* ". In modern speech one would rightly render : " brief extracts from the *Dominical Oracles* " .' Later he says (p. 30), ' To allege that this Christian philosopher is here referring to some unknown *collection* of Christ's sayings, or to an imaginary *manual* of messianic prophecy, or to *Testimonia*, is to ignore the normal value of this formula and to shut one's eyes to the context '. To this it is sufficient to reply that it is not necessary to make any of these allegations. It is only necessary to claim, what D. himself admits, that Justin is referring to the ' Dominical Oracles '. This phrase, in its plain and natural meaning, supplied by Justin in this very sentence—τα ὑπ' εκεινου του σωτηροσ ἡμων διδαχθεντα—is amply sufficient for the purposes of those who think that the document referred to by Papias or his informant is the Synoptic document Q.

But this is not sufficient for D. For him τα λογια του κυριου must be made to mean (p. 30) ' " Oracles concerning the Lord "—that is, God's Word or Revelation as couched in New Testament Scripture '. The subjective genitive —the natural and obvious construction—is quietly turned into an objective genitive. On what grounds ? That among the *sayings* of Jesus, which have just been quoted by Justin, there ' occurs one very precious item—a little portion of Gospel *narrative* '. Apparently D. would maintain that there are four Dominical Oracles in the passage :

Oracle 1. ὁ οικοσ μου οικοσ προσευχησ κτέ.
Oracle 2. και τασ τραπεζασ κτέ.
Oracle 3. ουαι ὑμιν, γραμματεισ και φαρισαιοι κτέ.
Oracle 4. ουαι ὑμιν, γραμματεισ κτέ.

There is no hint that he regards them otherwise than as separate items. But one has only to glance at the text of Justin to see that No. 2 is not a separate item at all, but a mere scrap of the narrative context of No. 1. No. 1 is an oracle uttered by the Lord *when* he overturned the tables of the money-changers in the Temple. The fact is that there are three oracles quoted by Justin from the Lord's Oracles ; and they are genuine oracles. Recognition of this fact saves us from the necessity of supposing that λογιον in the singular means one thing for Justin and something different in the plural, or that in talking to Jews he would describe the Gospels as τα λογια while in addressing the Roman Senate he would call them τα απομνημονευματα.

DIAL· cxxxiii. 5. (Otto I, ii. 474).
Quotation from Is. v. 24.

Tatian.

Orat. ad Graec. xli, 2 (ed. Schwartz, TU, IV, i. 42) : περι μεν ουν τησ καθ' ἑκαστον ⟨των⟩ λογιων πραγματειασ χρονων τε και αναγραφησ αυτων ὡσ οιμαι σφοδρα ✶ ✶ μετα πασησ ὑμιν ακριβειασ ανεγραψαμεν. Here the text is uncertain, the authorities being divided between λογιων and λογον. It is clear, however, that the passage sheds no light on the problem with which we are concerned.

6.

THE FOURTH GOSPEL.
(1947)

TO the searcher for materials for the Life of Jesus the
Fourth Gospel is either no problem at all or the most
baffling of all. We may say, for example, ' The question is
decided. The Gospel of John is inferior to the Synoptics as
a historical source just in proportion as it is more strongly
dominated than they by theological and apologetic interests ' ; [1]
or, in the words of one of the acutest and most learned New
Testament scholars of our time, ' John may contain a few remnants of true tradition, but in the main it is fiction '.[2]

If we take this line we may easily come to the conclusion
that the Fourth Gospel should be left on one side and that our
attempts to write the Life of Jesus should, in general, ignore
it. Alternatively we may decide to see what can be elicited
from this document and attempt to assess its value. We are
at once confronted by a series of puzzles, most of which still
await a convincing solution. The questions touch every side
of literary and historical criticism—date and place, authorship,
sources, original language, relation to the other Gospels, and
so on. To all these matters an immense amount of labour
and learning has been dedicated—so much so that a bare survey
of what has been done would easily occupy a whole series of
Rylands Lectures. For excellent accounts of the progress of
research on the problems we can refer to the works of Principal
W. F. Howard [3] and, more recently, Professor P. H. Menoud.[4]
I must be content with the more modest task of indicating some

---

[1] A. Schweitzer, *The Quest of the Historical Jesus*,[2] 1911, 87.

[2] Kirsopp Lake in *The Albert Schweitzer Jubilee Book*, 431.

[3] *The Fourth Gospel in Recent Criticism and Interpretation*.

[4] *L'Évangile de Jean d'après les recherches récentes* (Neuchâtel and Paris, 1943).

questions that seem to be worth asking and some lines of research that may produce useful results. I have no ready-made solution of the ' Johannine Problem ', only some paths on which we may travel hopefully, though without guarantees that they will not turn out to be blind alleys.

We have first to consider the external attestation of the Gospel, and we begin with the statement in the *Muratorian Canon*, which may be taken to give the views accepted in Rome at the end of the second century.[1] It is as follows :—

The fourth of the Gospels is that of John, one of the Disciples. He, when his fellow-disciples and bishops were urging him, said, ' Fast with me for three days beginning to-day, and let us report to each other what is revealed to each '. On that very night it was revealed to Andrew, one of the Apostles, that John should write the whole story in his own name with the authentication of them all.

And, therefore, even though the opening narratives are different in the individual Gospel books, nevertheless it makes no difference to the faith of believers, since by the one directing Spirit in all (four jointly) all (essentials) are set forth concerning the Nativity, the Passion, the Resurrection, the Intercourse with his Disciples, and his twofold Advent, the first in despised humility, which has taken place, the second in splendid kingly power, which is still to come.

What wonder, then, that John so deliberately gives prominence to these particulars in his Epistles, saying of himself, ' What we have seen with our eyes and heard with our ears, and our hands have handled, these things we have written to you '. For thus he claims to be not only an eyewitness and hearer but also the writer of an orderly account of all the wonderful doings of the Lord.

Elsewhere in the *Muratorianum* John is mentioned as the author of two Epistles [2] and the Apocalypse. It would seem

---

[1] I follow the text as edited by Zahn, *Geschichte des Neutestamentlichen Kanons*, ii. 139, with reference also to Lagrange, *Histoire Ancienne du Canon du Nouveau Testament*, 66-78, and *Évangile selon S. Jean*,[4] lxii. ff.

[2] On this see my article in *Journal of Theological Studies*, April 1947.

that the writer believed the Apocalypse to be earlier in date than the Pauline Epistles since he speaks of Paul's having followed the order of his predecessor John in writing by name to seven Churches only.

The first paragraph on the Fourth Gospel presents us with a picture of the Evangelist as a member, and perhaps the leading member, of a group of ' Disciples ' and ' Bishops '. As the whole emphasis of the passage is on the claim that the Gospel gives first-hand information about the Ministry, we should probably take ' Disciples ' to mean followers of Jesus during the Ministry. It may be supposed that ' Bishops ' means members of the group having definite ecclesiastical responsibilities at the relevant time. It would not follow that all former Disciples were now Bishops or that all the Bishops concerned were former Disciples, though doubtless it is implied that a number were both Disciples and Bishops. The request of these men that John should write a gospel is at once confirmed by a Divine revelation.[1] John is to write the book and they are to authenticate it. The second paragraph tackles the well-known problem created by the discrepancies between the Fourth Gospel and the Synoptics and points out that, however much the Gospels may differ about details, they combine to give the essentials of the Faith. The third paragraph, without saying it in so many words, suggests that John's order of events is to be preferred to the Synoptic, where they conflict. His personal relations with the Master may be presumed to give him the right to be heard both on the central matters of the kerygma and on the detailed course of events in the Ministry.

The passage as a whole gives one the impression that it is a defence of the Fourth Gospel against those who were attacking it. It is not difficult to guess who they were. In Rome it was one Gaius who, at the end of the second century or the beginning of the third, denied the authenticity of the Gospel in the course of his campaign against Montanism.[2] One of

[1] The prominent part assigned to Andrew in this matter is on all fours with his prominence in the Fourth Gospel itself as compared with his position in the Synoptics. See Moffatt, *Introd.*[3] 564.

[2] Lagrange, *L'Évangile selon S. Jean*, lv.-lxi. ; P. de Labriolle, *La Crise Montaniste*, 131-5, 191 f., 278-85 ; Bardenhewer, *Gesch. d. Altkirchl. Lit.*, i. 432 ff.

I

the objections urged by the critics of John was his disagreement with the Synoptics, a point which is taken up and answered in our text. And it is noteworthy that the main opposition to Gaius came from Hippolytus, who is now widely regarded as the author of the *Muratorianum*.[1]

The *Anti-Marcionite Prologues* also deal with the Fourth Gospel. The concluding paragraph of the Prologue to Luke states that the evangelist subsequently wrote the Acts of the Apostles. It continues : ' Afterwards John the Apostle ' [the Greek adds ' one of the Twelve '] ' wrote the Apocalypse in the island of Patmos, and after that the Gospel ' [the Latin adds ' in Asia ']. The John-Prologue proper is as follows :—

> The Gospel of John was published and given to the Churches by John still present in the body, as Papias, entitled Hierapolitanus, the beloved disciple of John related in the *Five Exegetical Books ;* indeed he (Papias) took down the Gospel, John dictating accurately. But the heretic Marcion, when he had been condemned by him (Papias) because he held opposed views, was expelled. He (Marcion) indeed had brought documents or letters to him (Papias) from the brethren who were in Pontus.

This Prologue, taken along with the closing sentence of the Luke-Prologue, maintains the Apostolic authorship of the Fourth Gospel. The work was completed and published during the lifetime of John. The emphatic *adhuc in corpore constituto* is pointless unless there were those who claimed that John was already dead before the publication of the Gospel attributed to him. The Prologue appeals to the writings of Papias, and mentions the Church of which he was Bishop, no doubt as evidence of his reliability as a witness. It remains odd that Eusebius, who quotes Papias on Gospel origins and had access to the *Five Exegetical Books*, does not mention any of the matters recorded in this Prologue. In any case it is most unlikely that the story of the dictation to Papias appeared in the *Exegeses*, or that it is true. The story about Marcion may well be Asian tradition ; and it may be surmised that the whole

[1] Altaner, *Patrologie*, 83.

Prologue gives traditions of Asian origin, and that the reference to the *Exegeses* is no more than a guess, and a wrong one.

From Alexandria the earliest testimony is that of Clement,[1] who is said to be reporting the tradition of ' the original elders ' (τῶν ἀνέκαθεν πρεσβυτέρων). According to this ' John was the last (to write), conscious that the matters of fact (τὰ σωματικά) had been set forth in the (other) Gospels, and, urged on by the disciples, under divine inspiration he produced a spiritual Gospel.'

Who the ' original elders ' were we can only guess. Their tradition may be the old tradition of the Alexandrian Church, or it may come from farther afield. The interesting thing is the agreement between Clement's tradition and that of the *Muratorianum* on the point that the composition of the Gospel was undertaken in response to an appeal from disciples.[2] The problem remains : whose disciples? The account in Clement would suggest that it was the Evangelist's own disciples who asked for a written Gospel. In the *Muratorianum*, on the other hand, the wording definitely favours the idea that it is disciples of the Lord who are meant.

Irenaeus, as quoted by Eusebius,[3] tells us of the composition of the first three Gospels, and then continues :

> Afterwards John, the disciple of the Lord, the same who leant back on his breast—he too set forth the Gospel, while residing at Ephesus in Asia.

Eusebius later [4] quotes from the letter of Irenaeus to Florinus a passage in which the Bishop of Lyons describes his boyhood in ' Lower Asia ', and how he saw and heard Polycarp the venerable Bishop of Smyrna, and in particular how Polycarp ' would tell of his intercourse with John and with the others who had seen the Lord, how he would relate from memory their words ; and what the things were which he had heard from them concerning the Lord, his mighty works and his teaching,

---

[1] Given by Eusebius, *H.E.* vi. 14. 7.

[2] So I translate τῶν γνωρίμων. Cf. Josephus, *B.J.* iv. 460 ; Justin, I *Apol.* 32. On the use of the term ' disciple ' in the early Church, Harnack, *Mission und Ausbreitung*,[3] i. 382-4.

[3] *H.E.* v. 8. 4 (Lawlor and Oulton's translation). Cf. *adu. Haer.* III. 1. 1.

[4] *H.E.* v. 20.

Polycarp, as having received them from the eyewitnesses of the Life of the Word, would declare altogether in accordance with the Scriptures '. It is clear from these passages that Irenaeus in his later life identified the John, of whom he had heard Polycarp speak in his boyhood, with the Apostle John, the son of Zebedee, and the disciple whom Jesus loved. The question is whether his memory is reliable, whether, in fact, the John of whom Polycarp spoke was the Apostle or another Christian leader who happened to have the same name.

The question becomes more acute when we consider the early quotations from and allusions to the Fourth Gospel.[1] The most striking fact is their scarcity, and that in places where we should have expected to find them. Polycarp [2] of Smyrna, who, according to Irenaeus, was a disciple of John, has nothing that can fairly be described as a quotation from the Fourth Gospel, and the one possible allusion does not carry conviction. Ignatius of Antioch, who wrote a letter to the Ephesians, failed to mention John in it, though if Irenaeus is right the work of John was both more recent and more prolonged at Ephesus than that of Paul, to whom he does refer. Moreover, while the letters of Ignatius are full of ideas of a Johannine cast there is nothing to show that he knew the Fourth Gospel. Mr. Sanders sums up a careful and detailed discussion by saying : [3]

> ' Nothing in these passages proves conclusively that Ignatius knew or used the Fourth Gospel as we have it, but it seems clear that there is a fairly close affinity between his theology and language and those of the Fourth Gospel. . . . But as against these points of similarity, there are significant differences, as for instance in the treatment of the Holy Spirit. There is enough agreement to make it probable that behind them both lies a common tradition of theological thought and language, perhaps even that Ignatius was acquainted with some written summary of

[1] These have recently been the subject of a fresh and illuminating study by J. N. Sanders (1943).

[2] For a detailed discussion of Polycarp's use of the New Testament see *The New Testament in the Apostolic Fathers*, 84-104 ; P. N. Harrison, *Polycarp's Two Epistles to the Philippians*, 285-310, 327-335.

[3] *Op. cit.* p. 14.   Cf. *N.T. in Apost. Fathers*, 63-83 ; Harrison, *op. cit.* 231-266.

our Lord's teaching used by the author of the Gospel (if any such work existed). But one cannot say with any certainty that Ignatius knew our Fourth Gospel.'

We move on into the middle of the second century. Polycarp (martyred A.D. 156), who according to Irenaeus was a disciple of John, does not mention him ; and, while his letter to the Philippians has one passage which looks like a quotation from 1 John, there is nothing to show that he was acquainted with the Gospel.

Justin (martyred about A.D. 165), born in Palestine, was converted to Christianity probably about A.D. 130 and, it may be, at Ephesus, the reputed home of the Fourth Gospel. Wherever his conversion took place we have the authority of Eusebius for saying that he was settled at Ephesus in the thirties of the second century.[1] His works show considerable affinity with Johannine thought ; but there are far-reaching differences.[2] Moreover, while Justin has frequent recourse to the Synoptic tradition, his references to the Fourth Gospel are few, slight, and not of a sort to suggest direct quotation.[3] As Mr. Sanders justly says, this ' relative scarcity of quotations from the Fourth Gospel is the more surprising as Justin misses many obvious opportunities of quoting or alluding to the Fourth Gospel in support of his conclusions, which in that case can hardly be derived from the Gospel '.[4]

The perplexing and important fact that emerges is that quotations are absent in those places where we should most confidently look for them if the Fourth Gospel was composed in Ephesus about A.D. 100 by John the Apostle. No theory about the Gospel that fails to give an explanation of the phenomena presented by the writings of Ignatius, Polycarp, and Justin has much chance of survival.

[1] *H.E.* iv. 18. 6. Cf. Justin, *Dial*, § 1.

[2] See, for example, Listzmann, *Geschichte der Alten Kirche*, ii. 182-6 ; Sanders, *op. cit.* 31 f.

[3] The nearest thing to a quotation is perhaps *I Apol.* lxi. 4 : καὶ γὰρ ὁ Χριστὸς εἶπεν. "Αν μὴ ἀναγεννηθῆτε οὐ μὴ εἰσέλθητε εἰς τὴν βασιλείαν τῶν οὐρανῶν, which may be a mixed reminiscence of John iii. 3 and 5. Other cases are less impressive.

[4] *Op. cit.* 32.

We have clear evidence of the existence of the Gospel from other sources. The Valentinian Gnostic Heracleon, who flourished about A.D. 145-180,[1] wrote a commentary on it, of which fragments survive. There is also good reason to think that the earliest form of Montanist teaching, including the oracles of Montanus himself, was dependent on the Fourth Gospel. The rise of Montanism belongs to the third quarter of the second century.[2] But perhaps the most interesting development in recent times is the way in which palæography has come to take a hand in the dating of the Gospel. I refer, of course, to the two papyrus fragments published shortly before the war. The one, P. Egerton 2, preserved in the British Museum, is a fragment of an apocryphal gospel, the author of which almost certainly made use of John.[3] The writing of this fragment is dated on palæographical grounds about the middle of the second century (A.D. 140-160). The composition of the Apocryphal Gospel is therefore earlier : the Editors of the fragment considered that it might be thirty years earlier (c. A.D. 110-130). The composition of the Fourth Gospel would then be earlier still.

The second papyrus fragment, P. Ryl. Gk. 457, is one of the chief treasures of this Library.[4] It contains verses of John xviii and is assigned by palæographers to the first half of the second century. That is to say, if we can trust the judgement of the experts—and there is no good reason why we should not —P. Ryl. Gk. 457, and probably a good many of its palæographical kinsfolk, was in existence during the lifetimes of Polycarp and Justin. If Justin does not quote from John it is not because there were no copies of the Gospel available.[5]

[1] Bardenhewer, G.A.L. i. 360. Cf. A. E. Brooke, The Fragments of Heracleon.

[2] On the chronology of Montanism cf. Harnack, Chronologie i. 363-381 ; P. de Labriolle, La Crise Montaniste, 569-589. On the Montanist appeal to the Fourth Gospel, Labriolle, op. cit. 38-43, 131-135.

[3] Bell and Skeat, Fragments of an Unknown Gospel (1935) and The New Gospel Fragments (1935) ; C. H. Dodd, A New Gospel in the BULLETIN OF THE JOHN RYLANDS LIBRARY, January 1936 ; T. W. Manson in the Journal of Egyptian Archæology, 1937, 130 ff.

[4] C. H. Roberts, An Unpublished Fragment of the Fourth Gospel (1935) ; Catalogue of the Greek Papyri in the Rylands Library, iii (1938), 1-3.

[5] I leave the case of Polycarp on one side as the question of the date of his correspondence with the Philippians is still in debate.

The results of a study of the external evidence are thus somewhat disappointing. It seems clear that the Gospel was in existence in the first half of the second century, how early in that period we cannot say with any certainty. It is probable that it was associated with the name of John, and certain that towards the end of the century Church opinion had settled down to the view that this John was to be identified with John the Apostle.[1]

I turn now to the internal evidence. Here there is a good deal of well-trodden ground, which I do not propose to go over again, as I have no fresh observations to make. I confine myself to those matters where there seems to be possibility of progress in our investigations. I take first the question of the literary unity of the Gospel. This was made the subject of a thorough and methodical study by Eduard Schweizer in a book published in 1939.[2] Schweizer began with a carefully selected set of characteristic marks of the Johannine style and then went

---

[1] This identification would at once break down if it could be shown that John the Apostle died a martyr's death at some time before the fall of Jerusalem in A.D. 70. The evidence for this is not of a very convincing kind; and I do not propose to go over it again here. I will make only two remarks. (1) What is often taken to be the strongest argument for the supposed martyrdom of John is the prophecy in Mk. x. 39; and it cannot be used to any purpose without committing a glaring *petitio principii*. For it is either a true prophecy (so R. H. Charles, *Revelation*, i. p. xlv, n. 2) or a *vaticinium ex eventu* (so many who use it to prove the early death of John) In either case the answer to the question ' How do we know that John was martyred ? ' is ' From Mk. x. 39 (a true prophecy or a prophecy after the event, as the case may be) '. ' Then how do we know that Mk. x. 39 is a true prophecy (or a *vaticinium ex eventu*) ? ' ' Because John was in fact martyred.' The argument is a perfect circle. The only escape from the circle is by producing independent evidence for the martyrdom of John. But if that can be done, the evidence of Mk. x. 39 at once becomes superfluous. There is no escape from the conclusion that the argument from Mk. x. 39 is either circular or unnecessary. (2) Although I think the evidence for an early martyrdom of the Apostle to be of very little value, I have no better opinion of the evidence for his prolonged residence, or indeed any residence at all, at Ephesus. That there was someone called John at Ephesus and that he played an influential part in the life of the Church in Asia, seems more than likely. That this person was the Apostle John, the son of Zebedee, I do not believe.

[2] E. Schweizer, *Ego Eimi*, Göttingen, Vandenhoeck und Rupprecht, 1939 (Forschungen zur Religion u. Literatur des Alten und Neuen Testaments, N.F., 38 Heft). The important part of the work for our present purpose is pp. 82-112.

on to examine their distribution in the Gospel. The results of the study can be set out in four propositions :

1. The style is in essentials one throughout the book. This stylistic unity lies not in an earlier document but in the final composition.

2. The author probably used traditional material which may have been in written form. But he has made it so much his own stylistically that it cannot be analysed out.

3. The Gospel as a whole is a unity on which the author has imposed his style and spirit.

4. These conclusions are only well-grounded working hypotheses, not settled and certain results.[1]

There are two other observations of Schweizer's which should be noted. First we have the areas of the Gospel where the stylistic characteristics are absent or scarce. These are the wedding at Cana (ii. 1-10) ; the cleansing of the Temple (ii. 13-19) ; the latter part of the conversation with the Samaritan woman and the stay in Galilee (iv. 16-53) ; the anointing at Bethany (xii. 1-8) ; the Triumphal Entry (xii. 12-15) ; and the *Pericope de Adultera* (vii. 53-viii. 11). The last of these is already rejected on textual grounds and the main interest of the stylistic test is that it confirms the decision of the textual critic. It will be noticed that almost all this material is narrative and that much of it has parallels in the Synoptics. The second point is the opinion expressed by Schweizer on page 107 that the Evangelist most probably used sources and that he may have had a collection of narratives and/or one of speeches. 'As the style of 1 John agrees with the elevated style of the speeches in the Gospel (and essentially with this alone) we should probably prefer to assume a source for the narratives, unless we are prepared to postulate a Discourse-source for the First Epistle as well as the Gospel.'

Schweizer's method has been carried further by P. H. Menoud [2] and E. Ruckstuhl.[3] The position seems now to be that we must think of the Gospel as bearing the impress throughout of a single mind expressing itself in a uniform Greek style.

---

[1] *Op. cit.*, 108.   [2] *Op. cit.*

[3] Literarkritik am Johannesevangelium und eucharistische Rede in *Divus Thomas*, 1945, pp. 153-190, 301-333.

This, of course, does not exclude the possibility that there may be interpolations (the *Pericope de Adultera* is the most notorious) and displacements. It is also allowed that the Evangelist probably made use of sources. If he did, it becomes extremely unlikely that he was the eyewitness Apostle.

To the question of sources one answer has been strongly urged in recent years, that of a single Aramaic document, of which the existing Greek Gospel is a translation. This hypothesis was put forward with many supporting arguments by C. F. Burney in 1922 in his book *The Aramaic Origin of the Fourth Gospel*.[1] The case was further fortified in *The Poetry of Our Lord* (1925), in which Burney argued that much of the teaching of Jesus was delivered in the forms of Semitic poetry, producing examples from the Synoptics and the Fourth Gospel. When Burney's first work was published it was observed that his evidences of Aramaism in John were not evenly distributed throughout the Gospel. They are found in the following blocks :—

i. 1-34 ; ii. 13-22 ; iii. 1-36 ; iv. 1-26, 31-38 ; v. 1-47 ; vi. 22-71 ; vii. 14-24, 32-52 ; viii. 12-59 ; ix. 8-41 ; x. 1-18, 22-39 ; xi. 1-44, 47-53 ; xii. 20-50 ; xiii. 1-30 ; xiv. 1-4, 8-21, 25-31 ; xv. 1-27 ; xvi. 1-15, 25-33 ; xvii. 1-26 ; xviii. 1-11, 19-24, 28-37 ; xix. 1-16, 31-37.

They are absent from :—

i. 35-ii. 12 ; ii. 23-25 ; iv. 27-30, 39-54 ; vi. 1-21 ;[2] vii. 1-13, 25-31 ; ix. 1-7 ; x. 19-21, 40-42 ; xi. 45-46, 54-57 ; xii. 1-19 ; xiii. 31-38 ; xiv. 5-7, 22-24 ; xvi. 16-24 ; xviii. 12-18, 25-27, 38-40 ; xix. 17-30, 38-42 ; xx. 1-xxi. 25.[3]

It is observed that a large proportion of the non-Aramaising sections are narrative and that many have parallels in the synoptic Gospels. Further we find that the vast majority of the

[1] The case for an Aramaic original is also argued by C. C. Torrey in "The Aramaic Origin of the Gospel of John" (*Harvard Theol. Rev.* xvi. (1923), 305–44 ; *The Four Gospels, a New Translation* ; and *Our Translated Gospels*.

[2] It is to be noted that if Chs. v. and vi. are transposed, iv. 39-54 and vi. 1-21 form a single block of material without Aramaisms.

[3] In order to avoid any arbitrariness the units into which I divide the Gospel for the purpose of reckoning presence or absence of Aramaisms are the paragraphs of Westcott and Hort's text. A block here may include several paragraphs of Westcott and Hort ; but no paragraph is divided between blocks.

passages which Burney adduces as evidence of Semitic poetic form in John come from the sections in which Aramaisms are recorded.

At this point we must take into account another element in the problem ; that of the relations between the Gospel and the First Epistle. The Epistle was examined by the Manchester University Hellenistic Seminar, and it was found that the Aramaisms discovered by Burney in the Gospel were absent from the Epistle. A further point to be noted is the fact that whereas quotations from the Old Testament are found in the Gospel, the Epistle shows none. Again, while the Gospel and the Epistle share many ideas and have many words and phrases in common, there is a not inconsiderable difference in their vocabulary. For example the following terms are frequently used in the Gospel, but not at all in the Epistle : ὁ υἱὸς τοῦ ἀνθρώπου, δόξα, δοξάζειν. The curious thing is that of the twenty Old Testament quotations in the Gospel no fewer than sixteen occur in sections marked by the presence of Aramaisms ; of the thirteen cases of ὁ υἱὸς τοῦ ἀνθρώπου, twelve are in such passages, as are eighteen of the nineteen examples of δόξα and twenty of the twenty-three cases of δοξάζειν.[1] That is to say, some of the most striking differences between the Gospel and

[1] For the sake of completeness I give the results of an examination of the long list of words found in the Gospel but not in the Epistle and brought forward by Professor Dodd as part of the case for separate authorship (RYLANDS BULLETIN, xxi. (1937), 139 f.). After each word or group of words I give the number of occurrences in the Aramaising sections of the Gospel and then, separated by an oblique stroke, the number of occurrences in non-Aramaising sections :—

σώζειν and σωτηρία 7/0 ; ἀπολλύναι and ἀπώλεια 10/1, ἀνιστάναι, ἀνάστασις, ζωοποιεῖν 14/1, εἰρήνη 3/3 (these three are all cases of the conventional greeting εἰρήνη ὑμῖν), χάρις 4/0, ἁγιάζειν 4/0, προσκύνειν 11/0, δεῖ 8/2, γραφή, γράμματα, γράφειν (of the Scriptures) 16/6, νόμος 13/1, κρίνειν, κρίσις 30/0, δόξα 18/1, δοξάζειν 20/3, ἀναβαίνειν 7/8, καταβαίνειν 12/6, ἄνω, ἄνωθεν 5/3, ὑψοῦν 5/0, θέλημα 11/0, ἐξουσία 8/0, πέμπειν 28/4, ῥῆμα 11/1, φιλεῖν, φίλος 13/6, τιμᾶν 6/0, ζητεῖν 24/10, καρπός 10/0, δοκεῖν 6/2, ἴδιος 12/3.

These figures seem to me to be highly significant. They greatly strengthen the case for regarding this division into Aramaising and non-Aramaising sections as fundamentally sound. I should add that I have left out of account one word in Dodd's list, κύριος. A very large proportion of the examples in the Gospel are the vocative κύριε in dialogue, for which there would, of course, be no need in the Epistle.

the Epistle turn out on closer examination to be differences between the Aramaising half of the Gospel and the Epistle ; and it is open to us to entertain the hypothesis that the Epistle is the work of a writer composing freely and the Gospel the work of the same writer with his style to some extent controlled by the material which he has to incorporate into his book. I venture to think that this is a possibility that deserves more detailed consideration than I am able to give to it here.

I have alluded to the fact that in a considerable number of cases the absence of Aramaisms and the presence of Synoptic parallels coincide. The whole question of the relation of John to the Synoptics has been reopened by the short but very important book by P. Gardner-Smith entitled *Saint John and the Synoptic Gospels* (1938). Here it is argued (and the argument, based as it is on detailed examination of all the parallelisms between John and the Synoptics, appears to be cogent) that ' when all the facts are taken into consideration it becomes difficult to believe that the author of the Fourth Gospel was familiar with those Gospels which are generally thought to have been written and given to the Church before he undertook his task '.[1] It follows that the Fourth Gospel may be regarded ' as an independent authority for the life of Jesus, or at least for the traditions current in the Christian Church in the second half of the first century '.[2] Similarities of a striking nature between Luke and John may be due to their common employment of the same developed traditions at certain points of the story. This also is a matter that deserves fuller consideration and investigation in the light of the points already brought forward in this paper.

In this connection there are a number of topics that call for discussion. Here it must suffice to indicate them in a general way.

First there is the question of the disagreements between John and the Synoptics. They are well known, so well known that there is no need to repeat them all once more. All that I want to emphasise is that it is no longer possible to say ' If the Fourth Gospel contradicts the Synoptics, so much the worse for the Fourth Gospel '. Each case must be considered purely

[1] *Op. cit.*, 88. [2] *Op. cit.*, 96.

on its merits. If this is done in the case of the cleansing of the Temple, which John places near the beginning of the Ministry, and Mark near the end, we shall probably reject the desperate solution of two cleansings ; and, when that is done, and we have to choose between John and Mark, I suppose that most scholars would give their votes in favour of Mark. On the other hand, when it comes to the question of the nature of the Last Supper, and the dating of the Crucifixion, a very strong case can be made for the view that John's dating is right.[1] But if John is right on a matter of capital importance such as this is, he has *eo ipso* established an indisputable claim to a full and unprejudiced hearing on every other point ; and his evidence must be seriously considered as possible independent confirmation, where it agrees with the Synoptic tradition, and as a possible alternative where it does not.

But if the Fourth Gospel contains an independent strain of tradition concerning the public career of our Lord, we are bound to enquire into its provenance. On this question we are not without indications : I mention a few which seem to me to be relevant and significant.

First I should put the growing conviction that the Fourth Gospel and the First Epistle of John are fundamentally Hebraic rather than Hellenic in character. To take a single and crucial example, the Johannine Logos doctrine : whatever branches may have been grafted in from the contemporary thought of the Graeco-Roman world, it is, I think, indisputable that the roots of the doctrine are in the Old Testament and that its main stem is the *d^ebar Yahweh*, the creative and revealing Word of God, by which the heavens and the earth were made and the prophets inspired. What is true of large matters is also true of points of detail. In an article on ' The Argument from Prophecy ',[2] I have argued that the use of the brazen serpent (Num. xxi. 9) as a type of the crucifixion goes back to the preaching of the Palestinian Christians, and that this argument,

---

[1] See the brief but masterly statement of the case by J. K. Fotheringham in *Journ. Theol. Stud.* xxxv. (1934), 155-162, and the fuller, more detailed, and equally decisive discussion by G. Ogg, *The Chronology of the Public Ministry of Jesus* (1940), 203-285.

[2] *J.T.S.* xlvi, (1945), 129-136.

along with a similar one derived from the story of Moses' hands
being held up during the battle between Israel and the Amale-
kites was replied to by R. Eliezer ben Hyrcanus (*fl. c.* A.D. 90).
The conclusion reached in that article was as follows : ' Since
Eliezer is a first-century Palestinian Rabbi, it seems clear that
we have to do in John iii. 14 and Mishnah *R.H.* iii. 8 with
Palestinian Christian proofs and Palestinian Jewish rebuttals.
So, whatever we may think about the authorship, date, and
place of writing of the Fourth Gospel, here is one more piece
of evidence of its dependence on Palestinian materials.'

Secondly, we have to consider a number of pieces of evidence
pointed out by Professor Dodd in his admirable commentary
on the Johannine Epistles.[1] As, unlike Dodd, I think the
Gospel and First Epistle to be the work of one man I have no
qualms about using this evidence here. He notes (1) the
similarity between the Confession of Faith in 1 John ii. 22 and
iv. 15 and the terms of Peter's Confession in Matt. xvi. 16
(p. 57) ; (2) the collocation of the ideas of sonship of God and
vision of God in 1 John iii. 1 f. and Matt. v. 8 f. ; (3) hatred and
murder linked in 1 John iii. 12-15 and Matt. v. 21 f. ; (4) the
idea of the easy yoke in 1 John v. 3*b* and Matt. xi. 30 (pp. 69 ff.).
It is to be emphasised that all these links are between 1 John
and Matthew, the (?) Antiochene Gospel, and, within the
Gospel, to passages or turns of expression that are peculiar to
it, and assignable to the M. strain of the Synoptic tradition.

Thirdly, I think we can point to another link between the
Johannine literature and Syria. I have discussed this at length
in an article appearing in the April issue of the *Journal of Theological Studies.* Briefly the point is that in the Acts of the Apostles
we are shown a variety of modes of entry into the Christian
Church, the main difference being on the question whether
reception of the Holy Spirit precedes or follows baptism. This
difference corresponds to a difference of liturgical usage between
the Syrian Church and the rest of Christendom. In the Syrian
Church the order of events in Christian initiation is unction
(or chrismation—what is later called confirmation), baptism,
admission to first communion ; elsewhere the order is baptism,

[1] C. H. Dodd, *The Johannine Epistles* (Moffatt Commentary), 1946.

unction, first communion. It is argued that in 1 John v. 7 f. the three witnesses, the Spirit, the water, and the blood, are a reference to the three stages of initiation—*in the Syrian order*. If this is so, we have another signpost pointing towards Antioch.

Fourthly, we have the remarkable affinity of theological ideas between the Johannine literature and the letters of Ignatius *of Antioch*, coupled with the equally striking absence from Ignatius of anything that can be confidently claimed as a quotation from the Fourth Gospel.

Fifthly, there is the remarkably Johannine-sounding passage, Matt. xi. 25-27 = Lk. x. 21-22, whose credentials as an integral part of Q are quite unimpeachable. There are independent grounds for thinking that Q was a document, perhaps the earliest document, of the Antiochene Church.

Sixthly, there is the fact that the oldest, and in some ways the most striking, support for the Johannine dating of the Last Supper and the Crucifixion comes from the first Epistle of St. Paul to the Corinthians,[1] a letter written at Ephesus by a missionary whose home base was Antioch.

All these lines of argument converge on a single conclusion : that we should seriously consider Sanday's suggestion [2] that there was ' an anticipatory stage of Johannean teaching, localised somewhere in Syria, before the Apostle reached his final home in Ephesus '. Probably we should now state the hypothesis in somewhat different terms. Very tentatively I should suggest that we have to reckon with a body of tradition of which the original home is Jerusalem, and for which the primary authority is an anonymous disciple of Jesus, not necessarily to be identified with John, the son of Zebedee, or any other of the Apostles. This tradition consisted of both matters of fact and teachings. It found its way, in the first instance to Antioch, where it left its mark on documents which we have reason to connect with that centre, on the liturgical usage of the Syrian Church, and on the teaching both of the missionaries who went out from Antioch (e.g. St. Paul) and of those who subsequently had the leadership of the Antiochene community itself (Ignatius).

[1] The passages in question are 1 Cor. v. 7 f. ; xv. 20.
[2] *The Criticism of the Fourth Gospel*, p. 199.

From Antioch it moved to Ephesus ; [1] and it is at Ephesus that
the final literary formulation was achieved in the Gospel and
Epistles attributed to John. How much of this long road was
travelled in person by the original custodian of the tradition ;
how much he (or his disciples) added on the way as the result
of meditation on what was given, or of contact with other
religious and philosophical ideas ;—these are questions to which
no cut-and-dried answer is possible. What is important is
that we should be prepared to reconsider our whole attitude to
the Fourth Gospel and to reckon seriously with the fact that
it contains some material, perhaps more than we yet realise,
whose value for historical purposes is as high as anything in
the Synoptics. The detailed examination of the Gospel in
search of such material will be a difficult and delicate task ;
but there is no longer any need to assume beforehand that it
will be wasted labour.

The upshot of the whole discussion conducted in this series
of Rylands Lectures may be stated somewhat as follows. We
are confronted in the first place by a Person and a Life of such
magnitude and power as to create a movement that has lasted
for two thousand years and appears still to have unlimited
resources for the renewal of its life and the reinvigoration of
its activity. One of the principal early by-products of this new
movement was a series of streams of tradition about the Founder-
Person and his public career. These streams of tradition have
their original sources in Galilee and Jerusalem (including
Judaea and Peraea), the scenes of the Ministry ; and in the
course of their flow they form, as it were, small lakes of standing
tradition at various centres of Christian Church life. The
first of these of which we have any clear trace was formed
probably at Antioch about A.D. 50. This we call Q. It may
be associated with the Apostle Matthew. At Antioch also we
can locate a body of ' Johannine ' tradition and (perhaps between

---

[1] I think we should look on Ephesus not simply as a place where Paul did
missionary work and therefore to be put in the same class as Athens, Corinth,
Philippi, and Thessalonica ; but rather as a second missionary base or advanced
headquarters and so to be classed with Antioch. If Paul's plans had matured
in the way he wished, there would have been a third base at Rome, from which
he would have pushed on to Spain.

60 and 70) another which supplied the material peculiar to Matthew (M). This M tradition along with Q, was used to produce the revised and enlarged edition of Mark which we know as the Gospel of Matthew, and may regard as the Antiochene Gospel. The earliest form of the Antiochene tradition reappears at Ephesus in Paul's letters : it may be that he brought it there in the first instance. Later on we find the Johannine tradition of Antioch taking literary form at Ephesus in the Fourth Gospel and the Johannine Epistles, and at Antioch in the letters of Ignatius. Another reservoir of tradition was formed, we may suppose, at Caesarea ; and it is a plausible suggestion that it was from this that Luke drew that part of his material that we call L. This in combination with Q may well have formed the first, and catechetical, draft of Luke's Gospel (Proto-Luke), which later (A.D. 70-75), by the addition of extracts from Mark, was to become the first part of a public apologia for the new religion. In Rome another body of tradition issued from the teaching of Peter and took literary form in the Gospel of Mark about A.D. 58.

In the result we have five streams of tradition :

(1) the ' Logia '-tradition (Q), which we can extract from Matthew and Luke, and reconstruct with fair confidence in the form which it probably had about A.D. 50 at Antioch ;

(2) the Petrine tradition embedded in Mark and giving us what was taught at Rome about A.D. 58 ;

(3) The L tradition which we may regard as Caesarean and date about A.D. 55-60 ;

(4) the M tradition, incorporated into Matthew in the form in which it was current in Antioch about A.D. 70 ;

(5) the ' Johannine ' tradition, now accessible to us only in the form which it assumes in the Fourth Gospel at the end of the first century or in the early decades of the second, but not without clear traces of an earlier phase of its history at Antioch.

These traditions sometimes confirm, sometimes supplement, sometimes contradict each other. None can be treated as infallible ; none can be neglected. Each has its own contribution to make to the story, a contribution which only painstaking and intelligent study can discover.

7.

THE SON OF MAN IN DANIEL, ENOCH
AND THE GOSPELS.
(1949)

EIGHTEEN years ago, in the course of an exposition of the leading ideas of the Synoptic Gospels, I devoted some pages to a discussion of the term Son of Man. [1] In taking up the subject again let me say at the outset that further reflection on the available evidence and consideration of the publications of other workers in this field have convinced me that the conclusions which I reached eighteen years ago are in general correct, though capable of considerable amendment in detail. I think that the time is ripe for a reconsideration of the problem and a restatement of my solution of it. The problem is the meaning of the term Son of Man in the sayings attributed to Jesus in the Synoptic Gospels : is it possible to find a meaning for the term which will (a) make sense in the passages of the Synoptic Gospels in which it occurs ; (b) show a reasonable connexion with the use of Son of Man in the Old Testament and other pre-Christian Jewish documents ; and (c) explain the later developments of Christian thought as we find them in St. Paul and St. John ?

I do not propose to spend any time on the discussion of the question whether *bar 'ĕnāsh* is a possible expression in Aramaic in the days of Jesus. We have the fact that it was used in the book of Daniel in the second century B.C., and the fact that *barnāsh* is in use in Christian Palestinian Aramaic ; and in between the two we have in the Synoptic tradition the Greek expression ὁ υἱὸς τοῦ ἀνθρώπου, which as Greek is as near meaningless as makes no matter, but which explains itself linguistically the moment we think of it as a literal rendering of an Aramaic original. In this context the presence of the

---

[1] *The Teaching of Jesus* (1931), 311-336.

term Son of Man in the Synoptics strikes me as excellent evidence that the term could be used in the first half of the first century A.D., that it was in fact used, and that it conveyed some meaning to those who heard it used.

That brings us to the really important question : what did the phrase mean ?   If we start from the Hebrew equivalent, *ben* *'ādām*, we can readily get the plain and literal meaning : ' a member of the human race ', ' an individual human being '.[1] This is clearly the meaning in any number of passages in the Old Testament.   It is the meaning in the book of Ezekiel, where the prophet is addressed as *ben 'ādām* eighty-seven times ; and what is emphasised by this mode of address is the contrast between the prophet as a man—one might almost say a mere man—and the God whose messages he receives.

The attempt has been made—most recently and most persuasively by Dr. Curtis [2]—to find the clue to the meaning of Son of Man in the Gospels in the use of *ben 'ādām* in Ezekiel. In his discussion of this self-designation of Jesus Dr. Curtis makes the important point that ' Jesus utters no such prohibition against its open use as He sternly directs against the divulging of His messiahship.   If " the Son of Man " was a not unfamiliar name for the Christ in popular expectancy, drawn from current apocalyptic, then His repeated use of it was utterly inconsistent with His attitude towards the latter title.' [3]   This argument seems to be valid against all who hold that ' Son of Man ' = ' Messiah ' and that Jesus concealed His messiahship, *unless* they are prepared to take the further step of maintaining that up to the end Jesus used the term Son of Man only in speaking to those who were already in the Messianic secret.   For the positive content of the term Dr. Curtis appeals to Ezekiel rather than Enoch, because ' we have no evidence either that He knew and valued the Enoch vision or that His hearers knew and were moved by it.' [4]   In Ezekiel what is stressed is the essential humanity of the ' Son of Man ' ; and in the teaching

---

[1] Cf. L. Köhler, *Lexicon in Veteris Testamenti Libros*, 133, where other examples of *ben* with collectives are given.

[2] *Jesus Christ the Teacher* (1943), 127-143.

[3] *Op. cit.*, 135.   [4] *Op. cit.*, 142.

of Jesus the ' Son of Man ' becomes the true representative of humanity, *the* Man *par excellence,* what Luther calls ' the Proper Man '. This Proper Man knows that his task is defined in the description of the Servant of the Lord in Deutero-Isaiah. So Jesus in combining Isaiah's Servant with Ezekiel's Son of Man produced not a Messianic title but a name perfectly adapted to his own purposes.

Attractive as this explanation is in many ways, I do not think it can be adopted. There are indeed two or three places in the words of Jesus where it is possible to see a reference to the book of Ezekiel ; but only one of them (Luke xix. 10) is directly concerned with the Son of Man, and in that case the corresponding passage in Ezekiel (xxxiv. 15 f.) speaks not of the activities of the Son of Man-prophet, but of the work of God himself. Moreover we are bound, I think, by the fact that the one explicit reference by Jesus to the Old Testament in a Son of Man saying is a reference to the Son of Man in Dan. vii. 13.[1] We should therefore begin the study of the term Son of Man in the Gospels by a consideration of its meaning in the one Old Testament passage to which we have an explicit reference, Dan. vii.

In this passage the meaning is not in doubt. The seer explains that he had a night-vision in which four great beasts came up out of the sea. The first three have a certain resemblance to real animals, lion, bear, leopard ; but the fourth is apparently so monstrous that there is nothing with which it can be compared. These four beasts are generally recognised to be symbolic figures representing the great powers that had dominated the Near East down to the time of the composition of the book of Daniel (c. 165 B.C.). After the first three have run their course, and while the fourth is still at work establishing new records in arrogance and brutality, the scene suddenly changes.

---

[1] Lk. xix. 10. ἦλθεν γὰρ ὁ υἱὸς τοῦ ἀνθρώπου ζητῆσαι καὶ σῶσαι τὸ ἀπολωλός.

Ez. xxxiv. 15 f. τάδε λέγει κύριος κύριος τὸ ἀπολωλὸς ζητήσω κτλ.

Mk. xiv. 62. ὄψεσθε τὸν υἱὸν τοῦ ἀνθρώπου ἐκ δεξιῶν καθήμενον τῆς δυνάμεως καὶ ἐρχόμενον μετὰ τῶν νεφελῶν τοῦ οὐρανοῦ.

Dan. vii. 13. (θ') ἐθεώρουν ἐν ὁράματι τῆς νυκτὸς καὶ ἰδοὺ μετὰ τῶν νεφελῶν τοῦ οὐρανοῦ ὡς υἱὸς ἀνθρώπου ἐρχόμενος ἦν.

Thrones are set up and the Ancient of Days takes his seat with all the accompaniments of supernatural power and glory. The records are opened and the judgment begins. It is the day of the Lord of which the prophets had spoken. After sentence has been passed on the great powers represented by the beasts, a new figure appears. He is described in terms similar to those used in describing the first three beasts. Of them it was said that one *resembled* a lion, another a bear, and the third a leopard: of the new figure it is said that he *resembles* a human being. This means, I take it, that we are meant to regard this figure as a symbol; and we must ask what the symbol represents. Daniel himself will furnish the answer in due course. Meanwhile we learn that this man-like figure arrives ' with the clouds of heaven '. What this expression means is clear from *Enoch* xiv. 8. The clouds are a means of transportation *from earth to heaven*.[1] The Danielic Son of Man is not a member of the heavenly court: he appears before it. So Daniel's narrative goes on to tell how this Son of Man makes his way towards the Ancient of Days and is ushered into the presence. The decision -of the court is in his favour and he receives ' dominion, and glory, and a kingdom, that all the peoples, nations, and languages should serve him : his dominion is an everlasting dominion, which shall not pass away, and his kingdom that which shall not be destroyed' (vii. 14). It cannot be too strongly emphasised that what Daniel portrays is not a divine, semi-divine, or angelic figure coming down from heaven, to bring deliverance, but a human figure going up to heaven to receive it. It must be equally emphasised that this figure is a symbol as the preceding monsters were. What the symbol stands for is made crystal clear in verses 18 and 27 of this same chapter, where we are told that ' the saints of the Most High shall receive the kingdom, and possess the kingdom for ever, even for ever and ever '; and again, ' The kingdom and the dominion, and the greatness of the kingdoms under the whole heaven, shall be given to the people of the saints of the Most High: his kingdom is an everlasting kingdom, and all dominions

[1] Cf. T. F. Glasson, *The Second Advent*, 14 ff. ; J. Munck, La Vocation de l'Apôtre Paul, *Studia Theologica*, I, 1-2 (1947), 141 ff.

shall serve and obey him '. Just as the beasts stood for the
pagan empires, so the Son of Man stands for Israel or for the
godly Remnant within Israel. In that case Son of Man in this
period is a new name for what in earlier times was called the
' Remnant ' or the ' Servant of Yahweh ', and later, as a result
of the ministry of Jesus, appears as the Church or the ' Body of
Christ ' or the ' Bride of Christ ' or the ' New Israel ', to name
only a few of the designations given a body of persons united
by a common loyalty and obligation to God.

But while it would be widely admitted that Son of Man in
Daniel is a symbol for a community, it is claimed that it very
soon became a personal title appropriated to the expected
Messiah, and in particular to a pre-existent heavenly Messiah.[1]
The evidence for this comes in the main from two sources.
First, it is held that in the *Similitudes of Enoch* Son of Man is
a Messianic title : I shall deal with the *Enoch* material in detail
presently. Secondly, some Rabbinic passages are adduced in
which Dan. vii. 13 is taken as a Messianic prophecy. But the
earliest of these [2] is attributed to R. Alexandrai (*c.* 270), and so
belongs to a period when the Messianic hope had ceased to be
a matter of daily practical politics, and had become much more
of a topic for academic theological speculation. There seems to
be no evidence that in Rabbinical circles Son of Man was used
as a name for the Messiah. The only possible case of this kind
is in a statement attributed to R. Abbahu (*c.* 300), which is
obviously a piece of anti-Christian polemic.[3] A third piece of
evidence for Jewish Messianic interpretation of Dan. vii. is
Justin's *Dialogue with Trypho*, § 32. In § 31 Justin has quoted
Dan. vii. 9-28 at length as a proof that the Old Testament
foretells the Second Coming of Christ. When the quotation is
ended, Trypho says : ' Sir, these scripture texts and others of
the same sort compel us to await someone great and glorious,
who " as Son of Man " receives " an eternal kingdom " from
" the Ancient of Days " ; but this so-called Christ of yours is
in fact so far dishonoured and discredited as to have fallen under

[1] See, for the evidence and the conclusions drawn from it, Billerbeck,
Komm., i. 485 ff., 956-959.
[2] *Sanh* 98ᵃ, cited Billerbeck, i. 486.   [3] Billerbeck, i. 959.

the final curse in the Law of God, for he was crucified '. I do not think that we can infer anything from this passage concerning the Jewish interpretation of Dan. vii. current in Justin's day. Justin himself has brought forward the passage and offered a Christian interpretation of it claiming (*a*) that it prophesies the coming of the Messiah in power and glory, and (*b*) that it refers to Christ. Trypho replies that he finds (*a*) proved, but not (*b*). I doubt whether his words should be taken to mean, ' We Jews already hold (*a*) ; but we must reject (*b*) '. In any case Justin here is only evidence for the second century A.D. For the interpretation of Dan. vii. a hundred years earlier we are driven back on the *Book of Enoch* and the New Testament. I turn now to *Enoch*.

The *Book of Enoch*, in the form in which it has come down to us, is a confused and bewildering mass of material. A great deal of pioneer work has been done on the text and the constituent elements have been more or less successfully isolated. Among the most important for our purposes is the section known as the Similitudes or Parables (chaps. xxxvii-lxxi), for in these chapters the Son of Man plays a large part. A good deal of what I have to say will be concerned with a recent and careful study, *Der Menschensohn im Äthiopischen Henochbuch* by Erik Sjöberg (Lund, 1946) ; and I should like to acknowledge how much I am indebted to this learned and thorough work, even though I am frequently compelled to take a different line of interpretation.

Before going into details it may be well to recapitulate briefly the basic facts which constitute the core of the problem. As we have seen, in the seventh chapter of Daniel the Son of Man is a symbolic figure representing ' the people of the saints of the Most High '.[1] In Dan. viii. 17 Daniel himself is addressed, and in the book of Ezekiel that prophet is addressed

---

[1] For this collective significance of Son of Man we have a good parallel in Ps. lxxx. 16, 18, on which see M. Black in *Exp. Times*, lx. (1948), 11 : ' The nation is personified as God's " right-hand man ", " the son of man whom thou madest strong for thyself " (or " securedst for thyself "), i.e. that branch of the human family appropriated by God for His Divine purpose in history. The " Son of Man " has become a collective symbol for Israel.' The Targum on these verses is instructive.

eighty-seven times, as ' Son of Man '. Again in Dan. x. 16 the seer is in contact with a being ' like the appearance of a son of man ' : the context makes it clear that this being is angelic. In *Enoch* ' the Son of Man ' is the name of a being who can also be described as ' the Elect One ', ' the Righteous One ', ' the Anointed One ', who, moreover, stands in a special relation to a body of people who can also be called ' the Righteous ' or ' the Elect '. In the Gospels we have a considerable number of sayings of Jesus which are susceptible of an individual or a corporate interpretation. In all these cases the first task is to determine as accurately as possible the sense of the term in the places where it appears and by reference to the context. Where ' Son of Man ' refers to an individual we must try to identify him ; where it refers to a group we must try to define the group.

So far as I can see there are no short cuts. We cannot say that there is any variation of language to show a difference of meaning. The symbolic figure of Dan. vii. who represents the people of the saints of the Most High is described as כְּבַר אֱנָשׁ. Daniel himself is addressed as בֶּן־אָדָם in viii. 17. In x. 16 his angelic visitor is described as בְּנֵי־אדם (or בֶּן) כִּדְמוּת. In vii. 13 ὡς υἱὸς ἀνθρώπου, oʹ and θʹ ; in viii. 17 υἱὲ ἀνθρώπου, oʹ and θʹ ; in x. 16 ὡς ὁμοίωσις υἱοῦ ἀνθρώπου, θʹ (strangely enough ὡς ὁμοίωσις χειρὸς ἀνθρώπου in oʹ) are all rendered in the Ethiopic version by *walda eguala ema ḥeyau*. All that can be said in a general way is something like this :

ἄνθρωπος is rendered by Eth. *be'esi* when a particular man is meant ;
  by *sab'e* when it is a man (indef.) or man (in general).

ἄνθρωποι is rendered by *sab'e* or *eguala ema ḥeyau*.

' Sons of men ' is rendered by *eg. em. ḥ* or *daqiqa eg. em. ḥ* or *weluda sab'e*.

ἀνήρ is normally rendered by *be'esi* and ἄνδρες by *sab'e* or *'adawu*.

Sab'e and *eguala ema ḥeyau* can be used as collective nouns for man in general. One way of indicating a single member of this group is to say *walda sab'e* or *walda eguala ema ḥeyau*. A number of such individuals is *weluda sab'e ;* but I have not seen a plural *weluda eguala ema ḥeyau*.

There is one further linguistic point. It has been noted that in Ethiopic *Enoch walda eg. em. ḥ.* is accompanied by the demonstrative pronoun. It is now, I think, widely agreed that this pronoun in the Ethiopic probably represents the Greek definite article. But there are two further points : (*a*) while the Similitudes of Enoch have ' that Son of Man ' they do not have ' that Elect One ' ; (*b*) in the Ethiopic Gospels we regularly find Son of Man without the demonstrative. That is to say, the translator of the Similitudes (assuming that he translated from Greek) used the demonstrative in the case of ὁ υἱὸς τοῦ ἀνθρώπου and not in the case of ὁ ἐκλεκτός : he, therefore, did not mechanically render the article by the demonstrative ; and we can only conjecture his reason for using it in these cases. The explanation may be that the demonstrative is used to indicate the translator's opinion that the term Son of Man is being used in a special sense. After all, *walda eguala ema ḥeyau* means simply ' the man '. The prefixing of the demonstrative may be meant to produce the effect that we should obtain by putting ' the man ' in inverted commas and writing man with a capital M. Expressions like ' Elect One ' or ' Lord of Spirits ' carry their meaning in themselves ; but ' the man ' will hardly convey any special meaning unless some hint is given that such a meaning is intended. The demonstrative may be a way of giving that hint.[1]

Son of Man, then, is an ordinary term which in certain contexts carries a special meaning. In Eth. *Enoch* it is the designation of a figure who makes his first appearance in chap. xlvi.

' And there I saw one who had a head of days.
And his head was white like wool.
And with him was another whose countenance had the appearance of a man.
And his face was full of graciousness like one of the holy angels.

---

[1] In the Ethiopic Gospels the demonstrative is not used with Son of Man because there the special meaning of the term is already firmly established and can be taken for granted.

And I asked the angel, who went with me and showed me all the hidden
things, concerning that Son of Man, who he was, and whence he was, and
why he went with the Head of Days.

And he answered and said unto me :

This is the Son of Man who hath righteousness.

With whom dwelleth righteousness,[1]

And who revealeth all the treasures of that which is hidden,

Because the Lord of Spirits hath chosen him,

And whose lot is pre-eminent before the Lord of Spirits.

And this Son of Man whom thou hast seen

Shall remove the kings and the mighty from their seats

And the strong from their thrones

And shall loosen the reins of the strong

And break the teeth of the sinners.

The description is most interesting. The seer is at pains to
indicate that the figure is a human-looking figure. Looking at
it you would say it was a man. It has also an expression of
countenance which can fairly be called angelic. A human figure
with the look of an angel : not a man or an angel. Evidently
it is a symbolic figure : the question is, what does it symbolise ?
The seer asks his angel guide for the information. The answer
given is not crystal clear. We must do the best we can with
the statements that are made.

(1) ' This is the Son of Man who possesses righteousness ;
with whom righteousness dwells.' I am inclined to think that
the true parallel to this is *Ecclus.* xxiv. 7-12, where wisdom is
the speaker :—

' With all these [i.e. every people and nation] I sought a resting place
And said : In whose inheritance shall I lodge ?
Then the Creator of all things gave me commandment
And he that created me fixed my dwelling place ;
And he said : Let thy dwelling-place be in Jacob
And in Israel take up thine inheritance. . . .
And I took root among an honoured people,
In the portion of the Lord (and) of his inheritance.'

When it is remembered that in *Ecclesiasticus* wisdom is identified
with the Torah and that the Torah is the righteousness of God,
the relevance of this text becomes clear.

[1] Cf. Dan. ix. 7, ' O Lord righteousness belongeth unto thee ' ; Is. i. 21,
' How is the faithful city become an harlot ! she that was full of judgment !
righteousness lodged in her, but now murderers.'

(2) 'He will reveal (or reveals) all the treasures of that which is hidden.' With this we may compare Prov. ii. 4 'If thou seekest her as silver, and searchest for her as for hid treasures', on which R. Phinehas, c. A.D. 300, said : 'If you seek after the words of the Law as for hid treasures, God will not withhold from you your reward.'

What the Son of Man possesses and reveals is the hidden treasure of God's wisdom and righteousness embodied in the Law.

(3) This Son of Man is further described as having been chosen by the Lord of Spirits ; and it is said that his lot is pre-eminent, or has prevailed, before the Lord of Spirits. This choice in heaven has certain consequences on earth in the putting down of tyrants and oppressors.

Sjöberg's conclusion after looking at these data that 'what is here envisaged is not in fact a man—at least not in the ordinary sense of the word' : and in that we must surely agree with him. But he goes on : ' It is rather a heavenly being, der ganz beson-dere *himmlische Mensch.*'[1]   At this point I think it is time to call a halt, and to say that 'heavenly man' is a question-begging term. (I leave on one side the question whether it is a term with any meaning at all in the framework of Hebrew and Jewish theology. I doubt it.) These bits of description of heavenly appointment to an earthly destiny no more justify us in thinking of 'a heavenly man' than the terms of Jeremiah's inaugural vision justify us in thinking of 'a heavenly Jeremiah'.

In *Enoch* xlviii we have a similar set of statements. First (vv. 2 f.) we are told :

> ' At that hour that Son of Man was named in the presence of the Lord of Spirits, and his name before the Head of Days, Yea, before the sun and the signs were created, Before the stars of the heaven were made, His name was named before the Lord of Spirits.'

In this Charles (*ad loc.*) found evidence for ' the pre-existence of the Son of Man '. Sjöberg (p. 53) recognises in this passage the reappearance of the Heavenly Man already mentioned in chap. xlii, and (p. 92) he regards this being as pre-existent. In this

---

[1] Sjöberg, *op. cit.*, 50.

view he is further fortified by v. 6 which tells us that the Son of Man

> ' has been chosen and hidden before him (the Lord of Spirits)
> before the creation of the world and for evermore.'

[Here let me say that I think it would not be a bad thing if the words ' pre-exist ', ' pre-existent ', and ' pre-existence ' could be quietly dropped. A pre-existent Son of Man is one who exists before. Before what ? The terms do not tell us. Nor do they tell us anything about the mode of the existence. Altogether they are thoroughly vague and ambiguous, and I cannot help thinking that we should get on better without them.]

But our immediate task is to discover what is meant by the naming of the name of the Son of Man before the Lord of Spirits. I can think of only two possibilities :—

(1) The Son of Man may be called into existence in this way. The nearest analogy would be the Primal Man in the Manichean myth. Here, as Burkitt says : ' The Father of Greatness neither espouses the Mother of Life nor begets the Primal Man, but calls (ﻣﺮ)—and they exist '.[1] Those who are interested in tracing connexions between the Son of Man and the ' Primal Man ' may also note the similarity between the name *walda eguala ema ḥeyau* and the name of the mother of the Primal Man in Theodore b. Khôni's account, احد ومتا ' the mother of life ' or ' mother of the living '. But it has to be borne in mind that the Manichean cosmogony is based upon ideas about the nature of the material would and of the processes that go on in it which are as far as possible from Old Testament and Jewish convictions. If there is anything at all in these parallels, they may well be regarded as evidence that the Similitudes have at some stage in their history come under Manichean influence.

But (2) we can find parallels a little nearer home. We have the proclamation of Sumerian kings by the god : " Bur Sin whose name was spoken in Nippur by Enlil the Lord of the

---

[1] *The Religion of the Manichees*, 23 f. Cf. F. Cumont, *La Cosmogonie Manichéenne d'après Théodore bar Khôni*, 14 ; H. J. Polotsky, art. Manichäismus in Pauly-Wissowa, *RE* Supplementbd. VI, Col. 251.

Earth " ; [1] and we have similarly Babylonian kings chosen and named by the god of the land. ' Anu and Enlil, the supreme gods, chose Marduk to be exalted over all the gods of the Earth, and at the same time pronounced the name of Babylon as a decree that it should be the head of all cities. Therewith they called the name of Hammurabi " so that I might cause justice to appear in the land and might destroy naughty and wicked men, so that the strong should not afflict the weak ".' [2]   In the Old Testament we have Is. xliii. 1, ' But now thus saith the Lord that created thee, O Jacob, and he that formed thee, O Israel : Fear not, for I have redeemed thee ; I have called thee by thy name, thou art mine ' ; Is. xlv. 3 f., addressed to Cyrus, ' I am the Lord, which call thee by thy name, even the God of Israel. For Jacob my servant's sake, and Israel my chosen, I have called thee by thy name ; I have summoned thee, though thou hast not known me '.[3] The naming of the name of a group or an individual can mean simply the designation of that group or individual to some high destiny. And this seems to me to be the most likely meaning in this passage in *Enoch*. We are told in v. 3 that this tremendous decision was taken before the creation of the world ; and in the remaining verses of the chapter the consequences of the decision are described. As in chap. xlii, they are to take place in the world as part and parcel of the history of mankind. The Son of Man is to be ' the staff of the righteous whereon to stay themselves and not fall ' (v. 4). Under him they are to have a complete triumph over ' the kings of the earth and the strong who possess the land because of the works of their hands ' (v. 8) ; and the elect, holy, and righteous ones will be left in undisputed possession ; and ' there shall be rest on the earth ' (v. 10). In this passage (as in the *Psalms of Solomon*) the expected hero of this story of the triumph of the righteous is called the Anointed One (Messiah) (v. 10). What the whole section gives is the story of pre-mundane decisions in heaven which are destined to have their fulfilment on earth.

[1] T. Fish, in *Bull. Ryl. Lib.*, xxi. (1937), 157 f.
[2] C. J. Gadd, *Ideas of Divine Rule in the Ancient East*, 43.
[3] The idea was still live in N.T. times. Cf. Phil. ii. 9 ff.

In this chapter we have two terms employed regarding the Son of Man ; and it is necessary to consider them briefly. In *v.* 6 we are told that the Son of Man

> ' has been chosen and hidden before him (the Lord of Spirits)
> before the creation of the world and for evermore '.

On this Sjöberg (p. 90) says that here, ' as is generally recognised, the idea of pre-existence is really present. The Son of Man is not only chosen before the creation of the world . . . but he is also hidden before God from that time on '. Similarly in lxii. 7 it is said that,

> from the beginning the Son of Man was hidden
> and the Most High preserved him in the presence of his might
> And revealed him to the elect.

And again in xxxix. 6 f.

> And in that place my eyes saw the elect one of righteousness and faithfulness,
> And righteousness shall be in his days
> And the righteous and elect ones shall be without number before him for ever
> And I saw their (v.l. his [1]) dwelling-place under the wings of the Lord of Spirits.
> And all the righteous and elect ones shall shine before him like the light of fire
> And their mouth shall be full of praise
> And their lips shall extol the name of the Lord of Spirits
> And righteousness before him shall not fail
> And uprightness before him shall not fail.

These passages are widely held to imply the ' heavenly pre-existence ' of the Son of Man. It may be remarked in passing that if the translation given by Beer and Flemming is right, xxxix. 6 f. would provide equally good evidence for the pre-existence of all the righteous and elect.

But will the texts in fact support a doctrine of pre-existence (whatever that may mean) ? I think the answer is that they

[1] his gm : their qtuβ. On the principle laid down by Charles (Introd., p. xxv) the reading ' their ' would have a fair chance of being right. The α MSS. are divided and the casting vote of β is in favour of qtu. Charles has made his choice of ' his ' seem more reasonable by transferring this line bodily into the context which speaks of the Elect One of righteousness and faithfulness, between ll. 1 and 2 of the passage. Dillmann read ' their '. Beer, Flemming, and Sjöberg follow Charles in reading ' his ' but not in the transposition of the lines.

clearly support a doctrine of pre-mundane election both of the Son of Man and of all the righteous and elect ones. (What the relation of the Son of Man and the righteous and elect ones is I shall discuss presently.) But pre-mundane election does not necessarily involve pre-mundane existence except as a project in the mind of God. The Hebrew and Jewish mind had no qualms about believing in the pre-mundane election of Israel.[1] *Ber. R.* 1. 2b (Theodor, p. 6) ' Six things preceded the creation of the world : some were actually created and some it was planned to create. The Torah and the Throne of Glory were created. . . . It was planned to create the Patriarchs, Israel (proof text Ps. lxxiv. 2, " Remember thy congregation, which thou hast purchased of old "), the Temple, and the name of the Messiah.' The pre-mundane election of Israel is implied and presupposed in St. Paul's argument in Rom. ix-xi. For the pre-mundane election of the Patriarchs we can refer to *Tanch.* (B) § 19 (17b),[2] and for that of the Messiah or the name of the Messiah to the passages collected by Billerbeck (*Komm.*, ii. 333 ff.). It is a natural development from the idea of the pre-mundane election of Israel, when the New Testament speaks of the pre-mundane election of the Church. This is quite explicit in Eph. i. 3 f., I Pet. i. 1 f., and is probably implied in I Cor. i. 27-29 and James ii. 5. What is quite clear is that the distinction was made between things that were actually brought into existence before creation and those whose future existence was decided upon before creation. The name—and in this connexion ' name ' probably means ' person '—of the Messiah belongs to the latter class.

Sjöberg and others lay greater stress on the ' hiding ' of the Son of Man before God as evidence of pre-existence ; but I do not think that the use of this term elsewhere gives much support to the contention. In the Old Testament various words are used to express the idea (חָבָא, Is. xlix. 2 ; צָפַן, Ps. xxvii. 5 ; Jb. xiv. 13 ; כָּסָה, Ps. cxliii. 9 ; סָתַר, Ps. xvii. 8 ; xxvii. 5 ;

---

[1] Billerbeck, i. 974 ; ii. 335. Ber. R. 1, 2b ed. Theodor, p. 6. ר' הונא ר' ירמיה
בשם ר' שמואל בר' יצחק (c.300) מחשבתן שלישראל קדמה לכל. Trans. Billerbeck, iii. 579 f. : Der Gedanke (die Idee) Israels ging allem andren voran.

[2] Quoted Billerbeck, *Komm.* ii. 335. Cf. Ac. xiii. 17.

xxxi. 20; lxiv. 2; and סֵתֶר, Ps. xxxii. 7; cxix. 114). In all
these cases the reference is to divine guidance and protection
amid the dangers and trials of this mortal life.[1] Similarly, the
references to dwelling under the wings of the Lord of Spirits
do not imply ' pre-existence '. To bring a person under the
wings of the Shekinah is a regular way of describing conversion
to Judaism and the large number of rabbinical passages collected
in Levy, *NHWB*, ii. 357 f. provides sufficient evidence that this
phrase means divine care and protection here and now.

I would emphasise again that what is set out in these passages is, it seems to me, the record of pre-mundane decisions
whose consequences in the created world of men and things
can then be " prophesied " in the best apocalyptic fashion. The
prophecies are as usual past history described in the future
tense until we come to the writer's own time : beyond that
they are wishful thinking.

It is noteworthy that when it comes to describing the mode
of the ' pre-existence ' of the Son of Man, all that Sjöberg can
say is this : ' Der präexistente Menschensohn ist *inaktiv* '
(p. 96, italics his). He is *most* inactive, not to say inert. He
does not even speak. He takes no part in the revelations made
to Enoch who has to rely for all his information on the angelic
interpreter who acts as his guide. The mystery of the Son of
Man is a mystery about him. In fact, he could more properly
be described as unborn than as pre-existent. Later he appears
on the stage of history and becomes active.

In describing this activity there is a tendency to stress the
word ' eschatology '. The Son of Man appears on the plane of
history only to inaugurate the great eschatological catastrophe,
in which he delivers the righteous and judges sinners. Properly
speaking there is no judgment of the righteous : their merits
are acknowledged and await only the appropriate reward of
complete happiness in a transformed world. The righteous are
united with the Son of Man in a classless society, in which all are
members of the aristocracy. In this scheme the righteous and
the sinners are already what they are. The Son of Man comes
not to seek and to save the lost but to vindicate and reward the

[1] Cf. A. Oepke in *ThWb*, III. 969.

good and to condemn and punish the evil. All the persons concerned already belong to one class or the other ; and the proceedings are political rather than judicial. (Rather like the triumphs of " democracy " of the Moscow pattern.) Those who need forgiveness cannot have it : they are marked down for liquidation. The others are due to receive rewards : they need no forgiveness other than a winking at their occasional slips in view of their general good character expressed in loyalty to Israel and Israel's God.

There seems to be something lacking here. The story is all beginning and end ; and the middle seems to have dropped out. At the beginning we have a ' pre-existent ' Son of Man, who for all practical purposes might as well be non-existent. At the end we have a very active Son of Man. In between we have hints of the oppression of the righteous and elect ones by the wicked. But I cannot help thinking that one object of the apocalyptic writers was to justify God's ways to man by making a sensible story of the whole course of history.

That brings us back to the problem of the relation of the Son of Man to the community which he vindicates at the end of the story, when they all live happily ever after. The problem is made more acute by the two chapters lxx. f., in which we have an account of the relations between Enoch himself and the Son of Man.

In Chapter lxx. it is said of Enoch :

> ' And it came to pass after this that his name (i.e. Enoch himself) during his lifetime was raised aloft to that Son of Man and to the Lord of Spirits from amongst those who dwell on the earth. And he was raised aloft on the chariots of the spirit (or wind) and his name (i.e. he) vanished from among them.'

This is clearly a reference to Enoch's translation as recorded in Gen. v. 24. Then Enoch carries on the story in the first person :

> ' And from that day I was no longer numbered amongst them ; and he set me between the two winds, between the north and the west, where the angels took the cords to measure for me the place for the elect and righteous. And there I saw the first fathers and the righteous who from the beginning dwell in that place.'

There follows a long poetical passage in which Enoch joins in the praises of the inhabitants of heaven. Then he tells us :

'And these blessings which went forth out of my mouth were well pleasing before that Head of Days and that Head of Days came with Michael and Gabriel, Raphael and Phanuel, thousands and ten thousands of angels without number.[1] And he came to me and greeted me with his voice and said to me: "Thou art the Son of Man (*walda be'esi*) who art born for righteousness and righteousness abides over thee, and the righteousness of the Head of Days forsakes thee not". And he said to me: "He proclaims peace to thee in the name of the world to come, for peace has gone out from here since the creation of the world, and so shall it be unto thee for ever and ever and ever. And all shall walk in thy ways for righteousness never forsakes thee. With thee shall be their dwelling-places and with thee their lot, and they shall never be separated from thee for ever." And so there shall be length of days with that Son of Man, and there shall be peace for the righteous and an upright way for the righteous in the name of the Lord of Spirits for ever and ever.'

What does all this mean? Sjöberg, after a careful survey of previous work, draws these conclusions. He says (p. 168): 'Two possibilities are open. *Either* the earthly Enoch is an incarnation of the Son of Man, and at his final translation is greeted as Son of Man because that is what he already was during his earthly life, *or* Enoch is first made Son of Man at his translation, and before that was only a man like other men. In the former case we have to do with the idea of incarnation, in the latter only with the idea of exaltation.' Of the two possibilities Sjöberg definitely chooses the latter (p. 171). 'What is here (i.e. in chaps. lxx. f.) portrayed, is not the return of an incarnate heavenly being to his original state, but the exaltation and transformation of a man into a heavenly being.' Again (p. 185 f.): '*Enoch* lxxi is to be understood in terms of the idea of exaltation, not of incarnation. . . . The relation between Enoch and the Son of Man is thus to be understood in terms of the idea of exaltation. At the end of his life Enoch is translated to heaven and identified with the pre-existent Son of Man.'

But here we come to the great difficulty, a difficulty of which Sjöberg is acutely aware: how is it possible at all to identify the exalted Enoch with the pre-existent Son of Man? (p. 187). It is not as if the two met and somehow fused into one. As Sjöberg points out the Son of Man does not appear at first. Enoch is met by God and hailed by him as Son of Man. Sjöberg

---

[1] Here we abandon Charles, who has rewritten the rest of the passage in accordance with his view of what Enoch ought to have said.

goes on to say : ' When this (the greeting) happens, the designation Son of Man is charged with the content which it has in the preceding account in the Similitudes. What is meant by it is the pre-existent heavenly Son of Man. As this (Son of Man) is the exalted Enoch hailed and takes his place in the heavenly world. We can form no concrete picture of how this is possible ' (p. 187). So the essential problem is stated and declared insoluble.

I venture to think that the problem is insoluble precisely because Sjöberg insists on retaining the conception of the Son of Man as a pre-existent heavenly being, a being something lower than God and something higher than the angels. I also think that the remedy is to recognise that the pre-mundane Son of Man in *Enoch* is, if I may so describe it, an idea in the mind of God. Now, what are the elements that go to make up the total conception indicated by the term Son of Man ? They are : divine election, divine protection and guidance, the possession of divinely given righteousness, and eventually divine vindication and everlasting happiness. There may be others that I have overlooked ; but these are the main ones. If we now ask how the conception thus made up is to be actualised, the obvious answer is in the field of history by human beings as individuals or as a group. And when we turn back to the Similitudes we do find some remarkable parallelism between ' the Elect one ' and ' the Elect ones '. They have certain common qualities and they share a common destiny. May it not be that we are here confronted by the ' oscillation ' between the individual and the corporate ?

I should like to suggest that there is in the Enoch picture a double oscillation, so to speak, for which there are parallels elsewhere. The group idea finds expression in the concept of the elect and righteous ones, i.e. the Israel within Israel, the Remnant. The individual idea finds expression in two personalities : at the beginning of the course of events in Enoch, who is regarded as the first human individual to embody the Son of Man idea, the nucleus of the group of the elect and righteous ones ; at the end it finds expression again in the figure of the Messiah who is to carry out the final vindication of the saints. But whether it be in Enoch, who is as it were the first-born of many brethren, or in the Messiah, or in the corporate body of the elect and righteous, it is the same idea that is embodied, an idea that formed part of the divine purpose before the creation of the world.

At this point I should like to introduce one or two bits of evidence which seem to me to illustrate the idea of oscillation between a group and its founder-member or first nucleus. The first is from *Ber. R.* 44, 27*a* (Theodor, p. 426) discussing the text Is. xli. 8 f. : ' But thou Israel, my servant, Jacob whom I have chosen, the seed of Abraham my friend. . . . I have chosen thee and not cast thee away.' On the last clause the comment is : ' " I have chosen thee "—in Abraham ; " and I have not cast thee away "—in Abraham '. You might almost say that Israel is the body of Abraham. Again, in Ps. lxxxix. 4 (LXX) we have

$$\delta\iota\epsilon\theta\acute{\epsilon}\mu\eta\nu \ \delta\iota\alpha\theta\acute{\eta}\kappa\eta\nu \ \tau o\hat{\iota}s \ \acute{\epsilon}\kappa\lambda\epsilon\kappa\tauo\hat{\iota}s \ \mu ov$$
$$\check{\omega}\mu o\sigma\alpha \ \varDelta\alpha\upsilon\grave{\iota}\delta \ \tau\hat{\omega} \ \deltao\acute{\upsilon}\lambda\omega \ \mu ov$$

and R. Kittel in his commentary on this verse (p. 296) remarked that ' der Erwählte ist wohl Israel das in David als dem König vertreten ist '. In the New Testament, Heb. vii. 1-10, we have an elaborate argument concerning Abraham's payment of tithes to Melchizedek, in which the nerve of the proof is the idea that Abraham represents the Levitical priesthood that would one day be descended from him, and that so the Levitical priesthood can be thought of as paying tithe to Melchizedek. In Eph. i. 4 we have the idea of the Church being chosen in Christ before the foundation of the world. In these cases we have an individual representing a community that does not yet exist in such a way that the community, when it does come into being, may be thought of as an extension of his personality. I am inclined to think that it is along these lines that we may find a solution of the problem of Enoch. Enoch incarnates, not a ' pre-existent heavenly being ' but a divine idea. He is hailed by God as the incarnation of the idea, *after* he has lived a life of righteousness on earth. He becomes the first actualisation in history of the Son of Man idea and the nucleus of the group of the elect and righteous. Some of these have died and are with

Enoch in Paradise ; others are still *militantes in saeculo*. The thing for which all wait is the manifestation of the Son of Man idea in triumph in the Messianic vindication of the elect and righteous.

Now an idea, a piece of God's purpose, which has been actualised in a famous man in the past, is actualised in the people of the saints of the Most High in the days of the Maccabees, and is destined to be more fully actualised in the expected Messiah, is something specially characteristic of the Hebrew way of looking at life and history. It has obvious points of contact with another characteristically Hebrew and Semitic idea, that of corporate personality. It is not possible here to do more than indicate the most important points.[1] Chief among these is one, to which I allowed too little weight in my earlier discussion of the Son of Man in the *Teaching of Jesus ;* that is the constant oscillation between the conception of the social unit as an association of individuals in the plural or as a corporate personality in the singular.[2] Along with this goes the fact that where the conception of corporate personality is dominant there is often a tendency to see the corporate personality as embodied in a person. The king in some sense embodies the corporate personality of his subjects.[3]

So when we come to study the use of the term Son of Man in the sayings of Jesus, we should be prepared to find that it

[1] For fuller treatment reference must be made to S. A. Cook in *Camb. Anct. Hist.,* iii. 437-444 ; in W. Robertson Smith's *Religion of the Semites*[3], 503 ff., 590 ff., 655 ff.; *The Old Testament ; a Reinterpretation,* 115 ff.; H. Wheeler Robinson, The Hebrew Conception of Corporate Personality, in *Werden und Wesen des Alten Testaments (B.Z.A.W.* 66), 49 ff. ; *Inspiration and Revelation in the Old Testament,* 70 f., 81-89, 264 ; J. Pedersen, *Israel* ; A. R. Johnson, *The One and the Many in the Israelite Conception of God,* 1-17 ; C. R. North, *The Suffering Servant in Deutero-Isaiah,* 103-110.

[2] Cf. A. R. Johnson, *op. cit.,* 15. Something of the same sort comes into our own thinking when we hesitate over ' The Committee were of the opinion . . .' or ' The Committee was of the opinion . . .', and solve the problem by saying ' The Committee came to the conclusion . . .'.

[3] Cf. N. A. Dahl, *Das Volk Gottes,* 20 ff. ; D. Daube, *Studies in Biblical Law,* 154-189. Something similar may be observed in the Roman Empire in the idea of the Emperor as carrying the person of the state. On this see C. N. Cochrane, *Christianity and Classical Culture,* 127 and cf. Seneca, *de Clementia,* i. 4 f. ' tu (Nero) animus rei publicae tuae es, illa corpus tuum '.

may stand for a community comparable to ' the people of the saints of the Most High ' in Dan. vii., and that sometimes this community may be thought of as an aggregate of individual disciples, at others as a single corporate entity. Again we should be prepared to find that this corporate entity is embodied *par excellence* in Jesus himself in such a way that his followers, who together with him constitute the Son of Man as a group, may be thought of as extensions of his personality, or, as St. Paul puts it later on, limbs of his body. And I think that all the authentic instances of the use of the term ' Son of Man ' in the Synoptic Gospels should be interpreted along these lines. When I wrote the *Teaching of Jesus*, I was prepared to make two exceptions, and to regard Son of Man in Mk. ii. 10 and 28 as signifying ' man ' in general. It now seems to me certain that in Mk. ii. 27 f. we should read, ' The Sabbath was made for the Son of Man and not the Son of Man for the Sabbath : and so the Son of Man is lord of the Sabbath '.[1] In the other and more perplexing saying about the right of the Son of Man to forgive sins on earth, I am more and more disposed to think that the essential thing about forgiveness of sins on earth is restoration to full fellowship with the community. Sin cuts off the member : forgiveness restores him. With whom, then, does the right of restoration and reintegration lie ? Mk. ii. 10 says that it lies with the community itself ; and the community in this matter acts through Jesus who embodies and represents it.

If now we look at the Gospel occurrences of ' Son of Man ' as a whole, I think we can lay down a number of propositions about them.

(1) Jesus took the term Son of Man, and with it its primary meaning, from Dan. vii. We have evidence in Mk. xiv. 62 that he knew the Daniel passage and was influenced by it. We have no good reason to suppose that he was aware of any other Son of Man than the Danielic.[2]

---

[1] For the proof of this see my article in *Coniectanea Neotestamentica*, xi. (1947), 138-146. I take the essential meaning of the saying to be that the Son of Man (= Jesus and his disciples) is engaged on a task whose requirements override those of the Sabbath laws.

[2] See T. F. Glasson, *The Second Advent*, 53 f.

(2) The Danielic Son of Man represents the people of the saints of the Most High ; and his destiny, which is theirs, is to ' receive the kingdom '. This reception of the kingdom I take to be a comprehensive expression covering all the popular hopes of the vindication of the Chosen People, all the ideas associated with the Divine promises made in favour of the dynasty of David, the kind of thing that is set out in detail in the *Psalms of Solomon* xvii. f., the *Magnificat*, and the *Benedictus*. The people of the saints of the Most High is the actualisation in history of the Israelite ideal. The concept of the Son of Man thus links the Davidic hope to the Israelite ideal.

(3) The tension in the Gospels between Jesus and his con-temporaries is in the interpretation of all this. The crucial questions are about the way in which the kingdom is to be transferred to its rightful owners, and about the nature of the Israelite ideal. In the days of Jesus there was a powerful inclination to answer the former question in terms of the acquisition of political power and economic advantage by Israel, and the latter in terms of the establishment of the Jewish Law as the supreme standard of behaviour.

(4) Jesus took a different line. He defined the ' Son of Man ' in terms of the ' Servant of the Lord '.[1] We can see this definition worked out in detail in the Son of Man sayings themselves, and in a series of sayings concerning the task of the disciples and the nature of the true greatness and power which a disciple may hope to attain. Above all we can see it in the nature and progress of the Messianic Ministry itself. The best reason for calling Jesus Son of Man *par excellence* is the fact that his Ministry reveals perfectly the true meaning of the term. If we say that the Son of Man must be the Servant of the Lord —and I think that is what Jesus said—it means that the Messiah must be the Servant of the Lord *and* that Israel (or the Remnant) must be the Servant of the Lord, *and* that the Israelite ideal must be the ideal portrayed in the picture of the Servant of the Lord. It means all three ; and we may add that the Messiah Jesus embodies the Israelite ideal and embodies Israel.

[1] On this vitally important point see W. Manson, *Jesus the Messiah*, 110 ff.

(5) Finally, it has to be said that the supreme and dominating figure in all this is the Ancient of Days or the Most High in Daniel, the Lord of Spirits in *Enoch* and the God and Father of Jesus Christ in the Gospels. The kingdom is his kingdom, and it comes as his gift. Its actualisation in history is a revelation of divine power. Similarly, the Israelite ideal is a God-given standard; whether as embodied in the Torah or in the Messianic Ministry it is a revelation of the Divine wisdom. So Paul can speak of Jesus as the power and wisdom of God, for in him the power and wisdom of God are actualised. In him the kingdom of God comes to Israel and the God-given Israelite ideal is realised.

PART TWO

THE EPISTLES OF ST. PAUL

8.

THE DATE OF THE EPISTLE TO THE PHILIPPIANS.
(1939)

IN this chapter I propose to discuss a single problem—that of the date of the Epistle to the Philippians. The traditional view is that the letter was written from Rome at some point in the period of two years during which Paul was awaiting trial there. In recent years this view has been seriously challenged by rival theories which would put the composition either during Paul's imprisonment at Caesarea (Acts xxiii-xxvi) or during a hypothetical imprisonment at Ephesus. The Caesarean theory seems to me to be open to fatal objections, so that the real issue is between Rome and Ephesus : it is that issue that I wish to consider.

So long as the traditional view held the field, it determined the exegesis of the Epistle. We knew from Acts that the Apostle was a prisoner in Rome, whither he had been sent by the Procurator of Judaea, Festus, after he had demanded to be tried in the Emperor's court (Acts xxv, 9-12). It is true that King Agrippa had expressed the opinion to Festus that, but for his appeal, Paul might well have been released there and then (Acts xxvi, 30-32). Nevertheless the appeal had been made, and a trial in Rome under Nero might well be only less perilous than an acquittal and release in Judaea. On any day during the Roman period Paul might be summoned to appear before a tribunal which had the power of life and death, and from whose sentence there was no appeal. On that background all the allusions in the letter had to be understood : references to bonds were obviously references to actual imprisonment which the apostle was undergoing at the time of writing ; allusions to death must refer to the possibility of condemnation by the Imperial Court.

Even when the place of composition was fixed at Ephesus instead of Rome, these presuppositions continued to dominate the interpretation of the text, and the upholders of the Ephesian hypothesis believed themselves compelled to posit an Ephesian imprisonment of the writer along with the Ephesian composition of the letter. But the evidence for an Ephesian imprisonment of Paul—apart from the internal evidence of Philippians itself —is so weak as to be negligible. The reference to fighting with wild beasts at Ephesus (I Cor. xv, 30-32) cannot be taken in any but a metaphorical sense without raising the most serious difficulties. Nor is the case any better with the allusions in Rom. xvi. There (vv. 3 f.) mention is made of Prisca and Aquila who had risked their necks when Paul was in danger of his life. This can hardly refer to an imprisonment on a capital charge. If Paul were in such a case, it is hard to see how his friends, by risking their necks, could protect his . the most they could do would be to share his fate, whatever it might be. Again in v. 7 Andronicus and Junias are called by Paul his ' fellow-prisoners ' ; but we do not know whether this is literally or metaphorically meant ; and even if it is literally meant, we have nothing to show that Paul, Andronicus, Junias (and perhaps Prisca and Aquila too ?) had all been in gaol together at Ephesus. We cannot allow much weight, if any, to the testimony of the Marcionite Prologue to Colossians, still less to the existence of a so-called φυλακὴ Παύλου at Ephesus. Acts knows nothing of an Ephesian imprisonment. In fact if it were not that we start with a preconceived idea that Philippians must have been written from prison, we should have little inducement to believe in an Ephesian imprisonment at all.

That leads to the first question for discussion : if the Roman origin of Philippians is given up, is there anything in the letter itself to compel the conclusion that it was written from prison ?

Repeated readings of the letter itself confirm me in the opinion that not only is there nothing in the letter to compel us to think that the writer was a prisoner, but also that there are several facts that seem to point in the opposite direction. Let us begin by examining the references to ' bonds ' and suffering for the Gospel.

The first is Phil. i, 7. καθώς ἐστι δίκαιον ἐμοὶ τοῦτο φρονεῖν ὑπὲρ πάντων ὑμῶν, διὰ τὸ ἔχειν με ἐν τῇ καρδίᾳ ὑμᾶς, ἔν τε τοῖς δεσμοῖς μου καὶ ἐν τῇ ἀπολογίᾳ καὶ βεβαιώσει τοῦ εὐαγγελίου συγκοινωνούς μου τῆς χάριτος πάντας ὑμᾶς ὄντας. The intimate union between Paul and the Philippian Christians has found expression in the way in which they have shared in his χάρις.[1] Χάρις here must be given the same meaning as in Rom. i, 5 ; xii, 3, 6 ; xv, 15 ; I Cor. iii, 10 ; Gal. ii, 9 ; Eph. iii, 2, 7, 8. It is the privilege of suffering for, defending, and establishing the Gospel. In this apostolic task the Philippians have taken their share from the beginning until now. Consequently when Paul speaks of his bonds and the successful defence of the Gospel, he must mean all experiences of that kind from his first day in Philippi to the time of writing ; and there is no reason why we should suppose that the phrase ἔν τε τοῖς δεσμοῖς μου refers specially to an imprisonment in Ephesus.

Phil. ii, 17 f. must, I think, be understood also in a general way. There, after exhorting them to live in such a way as to bring credit on his apostleship he goes on : ἀλλ' εἰ καὶ σπένδομαι ἐπὶ τῇ θυσίᾳ καὶ λειτουργίᾳ τῆς πίστεως ὑμῶν, χαίρω καὶ συγχαίρω πᾶσιν ὑμῖν· τὸ δ' αὐτὸ καὶ ὑμεῖς χαίρετε καὶ συγχαίρετέ μοι. The careful and conscious parallelism in the construction is surely meant to lead us to the simple and natural interpretation of the verses. In embracing the Gospel of the love of God both Paul and his converts have laid themselves open to the hatred and enmity of ' a crooked and perverse generation.' He and they have to pass through difficulties and dangers, to make sacrifices— perhaps the supreme sacrifice. The main point on which Paul

---

[1] I take ἔν τε τοῖς δεσμοῖς . . . εὐαγγελίου with what follows (so Light-foot and Dibelius). On the sense of χάρις see J. A. Robinson, *St. Paul's Epistle to the Ephesians*, 224 ff., and for βεβαίωσις, Deissmann, *Bible Studies*, 108.

insists is that like experiences call for like reactions. ' We are all,' he says in effect, ' in the same straits : let us show the same invincible joy in facing the odds against us.' Here again I do not see anything to compel us to think that, when he writes those words, Paul is actually in prison facing the imminent possibility of condemnation on a capital charge.

Similarly in iv, 14, καλῶς ἐποιήσατε συγκοινωνήσαντές μου τῇ θλίψει, the immediate reference is doubtless to a particular θλῖψις, where θλῖψις means the suffering which the enemies of the Cross of Christ are always ready to inflict upon the servants of Christ.[1] But there is nothing to indicate that this particular θλῖψις is imprisonment ; and indeed the context suggests that it is more likely to be the oft-repeated experience of being without food or shelter or friends among people indifferent or even hostile to his message. Paul, no doubt, found himself in that position often enough when he began in a new place ; and in such circumstances the help of his friends at Philippi would be doubly welcome.

The crucial passage, however, is i, 12-30. In this passage Paul is speaking about his own affairs. The first thing he has to say is that, contrary to expectation, events have turned out to the advantage of his missionary work in two ways. First it has become obvious ἐν ὅλῳ τῷ πραιτωρίῳ καὶ τοῖς λοιποῖς πᾶσι that Paul's imprisonment was on account of his religion (and, we are left to infer, *not* on account of any crime committed by him). I think that the phrase ἐν ὅλῳ τῷ πραιτωρίῳ must, in view of the following καὶ τοῖς λοιποῖς πᾶσι, be taken to mean a body of people ; and, in that case, the most natural view is that the *Praetorium* is the Roman court either at Rome itself or somewhere in the provinces. We are thus led to the view that Paul is writing about a trial that lies in the past. The most natural way to understand that it had helped on Paul's missionary work will be to suppose that, at the trial, he had been acquitted. If so, he is not likely to be writing from prison. In the second place the course of events has favoured the work by the fact that the majority of the brethren, filled with confidence by the proceedings against Paul, are themselves

[1] Cf. G. Kittel, *Lexicographia Sacra*, p. 23.

preaching the word with the utmost boldness. If Paul was, in fact, languishing in prison, it is not easy to see how that could be an encouragement to the brethren to go on with the preaching. If they did so, it would presumably be in spite of, not because of, what had happened to the Apostle. But if Paul had been acquitted, their confident boldness is at once explained.

The remainder of this long paragraph (*vv.* 19-30) is occupied with reflections of a more general character. If he thought only of himself, he would be happy to die and enter into the bliss of being with Christ. But the glory of his Master and the well-being of his converts alike demand that he should remain at his post. It is a work of difficulty and danger and suffering, but it has its own peculiar rewards. He and his Philippian converts have the privilege not only of believing in Christ, but also of suffering for Him. In all this there is nothing to suggest that Paul is in danger of sentence of death, any more than in the passage in II Cor. iv, 7-18.

Our conclusion so far is that the statements in the letter, which might seem to favour the view that it was written from prison, turn out on closer examination to support the opposite view. There are some further considerations, of a general nature, that seem to lead to the same conclusion.

(i) It may be taken for granted that if Philippians was written from Ephesus, it was written before I Cor., that is, at a relatively early date in the Ephesian ministry. But it is to be observed that in the accounts of Paul's missionary work in Acts, trouble with the authorities usually puts an end to his activities in a place, at any rate for the time being. On the hypothesis that Philippians was written from prison in Ephesus, we have to suppose that, on being released, Paul was able to resume the very activities which had been the cause of his imprisonment in the first instance. This seems very unlikely.

(ii) We have to remind ourselves that imprisonment in the Roman Empire of St. Paul's day is not to be thought of as on a par with imprisonment in modern times.[1] In Roman criminal

---

[1] Cf. *Digest*, xlviii, 19, 8, 9. *Carcer enim ad continendos homines, non ad puniendos haberi debet*, with Buckland's remarks in *Cambridge Anct. Hist.*, xi, 843 ;

law the primary purpose of a prison was to hold persons awaiting trial; and the use of imprisonment as a punishment was exceptional. If, however, Philippians was written from an Ephesian prison, we should have to regard Phil. i, 12-14 as an account of the trial and assume that Paul, at the time of writing, was 'serving his sentence.' This also seems very unlikely.

These general considerations would not tell against the Roman imprisonment as they do against the Ephesian; for in the case of Rome, Paul *is* awaiting trial; and, however the trial may have gone, he does not appear to have done any further mission work in Rome after it.

We may now pass to the next step in the argument. Not only is the evidence insufficient to prove that Philippians was written from prison: there are also positive indications in the

Greenidge, *Legal Procedure of Cicero's Time*, 513-16. Greenidge says that imprisonment was not recognised as a punishment; but preventive imprisonment is sometimes used as a penalty; and (p. 516) 'Thus it was that a part of the mere administrative machinery of the State became used for the ends of criminal justice. It was a use to which the Government was sometimes forced by the decline of corporal punishment and the growth of the theory of exile; for imprisonment was almost the only method which the later Republic possessed of securing the deterrent effects of punishment without resorting to extreme measures.' See also the articles *Carcer* and *Coercitio* in Pauly-Wissowa, and Mommsen, *Römisches Strafrecht*, 48 ff., 299 ff., 960 ff. In the provinces under the Empire, there does not seem to have been any lack of punishments apart from imprisonment. Paul tells us that he had been three times flogged at the time when he wrote II Cor. x-xiii (xi, 24 : τρὶς ἐραβδίσθην). There were also fines, various forms of exile, condemnation to penal servitude in the mines or quarries (*ad metalla*), and death.

If Paul was in prison at Ephesus, it would be before or after trial. If before trial, we have to explain away Phil. i, 12-14, which looks like the account of a trial that has already taken place. If after trial, it may be to await execution of some sentence that has been passed—and of this there is no trace whatever— or it may be a period of confinement imposed (by way of *coercitio*) by the provincial Governor. But in that case we have to take account of the fact that the object of *coercitio* is to compel obedience : and consequently if Paul had been put in prison to curb his missionary activities, he would not be likely to be released in order to resume them in the same place. And if, after his release, he was found doing the same things for which he had previously been committed, the treatment on the second occasion would not err on the side of leniency. Paul would probably have found it necessary to play his trump card—the appeal to Caesar—at Ephesus. Coercitio may be defined as the general police jurisdiction of magistrates. Cf. A. D. Nock in *CAH*, x. 491.

letter itself which strongly suggest, if they do not prove, that St. Paul was at liberty when he wrote. He speaks of his future plans, especially of a visit to Philippi, in the manner of one who is free to determine his own movements. He mentions the proposed visit in i, 26 f., and there is a suggestion that his arrival may be delayed. But any delay would seem to be due to general mission difficulties rather than to incarceration. St. Paul is too busy fighting against opposition of all kinds to be able to get away to Philippi.[1] In ii, 19-24 we are told that Timothy is to be sent first to Philippi to visit the Church there and report to Paul.[2] After that Paul hopes to go to Philippi in person, and there is no hint that the decision to set out will depend on anyone but the Apostle himself. The plans may be as yet rather indefinite, but they read like the plans of a free man.

If the argument up to this point is sound, it at once makes an end of the theories that the epistle was written from Rome or from Caesarea ; for in both places Paul was a prisoner, and our conclusion is that the writer of Philippians was not. It also makes an end of the theory that the letter was written from an Ephesian prison ; but it does not affect the hypothesis that it was written from Ephesus. We may now turn to examine this hypothesis more closely. There are several arguments in its favour.

(i) The travel plans fit in very well with what we are told in I Cor. In Philippians Paul and Timothy are still together

[1] Assuming that Philippians was written from Ephesus, I think that the real reason why Paul cannot leave the city immediately is not that he is in prison but that—as he says later in I Cor. xvi, 8 f.—ἐπιμενῶ δὲ ἐν Ἐφέσῳ ἕως τῆς Πεντηκοστῆς · θύρα γάρ μοι ἀνέῳγε μεγάλη καὶ ἐνεργής, καὶ ἀντικείμενοι πολλοί.

[2] The eulogies of Timothy should probably not be pressed, nor the somewhat depreciatory remarks about the others. These things may perhaps be partly explained by the fact that Timothy does not appear to have been a very forceful personality (cf. I Cor. xvi, 10 with II Tim. i, 6 ff. ; I Tim. iv, 12 : even if the Pastorals are spurious they should doubtless be regarded as reliable on this point, seeing that the natural tendency of the tradition would be to avoid disparaging the leaders in the great first missionary campaign of the Church). On the other side it may be that Paul—himself a very determined character—was beginning to find himself crossed by others who had minds and wills of their own (Phil i, 15 ff.). In that case the docility—if that is the right word—of Timothy would appear doubly virtuous in the eyes of his chief.

(i, 1) ; and Timothy is to be sent to Philippi soon. On his return Paul will come in person (ii, 19-24). Nothing is very definite and no times are set. In I Cor. xvi, 5-9, the arrangements are more precise. Paul writes from Ephesus that he will stay where he is until Pentecost, then visit Macedonia during the summer, and probably winter at Corinth. In I Cor. iv, 17 he says that he is sending Timothy to Corinth ; and in xvi, 10 the natural interpretation is that Timothy has already left for Macedonia on his way to Corinth [1] and that the letter to the Corinthians, being sent direct, will reach Corinth before him. The Philippian travel-plans thus seem to belong to an earlier stage than those in I Cor.

(ii) We note the absence from Philippians of any reference to the collection for the Jerusalem Church, which is so important by the time that I Cor. xvi, 1-4 was written. In I Cor. xvi, 1 Paul says that he has already given instructions to the Galatian churches. This may well have been done, as J. Weiss suggests, verbally during the Galatian visit recorded in Acts xviii, 23.[2] Now in II Cor. viii, 1-7 the collection has been completed in the Macedonian churches, and Paul speaks with high appreciation of the generosity that had been shown by them. The collection had been planned before I Cor. xvi was written, and probably before Paul's arrival in Ephesus : so far as Macedonia is concerned it is complete when he arrives in Macedonia at the end of the Ephesian period. A simple explanation of the absence of all reference to it in the letter would be that it was a matter that was to be arranged personally by Timothy when he went to Philippi.[3]   In that case Philippians would fit naturally into place before I Cor.

(iii) There are a number of expressions in Philippians that suggest that the interval between the foundation of the Church at Philippi and the writing of the letter has not been a very long one.

[1] Timothy did in fact leave Ephesus for Macedonia, along with Erastus, while Paul was still in Ephesus (Acts xix, 21 f.) ; and Paul followed later (Acts xx, 1 ; II Cor. ii, 12 f.).

[2] *Der erste Korintherbrief* (Meyer's *Kommentar*), p. 381.

[3] It may be that Paul felt a little shy about pressing the claims of the Jerusalem community at the moment when the Philippians had just made an effort on his own behalf.

(a) In i, 26 Paul uses the phrase τῆς ἐμῆς παρουσίας πάλιν πρὸς ὑμᾶς. Here it has been argued that the use of πάλιν is most suitable if the next visit of the Apostle to Philippi will be the second. In the same paragraph (vv. 29 f.) he tells the Philippians that they have been granted the favour not only of believing in Christ but also of suffering for Him, τὸν αὐτὸν ἀγῶνα ἔχοντες οἷον εἴδετε ἐν ἐμοί, καὶ νῦν ἀκούετε ἐν ἐμοί. It is unlikely that the Philippian Christians were in prison when Paul wrote to them; and the 'struggle' should doubtless be understood in a more general way of opposition to the Gospel. Paul had suffered from it when he was at Philippi. He now says to his converts: 'You saw my troubles in Philippi; now you hear of further troubles, which I have had to undergo.' This way of speaking is not very natural in a letter written during the Roman imprisonment. To say: 'You remember my troubles in Philippi; well, I am having the same troubles in Rome,' would suggest that the intervening ten or twelve years had been a period of unbroken calm. And we know that that was not the case. The sentence reads simply and naturally if we suppose that the interval between the two troubles is quite short.

(b) Again in ii, 12 Paul speaks of the obedience that is expected of his beloved Philippians not only when he was present with them, but now much more when he is away. Here, too, it looks as if there had only been one παρουσία of Paul's— that during which the Church at Philippi was founded—and that the ἀπουσία has not been extremely prolonged.

(iv) Lastly, there is the point that has been made so often that there is no need to repeat the arguments: that if Philippians was written from Rome, Paul's remarks on the subject of the gift sent from Philippi cannot be construed except as a rebuke, and a sarcastic rebuke at that. If the letter is dated before I Cor., this difficulty does not arise. The Philippians have had no opportunity to send a gift because Paul has been away to Syria in the interval between his departure from Corinth and the beginning of the Ephesian ministry (Acts xviii, 18-23).

It thus seems that there are good grounds for believing in

the Ephesian origin of the epistle, but not for believing in the Ephesian imprisonment. This brings us to the third and most adventurous part of the discussion, in which I must try to give an exegesis of Phil. i, 12-30 without putting St. Paul into an Ephesian gaol. The suggestion which I venture to make is that Paul, writing at a comparatively early date in the Ephesian ministry, is referring back to the events which put an end to his first stay in Corinth, and reporting the subsequent developments there (vv. 12-17). He then goes on to speak of his own reactions to these things (vv. 18-26), and of his hope that the Philippian Christians will not allow themselves to be intimidated by the opponents of the Gospel, but will stand fast in the faith even if it means struggle and suffering (vv. 27-30). Let us look a little more closely at vv. 12-17.

12 Γινώσκειν δὲ ὑμᾶς βούλομαι, ἀδελφοί, ὅτι τὰ κατ᾽ ἐμὲ μᾶλλον
13 εἰς προκοπὴν τοῦ εὐαγγελίου ἐλήλυθεν, ὥστε τοὺς δεσμούς μου
   φανεροὺς ἐν Χριστῷ γενέσθαι ἐν ὅλῳ τῷ πραιτωρίῳ καὶ τοῖς λοιποῖς
14 πᾶσι, καὶ τοὺς πλείονας τῶν ἀδελφῶν ἐν κυρίῳ πεποιθότας τοῖς
   δεσμοῖς μου περισσοτέρως τολμᾶν ἀφόβως τὸν λόγον τοῦ Θεοῦ λαλεῖν.

Paul begins to speak of his own affairs ; but at once, and characteristically, turns to consider their bearing on the progress of the Gospel, which is for him the one thing that really matters. From that point of view things have gone excellently with him. He has had a troublesome time, of course ; but it has served to help on the work, so that his troubles have really been blessings in disguise. There have been two principal results : the first concerns himself, the second his fellow-Christians. As to himself it has been made clear that his only offence—if it be an offence—is that of being a Christian.[1] This fact has been demonstrated to the general public (τοῖς λοιποῖς πᾶσι) as well as to a smaller circle (ἐν ὅλῳ τῷ πραιτωρίῳ). As we have

[1] I take ἐν Χριστῷ with τοὺς δεσμούς μου, and understand Paul to mean that it became obvious that he was under arrest in his capacity as an Apostle of Jesus Christ. The idea is similar to that which is set out more explicitly in I Pe. iv, 14-16. The point is clearly put by O. Linton in Coniectanea Neotestamentica, ii, 9-21 : 'Die Hauptsache ist dass es durch die Gerichtsverhandlung allen klar wird, dass er als Christ seine Fesseln trägt, dass er mit Christus stirbt oder lebt. Er steht und fällt mit dem Evangelium.'

abandoned the Roman origin of the letter, the *Praetorium* [1]
must be given the sense that it would have in the provinces ;
either the residence of the provincial Governor or the headquarters of the provincial administration. *Praetorium* is the
equivalent of our ' Government House.' And I think we may
go further and say that the context requires us to think of
Government House in its judicial capacity. ' It became clear
in the whole Praetorium ' means ' it became clear to the Pro-
consular court.' That implies a trial of some kind in the
course of which it was made evident that Paul was not a criminal
but, as Government House doubtless put it,[2] a crank. And
just such a trial is described for us in Acts xviii, 12-17. There
Paul is brought before the Proconsul Gallio by the Jews of
Corinth. The charge did not amount to much : teaching men
to worship God in ways not in accordance with the (Jewish)
Law ; but no doubt it was hoped that Gallio would regard
this teaching as—to use our own terms—' conduct likely to
cause a breach of the peace,' and deal with Paul accordingly.
This expectation was not realised. According to the account
in Acts Gallio said to the Jews :

Εἰ μὲν ἦν ἀδίκημά τι ἢ ῥᾳδιούργημα πονηρόν, ὦ Ἰουδαῖοι, κατὰ λόγον
ἂν ἠνεσχόμην ὑμῶν· εἰ δὲ ζητήματά ἐστι περὶ λόγου καὶ ὀνομάτων καὶ

---

[1] In the N.T. πραιτώριον is regularly used ' to denote the " palace " or
" official residence " of a Governor ' ; cf. Mk. xv, 16 ; Ac. xxiii, 35 ; and for
examples of this meaning in the Papyri see Moulton and Milligan, *Vocabulary*,
s.v. and the excursus in Dibelius's commentary in *HBNT*. The discussion
by Lightfoot in his commentary on the epistle, pp. 99-102, takes account only
of the possible senses of *praetorium* on the assumption that the letter is written
from Rome. The upholders of the Ephesian hypothesis argue, correctly enough,
that we must suppose that there was a *praetorium* at Ephesus since Ephesus was
the seat of the Proconsul of Asia ; but Corinth was equally the seat of the Proconsul of Achaea, and the arguments for the Ephesian *praetorium* are equally
valid for the Corinthian.

I may add here that on the theory which I propose, οἱ ἐκ τῆς καίσαρος οἰκίας
will be slaves and freedmen in the Imperial service (cf. Zahn, *Einleitung*, i, 391).
That such persons were to be found all over the Empire, and in particular at
Ephesus, may be taken as certain. In Phil. iv, 22, the reference will be to
members of this body in Ephesus, who have been converted to Christianity.
(See Michaelis, *Theol. Handkomm. ad loc.*)

[2] Cf. the verdict of Pliny, *Epp.* X, xcvi, 2 and 8. After examining Christian
deaconesses by torture : *nihil aliud inueni quam superstitionem prauam, immodicam.*

νόμου τοῦ καθ' ὑμᾶς, ὄψεσθε αὐτοί· κριτὴς ἐγὼ τούτων οὐ βούλομαι εἶναι.

With that the case was dismissed ; and, though the exasperated accusers did create a breach of the peace by beating the unfortunate Sosthenes, 'Gallio was not troubled at all by these things.' [1]

The essential judgement is : there is no crime here, only a dispute about some theological point, on which this court declines to adjudicate. The speech of Gallio and the words of Paul are, I venture to think, just two different ways of expressing that essential judgement ; the one, impatient and rather contemptuous, that of the busy Roman official with other and more important matters to think about ; the other, pleased and almost triumphant, that of the ardent missionary who sees in the finding of the Court a vindication of himself and his work.

The second result of the proceedings against Paul has been that the majority of the brethren have been filled with confidence and are boldly proclaiming the Gospel. I have already argued that Paul's acquittal would be the strongest possible stimulus to such activity on the part of the brethren. I now add that if I am right in thinking that the trial took place at Corinth, the brethren in question will be the members of the Corinthian Church. Now both Acts and the letters to the Corinthians bear witness that things were moving rapidly in Corinth, and from Corinth outwards through the province of Achaea, in the period after Paul's departure from the city (cf. II Cor. i, 1 ; Rom. xvi, 1). True, the developments were not all of the kind that Paul desired or approved ; but there was activity and zeal. In particular, Acts tells of a very effective mission carried on by Apollos (Acts xviii, 27 f.), and we know from I Cor. that there was a group in Corinth who were probably his converts. Also the Corinthian community had become sufficiently important to claim the attention of the authorities in Jerusalem ; and there was a party (the Cephas party) disposed to acknowledge the Petrine claims. We are entitled to think of the period after the trial before Gallio as one of great activity and rapid growth in the Corinthian Church.

[1] The translation is that of Lake and Cadbury. See their note *ad loc.*

Paul goes on (*vv.* 15-18) to speak further about this missionary activity :

15   τινὲς μὲν καὶ διὰ φθόνον καὶ ἔριν, τινὲς δὲ καὶ δι' εὐδοκίαν τὸν
16   Χριστὸν κηρύσσουσιν· οἱ μὲν ἐξ ἀγάπης, εἰδότες ὅτι εἰς ἀπολογίαν
17   τοῦ εὐαγγελίου κεῖμαι· οἱ δὲ ἐξ ἐριθείας τὸν Χριστὸν καταγγέλλουσιν,
18   οὐχ ἁγνῶς, οἰόμενοι θλῖψιν ἐγείρειν τοῖς δεσμοῖς μου. τί γάρ ; πλὴν
ὅτι παντὶ τρόπῳ, εἴτε προφάσει εἴτε ἀληθείᾳ, Χριστὸς καταγγέλλεται·
καὶ ἐν τούτῳ χαίρω, ἀλλὰ καὶ χαρήσομαι.

I suggest that the best commentary on these verses is to be found in the first four chapters of I Cor. It is in the Corinthian Church that there is faction and strife, and that at the very time when the letter to the Philippians is being written.[1] It is in Corinth that we find a party who are all for Paul, and others, no doubt equally zealous, who are all against him. We may be sure that all the parties in the Corinthian Church claimed to be good Christians, and that all believed themselves to be proclaiming the pure Gospel. We may go farther and suppose that at the time when he wrote Philippians, Paul did not yet fully realise the seriousness of the Corinthian situation. He has heard of some differences there, and even of opposition to himself ; but, after all, even those who are opposed to him personally, are nevertheless preaching the Gospel, and that is the main thing. Later, at the time of the Corinthian correspondence, he has become aware how deep are the rifts in the community, and how evil are the effects on the Christian life and witness of the Church.

Of his opponents Paul says that their purpose is to stir up trouble (θλῖψιν ἐγείρειν).[2] Since they are preaching Christianity in some form or other, as Paul himself admits, they can hardly mean to stir up trouble for the Church at large or for the local community where they are active. We can only suppose that it is Paul himself who is the object of their efforts. The question then is how we are to construe τοῖς δεσμοῖς μου. I think that we should take it as instrumental, and understand

---

[1] Is it possible that ' Chloe's people ' (I Cor. i, 11) had already arrived in Ephesus when Philippians was being written ? In any case there was certainly contact between Paul and Corinth before I Cor. was written.

[2] This, the more difficult reading, is to be preferred to θλῖψιν ἐπιφέρειν.

that the people in question use the fact that Paul had been under arrest (not for the first time) to undermine his authority in his churches. They could say, not without plausibility, that Paul was getting the Gospel a bad name. Wherever he goes, he seems to get himself involved in brawls which end up in court. He antagonises the synagogues and arouses the suspicions of the Roman authorities.

Now we know from the Corinthian correspondence (and I think that we should also bring in the letter to the Galatians) that during the Ephesian ministry Paul's position in the Gentile churches, and indeed his status as an Apostle, were both seriously challenged. There is no doubt whatever that the challenge came from the Jewish-Christian wing of the Church, and that its rallying cry—in Corinth at any rate—was the name of Cephas. It does not seem to me beyond the bounds of probability that, when he wrote Philippians, Paul had already heard the first rumblings of the approaching storm.

If that is so, we are in a better position to understand some striking features in the epistle.

(i) There is, first of all, the remarkable emphasis on unity which runs through the letter. The note is struck in the address to *all* the saints who are in Philippi. It is repeated in the four-fold ' all of you ' in i, 3-11, and again in i, 27, ὅτι στήκετε ἐν ἑνὶ πνεύματι, μιᾷ ψυχῇ συναθλοῦντες τῇ πίστει τοῦ εὐαγγελίου. Once more in ii, 2 f.: ἵνα τὸ αὐτὸ φρονῆτε, τὴν αὐτὴν ἀγάπην ἔχοντες, σύμψυχοι, τὸ ἓν φρονοῦντες· μηδὲν κατὰ ἐριθείαν μηδὲ κατὰ κενοδοξίαν . . . and ii, 14: πάντα ποιεῖτε χωρὶς γογγυσμῶν καὶ διαλογισμῶν. Finally in iv, 2: Εὐωδίαν παρακαλῶ, καὶ Συντύχην παρακαλῶ, τὸ αὐτὸ φρονεῖν ἐν κυρίῳ. These repeated exhortations to maintain peace and unity in the Philippian Church have added significance if we are right in thinking that Paul knew that there was faction in the Church at Corinth.

(ii) Then there is the remarkable outburst in Chapter iii which has led some commentators to think of interpolation. But there does not seem to be any serious difficulty if Philippians belongs to the early Ephesian period. The fierce warnings have their counterpart in II Cor. x-xiii, and in the letter to the churches of Galatia. In both these documents Paul is fighting desperately against those who attempted to depreciate him in the eyes of the Gentile churches and questioned his right to the title and privileges of an apostle. In Galatia the mischief has already been done when the letter is written : θαυμάζω ὅτι οὕτω ταχέως μετατίθεσθε ἀπὸ τοῦ καλέσαντος ὑμᾶς . . . (Gal. i, 6). In II Cor. x-xiii it is clear that a considerable section of the Corinthian Church is in revolt against the authority of Paul. At Philippi the situation is not, apparently, so alarming ; but it is necessary to deal with this kind of danger almost before it arises.

The nature of the challenge we can easily surmise. It came from persons of Jewish birth. Βλέπετε τὴν κατατομήν can hardly be meant as anything but a savage jest at the περιτομή. It is probable that they were also Christians claiming to stand in the original Palestinian tradition, to be in communion with the original Apostolate. Paul says bitterly (II Cor. xi, 5) : λογίζομαι γὰρ μηδὲν ὑστερηκέναι τῶν ὑπερλίαν ἀποστόλων ; and in xi. 13 : οἱ γὰρ τοιοῦτοι ψευδαπόστολοι, ἐργάται δόλιοι, μετασχηματιζόμενοι εἰς ἀποστόλους Χριστοῦ. He goes on (xi, 22-31) to declare with great emphasis that he is as good a Jew and as good a Christian missionary as any of them, and better than most. It is surely no accident that in Phil. iii, 2 we have the injunction, βλέπετε τοὺς κακοὺς ἐργάτας, and that in iii, 5 ff., we have an assertion by Paul of his whole-hearted devotion to Judaism before his conversion, and to Christ since that memorable day on the road to Damascus. It is difficult to compare Phil. iii with II Cor. xi, and we may add Gal. i, 11-17, without feeling convinced that they hang together, that the tension noticeable in Philippians is but a prelude to the crisis revealed by the Corinthian and Galatian correspondence.

This is perhaps the time to take into account Professor Dodd's theory of what may be called St. Paul's second conversion as it is reflected in II Cor. x-xiii. Accepting the theory in its main outlines, I cannot help thinking that it is more easily credible if Philippians was written before the spiritual experience which so profoundly affected the Apostle. I am unable to persuade myself that in Philippians there is any really serious change in Paul's general outlook and temper, such as is required by the theory of a second conversion. In particular

Chapter iii is more easily understood before the second conversion than after it.   Indeed if Philippians is to be dated after
the spiritual crisis, Chapter iii can only be regarded as either
a relapse or a misplaced survival from an earlier stage in Paul's
career.

Nor do I think that the eschatological views expressed in
our letter require a late date.   In discussing this question it
is important to bear in mind that from the time of the
Thessalonian correspondence onwards, the urgent problem is
to explain the delay of the Parousia.   The earliest form of
explanation, as given in II Thes. ii, is that a kind of Satanic
Parousia must come first, and then the second Advent of the
Lord Jesus will take place.   Later in I Cor. xv, 20-28, we are
told that Christ is risen from the dead and that He reigns until
He has subdued all enemies.   When the last enemy has been
put down the Parousia will take place.   Meanwhile Christians
are to be ' stedfast, unmoveable, always abounding in the work
of the Lord, for as much as ye know that your labour is not in
vain in the Lord ' (I Cor. xv, 58).   It seems to me that the
eschatological ideas of Philippians are akin to those of I Cor.
We may compare Phil. i, 6, ὁ ἐναρξάμενος ἐν ὑμῖν ἔργον ἀγαθὸν
ἐπιτελέσει ἄχρις ἡμέρας Ἰησοῦ Χριστοῦ, with I Cor. xv, 58.
Again the conclusion of the Christological passage (Phil. ii, 9-11)
expresses the same conviction as I Cor. xv, 25 f. :   every knee
must bow ;   and all enemies must be subdued.   Similarly in
Phil. iii, 20 f., the transformation which is to be effected by the
Lord Jesus Christ is precisely that which is described in I Cor.
xv, 50-54.   And it belongs to the power which He has of
subjecting all things to Himself (iii, 21 ;   cf. ii, 9-11 and I Cor.
xv, 25 f.).[1]   So in Philippians, as in I Cor., the Parousia is

---

[1] To Phil. iii, 20, ἡμῶν γὰρ τὸ πολίτευμα ἐν οὐρανοῖς ὑπάρχει the nearest
parallel is Gal. iv, 26, ἡ δὲ ἄνω Ἰερουσαλὴμ ἐλευθέρα ἐστίν, ἥτις ἐστὶ
μήτηρ ἡμῶν.   At the stage at which Philippians, I and II Corinthians, and
Galatians were written the coming of the heavenly kingdom with power, does
not seem to mean the negation of existing conditions so much as their
transfiguration.

I should like to suggest another link between Philippians and Galatians.
I think that the " enemies of the Cross of Christ " (Phil. iii, 18) means enemies
of the Messianic Cross—not enemies of Christ.   That is, it stands for those to

delayed, but not indefinitely. It is expected that it will come in the lifetime of Paul and his correspondents. Those who have already died in the Lord will be raised, and those who are still living will be changed.

It thus seems to me that Philippians fits in naturally with I Cor. and Gal.; and that the theory of a second conversion of Paul is strengthened if we can place the epistle before the conversion.

With that we may leave the pros and cons and attempt a reconstruction of the circumstances in which the letter was written. Paul, accompanied by Silas and Timothy, had made his way through Asia Minor and had arrived at Troas (Acts xv, 40-xvi, 8), where Paul in a vision by night was entreated by a man of Macedonia to bring the Gospel thither (xvi, 9). ' And when he had seen the vision, straightway we sought to go forth into Macedonia ' (xvi, 10). The appearance of the first person plural at this point may probably be taken to indicate the presence of Luke in the party. The journey by sea from Troas to Neapolis and thence by the Egnatian way to Philippi [1] is described in verses 11 and 12, and the adventures of the missionaries in verses 13-40. These events may probably be dated in the summer of 49. On leaving Philippi, Paul and Silas make their way to Thessalonica (xvii, 1-7) and thence to Beroea, where Timothy reappears. (As the use of " we " in narrative is not a feature of these sections, it may be assumed that Luke had been left behind at Philippi. This supposition is made the more likely by the fact that the use of " we " is resumed once more at Philippi (Acts xx, 5 f.). In that case it

whom the crucified Messiah is a stumbling-block (I. Cor. i, 23 f.). Linton puts it (op. cit. p. 18 f.) that it describes those who will not suffer for the Gospel, who want temporal safety as well as eternal salvation. It may be argued that to such persons Judaism (as a religio licita) presents such temporal safety; hence the temptation to get the Christian Church included in the Jewish fold. This is what seems to be meant in Gal. vi, 12, ὅσοι θέλουσιν εὐπροσωπῆσαι ἐν σαρκί, οὗτοι ἀναγκάζουσιν ὑμᾶς περιτέμνεσθαι, μόνον ἵνα τῷ σταυρῷ τοῦ Χριστοῦ μὴ διώκωνται.

[1] For a very full and interesting historical account of the city see Paul Collart, Philippes, ville de Macédoine, École Française d'Athènes, Travaux et Mémoires, Fasc. V (1937).

may be Luke who is addressed in Phil. iv, 3 as ' true yokefellow '.)
After a stay in Athens (xvii, 15-34), Paul came to Corinth where he
worked for some eighteen months (winter 49/50 to summer of 51).
In the summer of 51, soon after the arrival of Gallio as proconsul of Achaea, Paul was brought for trial on charges laid
by the Jews of Corinth. This trial and the results that followed
are described by Paul in Phil. i, 12-18 and by Luke in Acts
xviii, 12-17.

Some time later Paul left Corinth for Syria (Acts xviii, 18),
calling at Ephesus on his way. How long he spent in the East
we do not know, nor are we told how much time was occupied
in the journey through Asia Minor back to Ephesus (xviii, 22 f.).
It is, however, very improbable that the arrival in Ephesus was
earlier than the autumn of 52 or later than the early part of 55.

On returning to Ephesus Paul was able to come again into
close touch with the Philippian community ; and if we are
right in supposing that Luke was still at Philippi, there would
doubtless be a readiness on the part of the Philippians to get
into touch with Paul.[1]   It may be surmised that on hearing
that Paul was in Ephesus the Church of Philippi sent gifts and
greetings by the hand of their messenger Epaphroditus, of whom
Paul speaks in Phil. ii, 25-30.   I would hazard the conjecture
that Epaphroditus is to be identified with the Epaphras [2] who
is mentioned in Col. i, 7 ; iv, 12, and Phm. 23.   From what
Paul says in Phil. ii, 30 it would seem that he had been acting
as an assistant to the Apostle in his missionary work, and that
in the course of this work had contracted the illness which
almost ended fatally.   It is possible that later he returned to
this part of the field and made a place for himself in the Churches
of the Lycus valley.   Still later when Paul is a prisoner in Rome,
he comes there to seek the help of the Apostle against false
doctrines that are working mischief among his people.   The
lapse of time between the writing of Philippians and Colossians

---

[1] It may well be the case that the support of Paul by the Philippian Church
was due in the first instance to Luke's suggestion and encouragement.

[2] On the names, cf. Moulton-Howard, *Gramm. of N.T. Greek*, ii, 314, and
Moulton-Milligan, *Vocabulary*, 230a, where 'Επαφρᾶς is described as ' a pet
form of 'Επαφρόδειτος'.

would account for the change to the more familiar Epaphras in the later letters. But all this is guesswork.

What does seem fairly certain is that in the early fifties of the first century there was a definite attempt to bring the Gentile Christian communities—and Paul himself—into subjection to the central body in Palestine. Earlier attempts had traded on the name of James the Just—if indeed they had not had his approval.[1] The new movement put forward its claims in the name of Peter, and at the same time questioned the right of Paul to apostolic status. (We have, perhaps, the Palestinian side of the matter in Matt. xvi, 17-19.[2]) Soon we hear of a Cephas party at Corinth and of the defection of the Galatian Churches. It is in the early stages of this crisis that Paul writes to the Philippians. His letter is above all an expression of his love for them, and an appeal to them to preserve unity with one another and with him in the spirit of Christ. This appeal for unity and loyalty, with its climax in the great Christological passage (ii, 6-11), where Jesus Himself is set forth as the supreme example of self-effacing loyalty and devotion, stands between a report on the factions—as I think—in the Corinthian Church (i, 15-18), and a warning in the strongest terms against the Judaizing emissaries who were already beginning their attempt to undermine the loyalty of the Pauline communities to their Founder (iii, 2-21). It seems to me that this disposition of the material is conscious and deliberate on Paul's part. The last chapter deals with more personal matters, messages to individuals at Philippi, acknowledgement of the gift from the Church, greetings. The whole letter breathes a spirit of confidence in the love and loyalty of the Philippian community to the Apostle : we have no reason to think that that confidence was misplaced.

[1] Gal. ii, 12.
[2] I have discussed the interpretation of this passage in *The Mission and Message of Jesus*, 493-497.

9.

THE PROBLEM OF THE EPISTLE TO THE GALATIANS.
(1940)

MORE than any other of Paul's letters the Epistle to the Galatians has been interpreted in terms of the doctrine of Justification by Faith : more than any other it has been regarded as the scriptural basis of the doctrine. It is no accident that one of the key documents among Luther's writings is his Commentary on Galatians ; and his treatment of the Epistle is significant. At the outset he sets out briefly what he conceives to be the purport of Galatians :

'First of all it behoveth that we speak of the argument of this Epistle : that is to say, what matter St. Paul here chiefly treateth of. The argument, therefore, is this.

'St. Paul goeth about to establish the doctrine of faith, grace, forgiveness of sins, or Christian righteousness, to the end that we may have a perfect knowledge and difference between Christian righteousness and all other kinds of righteousness.'

There follow some seven closely packed pages of further explanation of this theme, and then at the end :

'Thus far concerning the argument of this Epistle, whereof Paul entreateth, taking occasion of false teachers who had darkened this righteousness of faith among the Galatians, against whom he setteth himself in defending and commending his authority and office.'[1]

---

[1] Luther, *A Commentary on Saint Paul's Epistle to the Galatians* (London, 1838), pp. xxxiii and xxxix.

Who, reading this argument as a whole, would ever suspect that almost half (about two-fifths to be more precise) of the letter is taken up with Paul's defence of himself and his apostolic status ?

Moreover, it is desirable to make clear to ourselves the central point in Paul's argument in this letter. If it is true to say that two-fifths are defence of Paul's status, it is equally true to say that at least another two-fifths are counter-attack. The nature of this counter-attack can be briefly indicated.

It is said to the Gentile Christians by Paul's rivals : ' You *must* be circumcised if you are to be true Christians '.

The logical contradictory of this is : ' You *need not* be circumcised in order to be true Christians.'

But Paul says : ' You *must not* be circumcised, if you are to be true Christians '. This is the contrary of the original contention. It carries the war into the enemy's camp. And it prepares us for the central argument of Galatians, which is not designed to prove the Law *unnecessary* for Gentile Christians, but to prove it *obsolete*, superseded. To go back to it is to be a traitor to the Gospel, to apostatise from Christianity. The violence of this opposition is in part to be explained by the fact that Paul is also facing a violent personal attack.

This gives the first indication for the dating of the Epistle. The only time when Paul appears to have had to face an attack of this kind and of this gravity is in the Ephesian period ; and the situation revealed in the Philippian and Corinthian letters is, I think, substantially that presupposed by Galatians. Only preoccupation with Justification *sola fide* obscures this fact for us. I shall therefore begin this investigation with the working hypothesis that Galatians belongs to the Ephesian period. I shall assume one other thing : that the persons addressed are those whom Paul and Barnabas evangelized on the First Missionary Journey, the Christians of South Galatia.[1]

---

[1] Note that Galatians is a circular letter. It is addressed ταῖς ἐκκλησίαις τῆς Γαλατίας. Presumably the copy sent was to circulate through the group of congregations and be read in each. It is most unlikely that " the Galatians " could ever have been together as a single unit. This makes it probable that any action which they seem to take as a united group, is suggested and engineered by the anti-Pauline agitators. This would apply especially to the composition and despatch of the hypothetical letter from " the Galatians " to Paul, for which I argue below.

So much by way of preface. We turn now to see what can be learned from Galatians about Paul and his missionary work.

The reader of our English versions, and still more the student of the Greek text, must be struck by the extraordinary jerkiness and abruptness of the style—extraordinary even for Paul. This is usually explained as being due to the strong emotion under which the Apostle was labouring when he composed the letter ; and this is no doubt a true explanation up to a point. But it is possible that there is another factor, which would help to account for this phenomenon. It may be that Paul is replying to a communication, oral or written, received from the Galatians (or about them). I should suggest that there are indications of the existence of such a communication in Gal. i. 6-9, 10 ; iii. 1-5 ; iv. 8-20 ; v. 7-12. And I should make a tentative reconstruction of its contents in this fashion.

The Galatians are receiving another account of Christianity ($\H{\epsilon}\tau\epsilon\rho\text{o}\nu$ $\epsilon\H{\nu}\alpha\gamma\gamma\H{\epsilon}\lambda\iota\text{o}\nu$) from missionaries who claim to be accredited from the Mother-Church in Jerusalem. They point out that Paul lacks these credentials.[1] The revised version of the Gospel ($\H{\epsilon}\tau\epsilon\rho\text{o}\nu$ $\epsilon\H{\nu}\alpha\gamma\gamma$.) involves, of course, circumcision and the adoption of other wholesome Jewish practices, including the ritual calendar (iv. 10). When the Galatians ask—as well they may—why they were not told about all these obligations when they were first converted by Paul, the answer given by their new ministers is that Paul is a somewhat easy-going missionary who accommodates his preaching to the tastes of his hearers, making himself and his Gospel agreeable to them (i. 10).[2] True, the preaching of Christ crucified is good and the gift of the Holy Spirit is a very great blessing ; but these things are not the whole story. The Galatians must complete the good work, and

---

[1] Paul's claim that his Apostleship is not $\H{\alpha}\pi$' $\H{\alpha}\nu\theta\rho\H{\omega}\pi\omega\nu$, $\text{o}\H{\nu}\delta\H{\epsilon}$ $\delta\iota$' $\H{\alpha}\nu\theta\rho\H{\omega}\pi\text{o}\nu$, and that his Gospel is not $\kappa\alpha\tau\H{\alpha}$ $\H{\alpha}\nu\theta\rho\omega\pi\text{o}\nu$, is double-edged. It means to say : (a) My opponents in Galatia claim to have Apostolic credentials and the authentic complete Jerusalem version of the Gospel. They say I lack these things. I don't want them, for (b) my authority and my Gospel are both derived from another (and a better) source.

[2] The foundation in fact on which this libel was based may be found in I Cor. ix. 20 ff.

the new missionaries are showing them the way (iii. 1-5). They do Paul no injustice by trying to improve themselves and adding to what he taught them (iv. 13). And if Paul chooses to take offence at this, it is he who is picking the quarrel, not the Galatians (iv. 16). But anyhow Paul is somewhat temperamental and liable to behave in quite incalculable ways. The new missionaries suggest that perhaps it is to be explained by his physical disabilities. If that is so, the Galatians will quite understand (iv. 13-15).

Something of this sort seems to lie behind Galatians as we know it; and bits of this communication flash before Paul's mind as he tries to produce something that will meet the emergency. That would explain why the composition is so jerky and disconnected. There is consequently no need to force logical cohesion all through the letter; and, indeed, it is probably a mistake to try.

It is the fact that his whole life's work is at stake that prompts the long autobiographical section in chapters i and ii. It bristles with difficulties, mostly (not all) arising from the necessity of fitting Paul's account into the narrative of Acts. In this matter three canons may be proposed:

(a) Where Acts and Galatians conflict, the preference should generally be given to Galatians.

(b) Any reconstruction of the events which involves tampering with the order in Gal. i, ii is to be regarded with suspicion. And, on the other hand, a reconstruction which allows us to preserve the Galatian order should have that fact accounted to it for righteousness.

(c) Never to forget Paul's purpose in writing the whole letter, and the first two chapters in particular. Galatians is Paul's *apologia pro vita sua*.

The autobiographical section opens with a picture of Saul of Tarsus persecuting the Church, a picture which has its counterpart in Acts (vii. 54-viii. 3; ix. 1 f.). It is not irrelevant to inquire how long this period in the Apostle's life lasted. I am inclined to think that it was very short, and, indeed, that the whole period covered by Acts i-ix was quite short too. The first five chapters of Acts speak in the main of the progress and popularity of the Christian community in Jerusalem. There is a certain amount of police action by the high officials of the Temple, but nothing that could be called systematic persecution. Acts vi. 1-6 describes the appointment of the Seven and vi. 7 mentions further progress. With vi. 8-viii 1ª troubles begin with the case of Stephen ; and, following upon the death of Stephen, we have (viii. 1ᵇ-40) an account of the dispersal of the persecuted Jerusalem Christians and the consequent spread of the Gospel.[1] Meanwhile Saul is persecuting the Jerusalem Church (viii. 3) and in chapter ix, we come to his expedition to Damascus and his conversion.

The inferences to be drawn from the narrative of Acts i-ix are these. (a) The Jerusalem Church begins, on the whole, prosperously. Serious trouble does not arise until the community has already grown too large for its affairs to be managed by the Twelve. Moreover, it is one of the Seven who awakes the spirit of persecution, and that among Diaspora Jews. Indeed the first serious persecution looks like a feud between Diaspora Jews and Diaspora Jewish-Christians. (b) Events move rapidly. Chapters i-v seem to me to be meant to give the impression of swift growth. And when persecution begins it, too, moves swiftly and fiercely. Consequently, when we are considering the time occupied by the events of Acts i-ix, we should think in terms of weeks rather than months and months rather than years. If, with Fotheringham, we date the Crucifixion at the Passover of A.D. 33, I should be inclined to place all the events described in Acts up to Paul's conversion before the end of A.D. 34.

(c) With regard to Saul's persecutions it is to be noted that in Acts he is shown as active in connexion with two places and two only, Jerusalem and Damascus. (This is a characteristic which reappears in Paul the Apostle : he goes for the strategic points every time.) That Saul's persecuting activity was thus restricted is confirmed by Gal. i. 22 where Paul says that after his conversion he was still unknown by face to the Churches of Judaea. Hence we may infer that his activity was neither widespread nor prolonged. It is probable that it amounts to a lightning campaign in Jerusalem, which was about to be

---

[1] This section is largely devoted to the missionary work of Philip.

followed by another in Damascus, when his conversion intervened.

Three years after his conversion Paul paid his first visit to the leaders of the Jerusalem community (Gal. i. 18-24). He says that the purpose of his visit was to get acquainted with Peter, presumably since Peter was the leader of the Twelve. He also saw James the Lord's brother. And that was all that happened in a stay of fifteen days. (Presumably Peter and James were the only leaders in residence at the time.) There is a parallel to this in Acts ix. 26-30. There are difficulties in reconciling the two stories: enough to cast doubt on some particulars in the Acts account, but not enough to bring in question the substantial identity of the two visits (G1 = A1).

Then after a lapse of fourteen years comes the second visit (G2) made by Paul, Barnabas, and Titus [1] (Gal. ii. 1-10). Since Barnabas is of the party it is most unlikely that the visit took place later than the commencement of the Second Missionary Journey. For at that point Paul and Barnabas parted company and do not seem to have joined forces again. Now Acts tells of *two* visits to Jerusalem by Paul and Barnabas before they fell out: one (A2) in Acts xi (the so-called Famine visit), the other (A3) in Acts xv (the Council visit). Supposing that the second visit described by Paul has a counterpart in Acts, the possibilities may be shown thus:

(i) G2 = A2 (A3 not described in Gal.).

(ii) G2 = A3 (A2 not described in Gal.).

(iii) G2 = A2 = A3 (all being different accounts of one and the same visit; G2 being Paul's, A2 that of the Church at Antioch, A3 that of the Jerusalem community). All three equations have been defended: (i) by Ramsay and by Lake (*Earlier Epistles of St. Paul*), (ii) by Lightfoot in his Commentary on Galatians, (iii) by Lake following Weizsäcker, McGiffert, and

---

[1] Titus does not appear at all in Acts. From the Pauline Epistles it appears that he was Paul's trusted lieutenant during the period covered by the Corinthian correspondence. Whence he came we do not know. He was a Gentile Christian, probably one of Paul's converts, and so presumably from one of the provinces in which Paul had worked—Syria, Cilicia, or even—if we put the second visit after the First Missionary Journey—Galatia. I am inclined to think that he was a member of the Church at Antioch.

Schwartz (*Beginnings of Christianity*, v. 195-212).[1]   It is in connexion with these identifications that the difficulties arise.[2] To appreciate them it is necessary to examine somewhat carefully Paul's own account of the visit.

' Then, after a lapse of fourteen years, I again went up to Jerusalem with Barnabas, taking Titus along also. And I went up in accordance with a revelation, and I laid before them the Gospel which I preach among the Gentiles (but privately before the men of repute) lest possibly I should run or had run in vain. But not even Titus, who was with me, Greek though he was, was compelled to be circumcised —but because of the interloping bogus Christians, who sneaked in to spy out our freedom which we have in Christ, that they may reduce us to slavery—to whom not for a moment did we yield in submission. And from those who were accounted to be something—what they once were matters nothing to me : God has no favourites—for to me the men of repute added nothing. But, on the contrary, seeing that I had been entrusted with the mission to the uncircumcised, as Peter with that to the circumcised—for he who empowered Peter for an apostleship to the circumcised empowered me also to the Gentiles—and realising the grace conferred upon me, James and Cephas and John, who were regarded as pillars, gave to me and Barnabas right hands of fellowship (agreeing) that we should go to the Gentiles, they to the circumcised. (The) only (other point settled was) that we should remember the poor, which very thing I have been zealous to do.'

This passage is very jerky and disconnected, and full of difficulties of interpretation ; but we can get some things reasonably clear.

(1) *The purpose of the visit.* To make sure that Paul and Barnabas on the one side and the Jerusalem leaders on the other

---

[1] The authors and works cited will give the English reader a clear statement of the case for each view.

[2] Stated most trenchantly by F. C. Baur, *Paulus* (2nd ed., 1866), i. 119-165. The main points in his argument against the identification of G2 and A3 seem to me to be unanswered and unanswerable.

were at one with regard to the fundamentals of the Gospel, so that Paul's converts would be recognised by the authorities in Jerusalem as genuine Christians and real members of the Church. This was vitally important for Paul just because he held such strong convictions about the unity of the Church as the Body of Christ. If, after a missionary campaign, his converts were re-fused the name of Christian and denied the status of members of Christ's Body, his work would be crippled and made ineffective. Such a calamity must not be allowed to happen and need not happen if there could be agreement on essentials.

(2) *The result of the visit.* (a) Paul tells us that he saw the Jerusalem leaders privately and that after a frank discussion they found that they were in agreement with him and had nothing to add to his Gospel. (b) The Jerusalem leaders recognised that Paul's status and appointment were from God in the same sense as their own. (c) Spheres of action were agreed upon. Paul and Barnabas, themselves Christians whose origin was from the Diaspora, were to go to the ' Foreign field ', the Twelve (or ' the Pillars ')—Palestinian Jews—were to take charge of the ' Home mission '. This was obvious common sense.[1] (d) Paul under-took to raise funds for the aid of the impoverished Jerusalem community.

This takes no account of Gal. ii. 3-5. These verses are usually taken as describing something that happened during the course of the conference. It is supposed that the issue of circumcision of Gentile Christians was raised in the case of Titus, thus providing a test case and a precedent for the future. The difficulty is that if Titus was a test case, Paul's account of it is utterly inept. Either Titus was circumcised or he was not. If he was not, it should have been simple to say so outright : ' Certain false breth-ren wanted to have Titus circumcised, but I put my foot down '. If he was circumcised, the fact would be well advertised in Galatia by Paul's opponents, and the involved and stumbling

---

[1] It is noteworthy that even now, at least fifteen years after the Crucifixion, the Jerusalem Apostles do not seem to have an idea beyond Home Mission work. (See Baur, *Paulus*, i. 142 ff.) I cannot accept Wrede's account (*Paul*, 68 f.) : ' The most that was attained was an agreement to differ. The union meant at the same time separation : Paul was to go to the Gentiles, Peter to the Jews.' It does not appear that there was any such feeling in Paul's mind at the time.

verbiage of these verses would be worse than useless as camouflage for that nasty fact.[1]

I believe there is a way of dealing with this passage that makes sense and allows us to keep our respect for Paul's intelligence. I venture to think that *v.* 3 belongs to the time of the conference, and that *vv.* 4 and 5 describe something that happened later. This later happening still rankles in Paul's mind, and the mere mention of circumcision brings it all back in awkward parentheses. The sense of the whole passage will then be something like this :

> ' The issue of compulsory circumcision did not arise on this occasion, though Titus who was with me was an obvious case being a Greek. When at a later date it was brought up it was through certain interlopers and bogus Christians . . . and *in your interests* we refused absolutely to make any concessions.'

The fact that stress is laid on Paul's refusal being in the interest of the Galatians ($\text{\"{\i}}\nu a \ \dot{\eta} \ \dot{a}\lambda\dot{\eta}\theta\epsilon\iota a \ \tau o\hat{v} \ \epsilon\dot{v}a\gamma\gamma\epsilon\lambda\dot{\iota}ov \ \delta\iota a\mu\epsilon\dot{\iota}\nu\eta \ \pi\rho\dot{o}s \ \dot{v}\mu\hat{a}s$) suggests that *vv.* 4 and 5 describe something posterior to the evangelization of the Galatians. As will appear presently, I think that the rest of the section describes a conference which took place before the First Missionary Journey.

(3) *The time of the visit.* The whole account seems to imply a private conference between leading men in the Churches of Antioch and Jerusalem, conducted in a friendly spirit, without any contentious matters arising, and ending in a friendly and sensible allocation of missionary tasks. This does not seem to me to resemble what is described either in Acts xi or in Acts xv.

---

[1] Against Burkitt, *Christian Beginnings*, 118 : ' Who can doubt that it was the knife that really did circumcise Titus that has cut the syntax of Gal. ii. 3-5 to pieces ? ' A. D. Nock's suggestion (*St. Paul*, 109) that ' Paul firmly refused to circumcise Titus, or to recommend him to be circumcised, but that . . . Titus, under pressure, but on his own initiative and without consulting Paul, had himself circumcised in the hope of easing a difficult situation ' is ingenious ; but it is open to the objection that if that is what actually happened, it would have been easy for Paul to say so : ' Titus was circumcised, I admit, but without my knowledge or consent. He did it with the best intentions ; and while I fully approve the motive that prompted the act I must repudiate the act itself.' But Paul does not say this or anything like it.

Further, the visit described here in Gal. ii does not fit the circumstances which occasioned either of the visits described in Acts. If we ask ourselves when such a visit as G2 might have been expected to take place, the obvious answer is : on the eve of some big new missionary enterprise. With that the place of the visit in the history of the Primitive Church is at once suggested : the period immediately before Paul and Barnabas set out for Cyprus and Asia Minor on the first deliberately planned piece of aggressive mission work of the Church. In that case it is possible to give a really satisfying meaning to the phrase ἀνέβην δὲ κατὰ ἀποκάλυψιν, for in Acts xiii. i f. we read : ' And there were in Antioch prophets and teachers. . . . And when they were engaged in service to the Lord and fasting the Holy Spirit said to them, " Come, separate to me Barnabas and Saul for the work to which I have called them " ' (Lake and Cadbury's translation). It is true that Acts does not record a visit by Paul and Barnabas in connexion with the First Missionary Journey ; but there are many other things that must have happened which are not recorded in Acts.

Supposing for the moment that this identification is correct, what is the probable date of the second Galatian visit (G2) ? It can be calculated to within a year or so by back-reckoning from the date of Paul's departure from Corinth. This should most probably be placed in the early summer of A.D. 51 or 52, which gives midwinter 49/50 or 50/51 for his arrival in the city. At the other end the date of the Famine visit (Acts xi) can also be determined with fair certainty. Evidence from Egypt shows that there was scarcity there—in one of the greatest grain-producing centres of the Roman Empire—from autumn 45 to spring 46.[1] There is evidence for a famine in Judaea during the procuratorship of Tiberius Alexander, i.e. in 46 or 47.[2] The sabbatical year fell to be observed in the twelve months beginning in the autumn (1 Tishri) of 47. Its effects would be felt most acutely from about Passover 48 to Passover 49. All these facts together suggest that there would be scarcity in greater or less degree from autumn 45 to spring 49 in Palestine.

[1] See the article on the Universal Famine under Claudius, by K. S. Gapp, in *Harvard Theological Review*, xxviii. 258-265.

[2] See Lake in *Beginnings of Christianity*, v. 452-455.

The Famine visit may well fall in 46 or early 47. In that case the events described in Acts xii. 25-xviii. 1 will fall in the years 47 to 49 or 50. They may be distributed thus :

First Missionary Journey 47 or 48.
Intervening events including Jerusalem Council 48 or 49.
Second Missionary Journey 49 or 50.

The second Galatian visit will then be placed in 47 or early in 48, about fourteen years after Paul's conversion.

Our theory is that this second Galatian visit was followed by the First Missionary Journey during which the Galatian Churches were founded. This journey was followed by a stay in Antioch during which we most probably should place the next incident recorded in Galatians (ii. 11-14).

> ' And when Cephas came to Antioch I resisted him to his face because he stood condemned. For before someone came from James he used to eat with the Gentiles ; but when (this person) came he backed down and separated himself, fearing those of the circumcision. And there joined him in this hypocrisy the rest of the Jews, so that even Barnabas was carried along with their hypocrisy. But when I saw that they were not advancing towards [1] the truth of the Gospel, I said to Cephas in the presence of everybody, " If you, though a Jew, live Gentile fashion and not as a Jew, how is it that you constrain the Gentiles to live as Jews ? " '

On this important passage there are some remarks to be made. First about the text. In v. 12[b] the best of the MS. authority is on the side of the singular verb $\mathring{\eta}\lambda\theta\epsilon\nu$ ' he came ' against $\mathring{\eta}\lambda\theta o\nu$ ' they came '. $\mathring{}H\lambda\theta\epsilon\nu$ is the reading of אBD*G and the Old Latin authorities d e g. It was certainly known to Origen who understood it to mean that James came down to Antioch in person. The difficulty is that in the preceding clause the accepted text speaks of ' certain persons ' (plural) as having come down from James, and one naturally expects a plural verb to follow. Alternatively, of course, one might have a singular subject in the first clause, and this reading was in fact presupposed by the Old Latin

---

[1] On the translation of $\mathring{o}\rho\theta o\pi o\delta o\mathring{v}\sigma\iota$ see the note by C. H. Roberts in J.T.S., xl (1939), 55 f.

texts *d e g* r**.   But this evidence by itself seemed insufficient to justify reading a singular subject in the first clause and a singular verb in the second.   The textual question is, however, reopened by the fact that the Chester Beatty codex of the Pauline Epistles (P[46]) supports both readings : in 12[a] it has TINA with *d e g* r**, and in 12[b] it has HAΘEN with אBD*G and the Old Latin.   We may also add Irenaeus' testimony : ' *cum* tamen *aduenisset quidam ab jacobo* '.[1]   I think that P[46] gives the true text of Galatians in *v.* 12 for the following reasons :—

(*a*) The weight of evidence in favour of ἦλθεν is very great—almost overwhelming : and if ἦλθεν be accepted, it automatically creates a presumption in favour of τινά.

(*b*) The supporters of τινά are now the very respectable company : P[46] *d e g* r** Irenaeus.

(*c*) The substitution of τινὰς for τινά may be explained as a confused reminiscence of Acts xv. 1 : καί τινες κατελθόντες ἀπὸ Ἰουδαίας ἐδίδασκον τοὺς ἀδελφοὺς ὅτι ἐὰν μὴ περιτμηθῆτε τῷ ἔθει τῷ Μωυσέως, οὐ δύνασθε σωθῆναι.

(*d*) The subsequent developments tell against the view that either James or a deputation of right-wing Jewish Christians arrived in Antioch.   For if such persons had been present, Paul could not have ignored their presence.   Yet in his own account of the matter he says that he tackled Peter (and apparently Peter only) in the presence of all.   If this was a public protest—and it clearly was—Paul must have attacked those who had stirred up the trouble as well as Peter.   That he did not do so indicates that they never existed except in the imagination of some scribe. Paul concentrates his attack on Peter because Peter is the leader, on the spot, of what is, from Paul's point of view, a retrograde movement which has swept away Barnabas and the rest of the Jews.

That being so, we accept the singular readings and understand that the ' somebody ' of 12[a] was a messenger (Paul describes him in this vague way most probably because he did not know or had forgotten the man's name).   He brought the message

---

[1] On the reading of Irenaeus at this point see Sanday and Turner, *Nouum Testamentum S. Irenaei*, p. 154, where the O.L. evidence is also given in a convenient form.

from James to Peter which broke up the happy relations till then subsisting between Jewish and Gentile Christians in Antioch. What was the purport of this message? We do not know. Perhaps Paul himself did not know. We can only conjecture what it was from its results. Paul mentions two. First it had the effect of throwing Peter into a panic—not for the first time. He feared ' those of the circumcision '. This phrase is used by Paul in Rom. iv. 12 ; Col. iv. 11, and it also appears in Acts x. 45 ; xi. 2. It means ' the circumcised ', ' the Jews '. This does not exclude the possibility that οἱ ἐκ περιτομῆς are converts to Christianity ; but it is not necessarily implied and it is certainly not stated by Paul. The most natural interpretation would be that οἱ ἐκ περιτομῆς were the occasion of James's message to Peter, and that they were either Jewish Christian members of the Jerusalem community (cf. Acts x. 45 ; xxi. 20 ff.) or Jews outside who could find in Peter's behaviour a new ground of complaint against the Church, namely that its leaders were apostatising from Judaism. And the alternatives are not mutually exclusive : both factors could well have been operative, and the language of Galatians excludes neither.[1] In this connexion it must be borne in mind that Peter as head of the ' Home Mission ' work of the Church had to consider the feelings of those whom he was evangelising.

The second result of James's communication is that Peter ' backed down and withdrew ' (or perhaps ' played the Pharisee ').[2] This doubtless means that he discontinued his practice of table-fellowship with Gentile Christians. Why? The only really probable answer is that the Gentile Christians were suspected— no doubt rightly—of not observing the Jewish dietary laws [3] in the selection and preparation of the food which was set before the mixed company of Jewish and Gentile Christians. There is abundant evidence, before as well as after the Christian Era, to show how suspicious was the devout Jew of partaking of Gentile

[1] The fact that the objections were apparently being made at Jerusalem and to James may be regarded as an indication of his position in the community there.

[2] See my *Teaching of Jesus*, 241 f.

[3] On these laws see Moore, *Judaism*, ii. 74 f. ; Schürer, *Geschichte des jüdischen Volkes im ZA. Jesu Christi*[4], ii. 91-94 ; L. Finkelstein, *The Pharisees*, 534 f. ; S. R. Driver, Commentary on Daniel (*Cambridge Bible*), note on Dan. i. 8-10.

hospitality because of the danger of consuming food that had been offered on heathen altars or that had not been slaughtered in the proper way.[1] It would be a great mistake to regard this as a mere superstitious fad. The truth is that, whatever the origins of the dietary customs, they had been clothed with a special sanctity in the second century B.C. Then, in the attempt to hellenize the Jews, unclean foods had been forced upon them and the Maccabaean martyrs had resisted unto death.[2]

All that has to be added is that as a result of Peter's abstention Barnabas and the other Christians of Jewish origin also withdrew from table-fellowship with their Gentile brethren. And with that Peter destroyed something valuable—a spirit born of the Gospel, which had made Jews and Gentiles (Aryans and non-Aryans) forget their mutual prejudices and suspicions and sit down together as brethren. What was worse, in all probability he destroyed something that he had not himself created, something that was already in existence before he came to Antioch.

Taking all these facts into account we may suppose that the message from James was to this effect :

' News has come to Jerusalem that you are eating Gentile food at Gentile tables, and this is causing great scandal to many devout brethren besides laying us open to serious criticism from the Scribes and Pharisees. Pray discontinue this practice, which will surely do great harm to our work among our fellow-countrymen.'

If we now turn to Acts and ask ourselves where is the most natural setting for all this, the obvious answer is that the decisions of the Council of Jerusalem (Acts xv) seem to contemplate just such a situation as that which had arisen at Antioch. At least that is so on what appears to me to be the most reasonable interpretation of the Council's decisions. However, as there is difference of opinion among scholars, it is necessary to examine the proceedings of the Council. It will be convenient to begin at

---

[1] Dan. i. 8-10 ; Esther, LXX, iv. 17^x (ed. Rahlfs, i. p. 961) ; *Judith*, xii. 1, 2 ; *Tobit*, i. 10, 11 ; *Jub.* xxii. 16 ; Josephus, *Life*, ch. 3 (§§ 13 f.) ; *Ant.* iv. 137 ; Posidonius, cited by Th. Reinach, *Textes d'auteurs grecs et romains relatifs au Judaïsme* (1895), p. 57.

[2] *I Macc.* i. 47-49, 62-64 ; *II Macc.* vi. 18-vii. 41.

the end and work backwards. The business of the Council terminated with the dispatch of two official delegates bearing a letter containing the findings of the Council. The crux of the matter lies in Acts xv. 28 f. :

> ' It was decided by the Holy Spirit and by us to put no further burden on you than these essentials—to abstain from things offered to idols and blood and that which is strangled and fornication. And if you keep yourselves from them you will be doing right.'

This embodies a proposal which had already been put forward in the speech of James the Lord's brother (xv. 19 f.). The terms are later repeated in a conversation between Paul and the Jerusalem authorities recorded in Acts xxi. 20-25.

There are two well-worn problems here. The first concerns the text, the second the interpretation, of the decrees : and the two hang together.[1]

First the text. In the translation given above four things are forbidden. These four appear in all three places (Acts xv. 20 ; xv. 29 ; xxi. 25) in the MSS. of the B family, in the Peshiṭta, and (for xv. 29) in Clement of Alexandria. The so-called Western text differs in two respects : (a) it has only three forbidden things, omitting ' that which is strangled ' ; (b) all the authorities for this type of text, except Tertullian, add a form of the Golden Rule at the end of the list, and three of them (Codex Bezae, Irenaeus, and Tertullian) add a reference to the Holy Spirit after the words ' you will be doing right ' in xv. 29. A smaller group of authorities comprising Origen (C. Cels. viii. 29), the Harris MS. of the Syriac Didascalia (cited by Preuschen in his commentary on Acts), and (for xv. 20)[2] the Chester Beatty codex P⁴⁵, omit ' fornication ' from the list. There is a further point. In the three places in Acts the order of the items in the

---

[1] For the text see the discussions by Ropes, *Beginnings of Christianity*, iii. 265-269 ; Clark, *The Acts of the Apostles*, 360 f. (earlier literature cited by Ropes, *op. cit.*, p. 269). For the exegesis of the decree see especially Lake, *Beginning of Christianity*, v, 204-212 ; Harnack, *Die Apostelgeschichte* (1908), pp. 188-198.

[2] a]λλ επιστειλαι αυτοις του απεχεσθαι των αλι[σγηματων των ειδω]λων· και του πνικτου· και του αιματος μωση[s γαρ εκ. The papyrus is unfortunately not extant for the other two places.

list is different : in xv. 20 it is ' idol offerings, fornication, things strangled, blood ' ; in xv. 29 and xxi. 25 it is ' idol-offerings, blood, things strangled, fornication '. The undisputed members of the list are ' idol-offerings ' and ' blood ' ; the other two appear now before ' blood ', now after it.

It will be observed that the effect of the peculiar ' Western ' readings is to exclude any food-law explanation, and virtually to compel the reading of the decrees as a compendium of moral requirements. That in itself makes these readings suspect. Consequently, if we judge that the Western authorities are wrong in adding the Golden Rule and the reference to the Holy Spirit, we are bound to ask whether they are not also wrong in omitting ' the thing that is strangled '. Nor can we stop there. In the light of the reading of P⁴⁵ and Origen we must ask whether the appearance of the word ' fornication ' in the list is not one of the first steps in the process of moralisation. For it is well known that the Western text can be interpreted in a sense which makes it practically equivalent to the decisions of the Jewish Council of Lydda held after the rebellion under Hadrian (A.D. 132-135). There it was decided that, *if his life were at stake*, a Jew might break any commandment of the Law except those prohibiting idolatry (עבודה זרה), sexual immorality (גלוי עריות), and murder (שפיכות דמים).[1] It is simple and tempting to equate ἀλισγήματα τῶν εἰδώλων with עבודה זרה, πορνεία with גלוי עריות, and αἷμα with שפיכום דמים. But it cannot be done without reducing the findings of the Jerusalem Council to absurdity.

For the situations are not parallel. The Jewish Council of Lydda was legislating for Jews in peril of their lives in a time of fierce and relentless persecution, and the three things mentioned are things which a Jew must not do even to save his life. But no such dreadful dilemma faces the Gentile convert to Christianity. The Council of Jerusalem is not legislating for Gentile Christians confronted with the alternatives : eat idol-offerings or be slain. And for a gathering of Apostles and elders to lay down in solemn form that well-behaved Christians will abstain from idolatry, fornication, and murder is simply to make fools of themselves. Ecclesiastical gatherings have before now achieved

[1] On this see the article by Dr. J. W. Hunkin in *J.T.S.*, xxvii (1926), 272-283.

remarkable results in the way of pompous platitude ; but it is asking too much to expect us to believe that the Fathers at Jerusalem (who were presumably in possession of those ' sayings of Jesus ' which went to make up such a document as Q) perpetrated this, or that the Paul, who wrote I Cor. xiii and Rom. xii, could ever have allowed it to pass. For it would fix for the Gentile Christian a lower minimum standard of conduct than the Jewish Law normally required from the resident alien.[1] And, in its context, the finding could only mean : ' We Jewish Christians have, of course, to maintain a somewhat high standard to which you converts from heathenism cannot be expected to attain. Consequently we must overlook such peccadilloes as lying, thieving, fraud, bullying, and backbiting, but we do draw the line at idolatry, fornication, and murder.' Neither the legalistic Jewish Christians nor the anti-legalist Paul could ever have supposed that you solve the problems created by the existence of the Mosaic Law by the whittling down of moral standards. It is too much like the imaginary examination paper which consisted of the Ten Commandments together with the rubric : ' Candidates are advised not to attempt more than six of these '—except that in this case the requirement for a pass is reduced to three. It is too ridiculous to be credible.

But if the ' ethical ' interpretation breaks down, the only real alternative is that which understands the prohibitions in connexion with Jewish dietary practice. And in that case ' fornication ' is quite out of place in the list and should be removed from the text. This leaves us with idol-offerings, that which is strangled, and blood. The only textual evidence against τοῦ πνικτοῦ (τῶν πνικτῶν) is its absence from the Western authorities. (Perhaps we should add here its variable position in the lists.) But its absence from the Western text is somewhat discounted by the consideration that it was absolutely necessary if the decree was to be understood in a purely ' ethical ' sense. It may, therefore, have been ejected in the process of moralisation which produced the Western text. On the other hand it may be argued that if it was absent from the original form of the decree, anyone who was bent on an ethical interpretation would find no obstacle

---

[1] See Moore, *Judaism*, i. 338 f., for these requirements.

in his path, since the remaining two items might be taken in either way.

There is one other objection to the genuineness of τοῦ πνικτοῦ. It was raised by Wellhausen and relied upon by Harnack.[1] It is that πνικτόν is included under αἷμα, so that if αἷμα, in the sense of ' eating meat with blood in it ' is forbidden, πνικτόν is automatically forbidden at the same time. In strict logic no doubt this is so. It would seem that πνικτόν is a comprehensive term for meat from animals not slaughtered in accordance with Jewish rules. But one might obtain meat that conformed to all the Jewish rules in regard to slaughtering, and still be guilty of the αἷμα by failing to prepare it properly before cooking. It is perhaps possible that πνικτόν is meant to cover the slaughter of the animal, and αἷμα the preparation of the meat for the table.[2] This would be the more plausible if the order πνικτὸν αἷμα, as in xv. 20, were the original. But all this is highly conjectural, and we cannot exclude the possibility that πνικτόν is an early gloss on αἷμα. I do not attempt to decide the question here, and am content with the conclusion that, whether the decree covered idol-offerings, things strangled, and blood, or idol-offerings and blood only, it was a provision regulating the dinner tables of the Gentile Christians.[3]

The difficulties begin when we attempt to relate this result to what has gone before in the Acts account of the Council. The essence of the matter is that the Council was ostensibly convened to deal with the question of the circumcision of Gentile Christians and that it ended by issuing regulations about the common table of Jewish and Gentile Christians. The decrees are

[1] *Die Apostelgeschichte*, 191.

[2] See Krauss, *Talmudische Archäologie*, i. 120, 502 ; Billerbeck, *Kommentar*, ii. 735 ff.

[3] There is a good deal of evidence to show that the decrees regarded as a food law continued to be observed in the Church in post-apostolic times. In particular, abstinence from blood appears as the rule in Gaul (Eusebius, *H.E.*, v. 1, 26) and Africa (Tertullian, *Apol.*, ix. 13). In the Eastern Church the ' eating of blood ' was regarded as a serious ecclesiastical offence punishable in the case of clergy by deposition, and in the case of a layman by excommunication (Conc. in Trullo, Canon 67 ; see Hefele-Leclercq, *Histoire des Conciles*, iii. 571). See further, Suicer, *Thesaurus Ecclesiasticus* (1682), i. 113 (*s.v.* αἷμα) ; Grotius, *Annotationes in Nouum Testamentum*, ii (1646), 80 ff.

the answer to the question raised in Gal. ii. 11-14 : they are not, *and cannot be*, the answer to the issue raised in Acts xv. 1. That is the fundamental internal difficulty in Acts xv. We have also to face the following facts.

(*a*) If G2 = A3 we have to explain the inexplicable behaviour of Peter at Antioch (Gal. ii. 11 ff.), which can only be done by supposing that Paul has told his story out of order.

(*b*) In I Thess. ii. 13-16 Paul speaks very kindly and appreciatively of ' the Churches of God which are in Judaea in Jesus Christ '; and there is no word of any demand for circumcision. The only difficulty is the opposition of the Jews (*not* Jewish Christians) to any mission work at all among the Gentiles.

(*c*) The demand for circumcision of Gentile Christians is being made insistently at the time when Galatians is written, and it appears as a live question in I Corinthians, Philippians, and Romans. That is to say, the question which, in Acts, is supposed to have been settled for ever before the Second Missionary Journey appears as a live issue for the first time in the Pauline letters in documents which we may assign to the time of the Third Missionary Journey.

When all these data are considered together they at least suggest the possibility that the narrative of Acts xv is composite, and that the demand for circumcision of Gentile Christians reported in Acts xv. 1 and 5 *may* have been first made at a later time, perhaps on the visit recorded in Acts xviii. 22. But it is not possible to enter into the detailed consideration of these possibilities here. All that can be done is to reconstruct the probable course of events, taking Paul's narrative as the foundation. On that basis it may be said that the incident at Antioch as described by Paul furnished the occasion for the Council meeting whose decisions are given in Acts xv. I think it probable that Paul and Barnabas were present at that meeting. Whether or not the issue of circumcision was raised on this occasion, as related in Acts xv, we cannot say. If it was, it was a side issue and was ignored.[1] The matter of table-fellowship

---

[1] It is to be noted that circumcision is not even mentioned in the Apostolic letter. This is very remarkable if the Council had been summoned expressly to deal with this very question.

was settled by the decree.   In this way table-fellowship was
restored, which was what Paul wanted ; but it was a *kosher*
table, which was what James wanted.

There remains one difficulty.   If the decree is the answer to
the question raised in Gal. ii. 11-14 why does not Paul state the
Jerusalem decision, which we may presume that he accepted as
a fair settlement of the difficulty ?   It seems to me that there
are two possible answers to this question.   Either Paul does not
quote the decree because there is as yet no decree to quote, which
would, of course, mean that Galatians was written before the
Council of Jerusalem ; or he does not quote the decree because
he no longer regards it as binding, in which case we may date
Galatians at any time after (but not too soon after) the Council.
There are reasons which incline one to prefer the second
alternative.

We call the outcome of the Council a decree ; but in fact it was
a working compromise.   The end to be served by the observance
of the prohibitions was the restoration of the table-fellowship between Jewish and Gentile Christians which had been interrupted at
Antioch.   It was a reasonable request that where Jewish Christian
Apostles were the guests of Gentile Christians, they should not
be—so to speak—unjewed, and their work among their Jewish
brethren thus jeopardised.   Further, it could be represented that
it would be an act of Christian courtesy on the part of the Gentile
converts to make this concession to the needs of the Jewish
Christian members of the Church.   There is no reason why
Paul and Barnabas should not have accepted an agreement of this
kind and have done their best to get it observed by the Gentile
Christians.   It involved no sacrifice of principle.

A few years pass and the situation is changed.   The agreement described in Gal. ii. 9 is broken, and Paul's mission field
is invaded by emissaries from the Jewish Christian side.   This
appears clearly not only in Galatians, but also in Philippians and
in the Corinthian letters.   Secondly the apostolic authority of
Paul is questioned.   This also appears clearly in these same
documents.   It seems fairly certain that part of the propaganda
against Paul consisted in asserting that his Gospel was based on
instruction received from Jewish Christian sources, and that his

o

missionary work had always been under the supervision and orders of the Jerusalem Apostles. In particular it could be urged that Paul had submitted to the authority of Jerusalem in the matter of the common table for Jewish and Gentile Christians. For, admittedly, the practice in Antioch had been very free and easy until James intervened to restore order ; and the Council of Jerusalem had in fact upheld James (and Peter) against Paul by imposing the dietary requirements on the Gentile Christians. So it could be represented.

Moreover, it seems likely that the acceptance by Paul of the dietary regulations had been made—as concessions so often are— the basis for new and more far-reaching demands. The Galatians are now asked to observe the Jewish calendar with all its high days and holidays (Gal. iv. 8-11) and to be circumcised (Gal. vi. 11-13).

Paul's response to this is two-fold. The radical retort is made here in Galatians. In effect it is this : ' So far from submitting to Jewish Christian requirements, I deny their right to exist. They are based upon the Jewish Law, and that Law is now obsolete, its place having been taken by the Gospel.' This is the central argument of the Epistle, announced in unmistakable and uncompromising terms in ii. 15 f. : ' I though a Jew by birth and not a " Gentile sinner ", yet knowing that a man is not justified by works of the Law, but only through faith in Jesus Christ, even I believed in Christ Jesus that I might be justified by faith in Christ and not by works of the Law ; because by works of Law " shall no flesh be justified ".'

It follows that circumcision, fasts and feasts, clean and unclean meats, are, all of them, *irrelevant to Christianity.*

But—and this is Paul's second point—it is still true that large numbers of sincere Christians, who have been brought up under the Law, have a sentimental attachment to these traditional customs. What should the Gentile Christian do about it ? Paul's answer to that question is that the Jewish Christian *may* observe Jewish customs ; but that the Gentile Christian *must not accept any positive obligation that limits his liberty as a Christian.* On the other hand, he may, and should, abstain from exercising his undoubted rights in order to avoid wounding the suscepti-

bilities of his less emancipated brother (I Cor. viii-x ; Rom. xiv).
The genuine Pauline position is stated briefly in Gal. v. 1 and
13-15 (and the two passages must be held together) :—

'Christ set us free : stand, therefore, and be not en-
tangled again in a yoke of bondage. . . .

'Ye were called for freedom brethren. Only do not
turn your freedom into an opportunity for the flesh, but
through love be servants of one another. For the whole
Law (about which you have heard so much of late) is fulfilled
in a single " word " [" One word " not " Ten words " ;
a μονόλογος rather than a δεκάλογος], namely, " Thou shalt
love thy neighbour as thyself ".'

10

THE CORINTHIAN CORRESPONDENCE. (1)
(1941)

IN the two previous lectures in this series I have dealt with the letters to the Philippians and the Galatians. For this one I have set down the Corinthian correspondence, a subject of great complexity and difficulty, yet one of endless fascination, and to the serious student greatly rewarding in the light it sheds on the day to day life of the Gentile Church.

The materials for our study are the two canonical Epistles in the New Testament. From evidence supplied by these documents we know that Paul wrote at least four letters to the Church at Corinth during the period with which we are concerned. To avoid confusion I refer to our existing canonical Epistles by the customary names, First and Second Corinthians, while the four letters I call Corinthians A, B, C, and D. The following conclusions about the relations of I and II Cor. to Cor. A, B, C, and D are fairly widely accepted.

Cor. A was written before I Cor. It is possible that a fragment of Cor. A survives embedded in II Cor. vi. 14-vii. 1.

Cor. B is identical with I Cor.

I Cor. was followed by a personal visit to Corinth, which ended in a complete and devastating rebuff for the Apostle. On his return to Ephesus from this ' Painful Visit ' he wrote Cor. C, the ' Severe Letter '. It is possible that II Cor. x-xiii is part of this letter.

Cor. D was written on hearing that the severe letter had produced a better frame of mind among the Corinthians and

that relations between them and him were once more to be on
the old footing of mutual confidence and affection.   If II Cor.
x-xiii is part of Cor. C, as I am inclined to think, then II Cor.
i-ix will belong to Cor. D.   Otherwise our II Cor. as a whole
will be identical with Cor. D.

Now it is clear that one lecture is not enough to deal adequately
with the whole of this correspondence, which is spread over a
considerable period of time and covers a great variety of topics.
I therefore propose a limited objective, namely, the attempt
to picture from the evidence supplied by I Cor. the state of
affairs in Corinth at the time when Paul wrote the letter, and in
particular the divisions within the community and the relation
of those divisions to Paul's own dealings with the Church of
Jerusalem and its leaders.   I think that any light we may gain
on conditions at Corinth will also serve to illuminate the much
more obscure and difficult problem of the relations between
Paul and his colleagues at Jerusalem and elsewhere.   It seems to
me certain that this period was a critical one for the Apostle,
whose authority and status were constantly being challenged
within and without his Churches, and here in I Cor. as in
Philippians and Galatians we may see many signs that Paul is
on his defence against attempts to question his calling or to
belittle his achievements as a missionary. The defence of Paul's
status, of Paul's Gospel, and of Paul's Churches tends to become
a single and indivisible undertaking.

I shall consequently leave on one side all the rare and refresh-
ing fruit that might be gathered if we approached I Cor. asking
only what we could learn from it about the fundamental principles
of Christian dogma and Christian ethics.   Instead I shall try
to relate each part of the letter to the actual situation in which
it was written, in the hope that the situation may help to explain
the letter and that the letter may illuminate the situation and
focus more clearly for us the issues that were at stake.   The
letter lends itself readily to this kind of treatment.   As you know,
it breaks up on analysis into a number of separate and self-
contained sections, each of which deals with a single topic.   It
is clear from the way in which many of these topics are introduced [1]

---

[1] Περὶ δὲ ὧν ἐγράψατε (vii. 1), cf. vii. 25 ; viii. 1 ; xii. 1 ; xvi. 1, 12.

that Paul is answering questions raised in Corinth. In each case we must try to get behind Paul's answer to the minds of those who put the question, to discover what purpose lay behind the enquiry, what answer they hoped to receive, how the question and Paul's answer square with Jewish, Jewish-Christian, and Gentile (Græco-Roman) sentiments and convictions. I venture to think that this method will produce some interesting results. It will raise more questions than it answers, but both questions and answers will be, I hope, worth while.

I Cor. like other Pauline letters opens with the prescript, which runs as follows :

> ' Paul called to be an Apostle of Jesus Christ by the will of God, with brother Sosthenes, to the Church of God which is at Corinth, consecrated in Jesus Christ, called as Saints, with all who call upon the name of our Lord Jesus Christ in every place, theirs and ours, grace to you and peace from God our Father and the Lord Jesus Christ.'

The difficulty, and the point of interest, lies in the strange phrase ' with all who call . . . theirs and ours '. I think it right to take τόπος in the sense which it has in Jewish Synagogue inscriptions—' place of worship '.[1] What Paul means is ' in every church, theirs and ours '. There can be little doubt as to what Paul means by ' ours ' : it is the churches of his own founding. ' Theirs ' will then apply to the other Christian communities founded by other Apostles but owning the same Lord Jesus Christ. The force of the whole prescript is thus to stress the unity of the Church as a whole, and at the same time to insist on the equality of the different communities comprised in the unity. The Corinthian Christians are Saints by calling along with all the others and on precisely the same footing as the others.

The thanksgiving which follows (i. 4-9) again underlines the equal status of the Corinthian Church with the other communities of Christians, this time in respect of gifts and graces. They lack no spiritual endowment (7). This may seem a very odd assertion when we reflect how Paul goes on in this letter to

---

[1] I am glad to see that Dr. Moffatt assigns the same meaning to the word τόπος. (See his *Commentary*, p. xxiii.) On the Jewish use of the term see the detached note at the end of this article.

rebuke unsparingly the faults and shortcomings of these same Corinthian Christians. But it is not so strange after all. It is a reminder that we are dealing with a real man who would defend his own against all comers without surrendering his own right to deal faithfully with their faults.

The root of the matter is that all the time Paul is fighting on two fronts. He struggles against those who would assign to the Gentile Christian an inferior status in the Church. As against all such he insists on the absolute equality of all Christians before Christ. On the other hand, he has to contend with those inside the Gentile Christian community who are inclined to play fast and loose with the precious privileges that are theirs as Christians. He fights against those who value Christianity so highly that they grudge its full benefits to the Gentile, and against those Gentiles who fail to realise just how valuable Christianity is, and try to eke it out with remnants of their old pagan inheritance. Against those who cling blindly to the pride and prejudice which they have from the past he declares that Christianity is not primarily a new form of Jewish nation-alism or a new development of Greek culture, but an act of God : a proclamation of God's saving intervention in human affairs, leading to faith in God, which in its turn issues in man's con-fession of his faith in God through Jesus Christ, and a new life proper to those who stand in a new relation to God. That is the fundamental thing which is never allowed to get out of the centre of Paul's picture, and it is an essential part of his greatness that he knows how to keep it in the centre.

But it is a difficult task, the more difficult because of the petty jealousies and divisions that threaten the unity of the Church. To these divisions we are introduced at the beginning of the letter. There is mention of four parties, who take as their rallying cries the names of Paul, Apollos, Cephas, and Christ. Paul we know, Apollos we know, Cephas we know (it is the Aramaic name of Peter). But who is the ' Christ ' who is invoked as the head of a clique in Corinth ? The most various answers have been given, and the problem seems as far as ever from solution. It may be that study along the lines already suggested will do something towards clearing up the obscurity.

One party division can, I think, be disposed of fairly easily. The Apollos party does not represent a real split in the community. No doubt there were members of the Corinthian Church who looked to Apollos as their father in the Gospel in the sense that they owed their conversion to Christianity to his preaching. But that did not in any way trench on the authority of Paul. On the contrary, Paul himself recognises Apollos as a useful and valued colleague. ' I planted, Apollos watered.' Here there is no rivalry or jealousy : Paul and Apollos collaborate in the work. This is the clear inference to be drawn from iii. 1-9. But in iii. 10-17 there is another, whose name is not mentioned, who is represented as trying to build on Paul's foundations.[1] What is to be built is the Temple of God, and Paul makes it clear that the community is in fact the Temple. In the community the Spirit dwells. But is this other, who is using Paul's foundations, really building the Temple or only marring work already done ? Paul's language strongly suggests that he holds the latter view. It also suggests that the mischief is being done where Paul's work has already been put in—on the foundation. That seems to be the purport of the statement : ' Other foundation can no man lay than that is laid, even Christ '. What other foundation would anyone think of laying ? There is only one alternative, so far as I know, and that is the one mentioned in Matt. xvi. 18, where Peter is the Rock on which the Church is to be built. Were the Petrine claims already being made in Corinth ? And is this ' other ', who is trying to lay another foundation for the Church, Peter himself or someone acting on his behalf ?

These questions at once bring us face to face with the thorny problem of leadership in the primitive community. It is obviously not possible to discuss this adequately here, and I must be content to state briefly some points that seem to be relevant to our main subject.

During the ministry of Jesus the question of leadership did not get past the academic stage. There was only one Leader, whose authority was never questioned from within the group of

---

[1] That Paul regarded this as a somewhat reprehensible practice is clear from the pains he takes to clear himself of any similar charge in II Cor. x. 12-18 and Rom. xv. 15-24.

His followers. The only disciple to turn against Him had to
stab Him in the back. At the same time there was keen interest
in the question who should have the second and succeeding
places after Jesus, as we learn from the story of the Sons of
Zebedee in Mark x. And it is not without significance that
John has a leading place in the early chapters of Acts, while
James is singled out for destruction by Agrippa. The Sons of
Zebedee were clearly not destined to live in obscurity at any
time, least of all when Jesus was no longer there in the flesh to
hold an undisputed and indisputable primacy.

In the earliest days of the Jerusalem community Peter takes
a leading place, and this does not seem to be any merely official
status. Rather he is outstanding in virtue of two things : (1) He
is the first witness to the Resurrection. For this we have the
testimony of Paul, who, when he gave it, had no inducement to
go out of his way to add to the prestige of Peter ; (2) In the
critical early days of the infant Church he displayed high qualities
of leadership and personal courage, which doubtless earned for
him the confidence of the whole community.

In the record of Acts Peter appears as a leader all through
the first half, the last mention of him being at xv. 7. In the earlier
chapters he is associated frequently with John, the last mention
of the pair being at viii.14. The order of the names is always
Peter, John in the Acts, and this is the case also in Gal. ii. 9.
This, for what it is worth, suggests the precedence of Peter over
John in the early days.

So far we have not moved outside the circle of the Twelve.
A further complication was provided by the fact that Jesus had
brothers and sisters, and that the brothers, headed by the eldest,
James, joined the Christian community in Jerusalem. The
question where in the order of precedence the blood-relations
of the Lord should find their place could not be shelved, and it
seems to have been settled on the most favourable terms for James
and his brethren. In I Cor. ix. 5 Paul speaks of ' the brethren
of the Lord and Cephas ', and in Gal. ii. 9 he names James and
Cephas and John, in that order, as the reputed pillars of the
Jerusalem community. Both these letters belong to the time
round about A.D. 55. But it is clear that James had taken an

important, and eventually perhaps the most important, place in the Church before this date. He appears first at Acts xii. 17, in the story of the imprisonment of Peter by Agrippa and his wonderful escape. This event must fall before A.D. 44, the year of Agrippa's death. It is noteworthy that in the story it is Peter himself who directs that the news of his escape is to be communicated to 'James and the brethren'. In the account of the Jerusalem Council in Acts xv the position of James is unchallenged, and the status which he enjoys there seems to me to be confirmed by what Paul writes in Gal. ii. 11 ff., where Peter is thrown into a panic by a message from James.[1] It is, I think, possible that one factor that helped to establish the primacy of James was the fact that Peter was a good deal out of Jerusalem, whereas James was always on the spot.

The primacy of James was, I think, established by 48 or 49, the date of the Jerusalem Council. I do not think that it can be traced back to a much earlier time. Paul tells us in Gal. i. 18 that some three years after his conversion he went up to Jerusalem to make the acquaintance of Peter, and then mentions almost casually that he also saw James, whom he lumps with the 'other Apostles'. The natural interpretation of the text requires us to presume that at that time Peter was still the principal man in the community. If it is right to date the conversion of Paul about A.D. 34, the first visit will fall about 37, and it would seem that by that time James was reckoned with the Apostles : before 44 he had reached such a position that Peter regarded him as *at least* the second in command : by 48 or 49 he seems to be clearly first among the Apostles. This primacy was, I think, already established in 47 or 48, the date I assign to the second visit of Paul recorded in Gal. ii.

It may be mere coincidence, though I think it is more than that, that soon after we get the evidence of the primacy of James, we also get the evidence of attempts to assert the authority of Peter in the sphere of Paul's work. Whether Peter in this was seeking a new sphere for himself outside the supervision of James, or acting as James's agent, I do not attempt to determine. It

---

[1] See Chapter 9, above.

does, however, seem fairly clear that it was only the fall of Jerusalem and the consequent dispersal of the Jerusalem community
that stopped the foundation of a regular Christian Caliphate with
its headquarters in the Holy City. We know how vigorously
Paul resisted any attempt to encroach on his authority : we do
not know how the struggle went in Palestine, or indeed whether
there was any struggle at all. What we do know is that at the
beginning the initiative is in the hands of Peter, and that later it
has passed to James.

With this by way of preface we may proceed to consider
some of the matters dealt with in the body of the letter.

We may begin with the reference to the ' Previous letter '
which I call Cor. A (I Cor. v. 9-13). This reference comes in
the course of Paul's remarks on the case of sexual immorality
in the Corinthian Church ; but I very much doubt whether it
was prompted by any knowledge of this particular case. Indeed
I should be inclined to doubt whether it was written during
the Ephesian period. It is more probable that what Paul said
in Cor. A was based on his general knowledge of the Christians
in Corinth. Then the letter may have been written at any time
after the Apostle's departure from Corinth in about A.D. 51.
There is one remark that may be significant. It comes in v. 11,
where Paul forbids association with Church members of bad
character and will not sanction even sitting down to a meal in
their company. Is it too hazardous to suggest that we may have
here an echo of the controversy that shook the Church at Antioch
a short time before and required a Council to settle it (Gal. ii.
11 ff. ; Acts xv. 28 f.) ? May it not be that Paul was giving in
this letter *his* idea of what constituted a ' kosher ' table for
Christians, with all the emphasis on the company rather than the
viands ? The matter comes up again later in I Cor.

Next we may consider the question (vi. 1-8) of Church
members suing one another before civil courts. In protesting
against this practice Paul is at one with Jewish sentiment and
custom. The authoritative Rabbinical rulings on the subject
are conveniently given by Billerbeck[1] while the actual practice
can be learned from Juster.[2] As to the former, it was laid down

---

[1] *Kommentar*, iii. 362 ff.   [2] *Les Juifs dans l'Empire Romain*, ii. 93-126.

by R. Tarphon and R. Eleazar b. Azariah (both c. A.D. 100)
that Jews must not sue one another before pagan courts. The
proof text was found in Exod. xxi. 1, and it is clear that the
Rabbis were only declaring what had long been the rule. For in
Palestine before A.D. 70 ' Jewish tribunals had exclusive competence in civil cases where both parties were Jews '.[1] In the
Diaspora it seems clear that Jews went to their own courts,
which had competence to deal with civil cases where both parties
were Jews. It is true that in the pagan world there were mutual
benefit societies whose members were bound to abstain from
suing one another in the courts, as well as religious brotherhoods
in which all disputes between members were resolved by arbitra-
tion within the fellowship.[2] It does not appear, however, that
these admirable bodies had had much influence on the practice
of the Corinthian Christians, for they *had* had a lawsuit, and the
case against these actions in pagan courts is argued from the Jewish
and Christian standpoint with no appeal to the example offered
by *eranoi, sodalitates,* and *sunodoi.* In fact, vi. 1-6 is the kind of
criticism that could have been passed by any Jew or Jewish
Christian—including of course, Paul himself—on the doings at
Corinth. The characteristic voice of Paul is heard in *vv.* 7-8,
where he protests that the real scandal is not that they go to
law before the heathen, but that they need to go to law at all.
It seems to me likely that in *vv.* 1-6 we have the kind of criticism
that was passed by the Cephas party speaking from the Jewish
Christian standpoint. Paul feels bound to agree with the
criticism, but himself goes much further. There should be
no dispute to bring before any tribunal, domestic or external.
There are thus two distinct points :

(*a*) Christian cases should be tried by Christian courts.
(Cf. Matt. xviii. 15-18, which belongs to the strongly Jewish
Christian stratum of the Gospel.)

(*b*) There should be no cases : Christian courts should have
perpetual white gloves. This, I think, is Paul's own view.

With chapter vii begin Paul's answers to a series of queries
put to him by the Corinthian Church or some part or parts of it.
It is in the study of these topics especially that we may hope for

[1] Juster, *op. cit.,* ii. 95.   [2] See Moffatt's *Commentary, in loc.*

some light on what was going on behind the scenes at Corinth.
Two points are discussed in chapter vii, family life in general,
with special regard to the relations of husband and wife, and the
peculiar form of family then coming into vogue in which couples
lived together in a relation of brother and sister rather than
husband and wife. On matters of this sort Jewish principles
were well defined. Marriage and the begetting of children
were the norm. Mixed marriages between Jews and non-Jews
were frowned upon. The husband was the head of the family.
In this discussion Paul is clearly moving away from the Jewish
dislike of mixed marriages. He is equally clearly engaged in an
internal conflict between his inherited conviction that the husband
has the last word and the new principle, which I think goes back
to Jesus himself,[1] that husband and wife in marriage meet on
a footing of real equality. Similarly, in the treatment of the
question about the *parthenoi*. The thing itself seems to be
contrary to Jewish sentiment, for which the normal sex-relation
of husband and wife is a real good, a privilege accorded and
a duty imposed by God. The best non-Jewish opinion, on the
other hand, as represented by Stoicism, recognised the natural-
ness of the biological functions involved but deprecated the
engagement of the feelings and the consequent loss of the self-
contained, self-possessed calm of the philosopher. Paul takes
up a position that is in part eschatological : the fashion of this
world is passing away and Christians must adapt themselves to
that fact. But there is also the recognition of a tension between
the claims of family life and the claims of the Lord—between
the ' morality of my station and its duties ' and the ' morality of
grace '. That tension we are still trying to reduce. We may
ask who wanted Paul's guidance about *parthenoi*. It seems unlikely that the request would come from those with Jewish-
Christian sympathies. One is tempted to think that it was the
followers of Apollos or the members of the ' Christ ' party who
were concerned about the matter. It may be suggested that at
Corinth there was a movement to establish these ' spiritual '
unions, and that it was being criticised from the Jewish standpoint by the Cephas party. The same party may well have had

[1] See *The Mission and Message of Jesus*, pp. 428-430.

a good deal to say about the evil of mixed marriages.   Paul has
to decide between these conflicting views, and he does it in a way
of his own.

Next comes the question of meat that had come to the
butcher's block by way of the heathen altar.   As we well know
the Jewish conscience was extremely sensitive about anything
connected with idolatry, and there is an *a priori* presumption
that where this question is raised, Jewish or Jewish-Christian
scruples are involved.   I have argued elsewhere [1] that this
question had been raised at Antioch, as described in Gal. ii. 11 ff.,
and that the answer had been given in the finding of the Jerusalem
Council in Acts xv.   These events are prior to the writing of
I Cor.   Why does Paul now discuss the problem as if the Jerusalem Council had never met ?   I cannot help thinking that the
question was raised at Corinth by the Cephas party, and that
Paul's way of dealing with it is, and is meant to be, a snub.   He
takes it as a matter of purely domestic concern within the Gentile-
Christian community, the implication being that the Jerusalem
compromise is doubtless suitable for Churches like that of
Antioch with a mixed membership, but that in predominantly
Gentile-Christian communities Jewish taboos do not count and
Jewish-Christian visitors cannot presume to legislate in these
matters for Gentile-Christian Churches.

At this point Paul breaks off into an impassioned defence of
himself, his status as an Apostle, and his missionary methods
(ch. ix), returning to close the discussion about meats sacrificed
to idols in chapter x.   It is highly significant that the status of
the Apostle is intruded in this way : it means that it is something
of critical moment to Paul, something that is very much on his
mind, something that touches his deepest feelings.   He takes
his stand on two facts : the fact that he has seen the Lord and
the fact that his mission has produced results.   In virtue of these
facts he claims equality of status with the other Apostles.   He
claims rights even though in actual practice he refrains from
exercising them.   In particular there is the matter of sustentation.
Paul lays down the principle that the Apostle is entitled to be
maintained by those to whom he ministers.   The army lives on

---

[1] In *The Problem of the Epistle to the Galatians.*

the country it conquers. This is in accordance with the procedure laid down by Jesus when He sent out the Disciples during
the Ministry. (The abuse of this privilege is implied in the
Didache, xi ff.) Against this we may set the slight indications
that at Jerusalem there was a central fund for the maintenance
of the Church personnel there. The tendency seems to have
been to replenish this fund by means of tribute paid by other
Churches in somewhat the same way that the synagogues of the
Diaspora sent their annual tribute to the Temple authorities in
Jerusalem. Paul could claim that he stood nearer to the intention
of Jesus in this matter.[1]

After this long digression about apostolic status, the Apostle
returns to the question of meats offered to idols and solves it in
his own way. As he sees it, the essential point is not the defence
of the abstract principle of pure monotheism but the assertion
of the exacting demands of the Christian's fellowship with Christ
and His Church. ' Ye cannot drink the cup of the Lord, and
the cup of demons : ye cannot partake of the table of the Lord,
and of the table of demons ' (x. 21). There is given in Christianity a relation to Christ so intimate that it can be adequately
figured only by the relation between the body and its component
limbs. Such an intimacy excludes other fellowships. It is not
merely that they are wrong : it is that they are impossible, so
long as fellowship with Christ continues to be a reality. It is
possible to have one or the other, but not both. In stressing
this point Paul emphasises what is the specifically Christian

---

[1] It may be noted here that ix. 5 breaks the thread of the argument—in
characteristic Pauline fashion. Here is something else that Paul is entitled to
but does not take. It is interesting to note how the other Christian leaders are
named : (1) The other *apostoloi ;* (2) The Lord's Brethren ; (3) Cephas. Why
is Cephas singled out from the *apostoloi ?* Is it that he does in fact stand apart
—the rival of the blood-kindred of the Lord ? Or is it that he is actually present
in Corinth ? Or that special claims are being made for him there ? Or some
combination of these possibilities ?

Another interesting point is in ix. 20-23, where Paul deals with the question
of what may be called ' missionary tactics '. We may compare and contrast
Gal. ii. 14. What criticism is Paul meeting in ix. 20-23 ? Was it being urged,
for example, that missionaries of Jewish origin were not free to abandon the Law,
whatever might be the case with their converts ? Or that all genuine Apostles
strictly observe the Law themselves, whatever concessions they may make to
others ?

objection to idolatrous practices, as distinct from the general monotheistic position common to Judaism, Christianity, and— later—Islam. Here as elsewhere Paul, even when accepting the Jewish-Christian conclusion, insists on supplying it with an entirely Christian basis. It is fortunate for us that he chose to do so ; otherwise we might never have had the glorious digression about the Lord's Supper in chapter xi, a passage which seems to be suggested to the Apostle by his previous reflections on the subject of communion.

The Eucharist is discussed in xi. 17-34, and in the course of the discussion Paul gives us the oldest account of the Institution of the Sacrament in existence. We cannot, however, stay to discuss Eucharistic origins : we must rather try to see what Paul was fighting against at Corinth. In this passage he arraigns those who treat the Supper as a jollification. Against these he insists on its connexion with the Passion. The following phrases are significant :—

> ἐν τῇ νυκτὶ ῇ παρεδίδοτο.
> εἰς τὴν ἐμὴν ἀνάμνησιν.
> ἐν τῷ ἐμῷ αἵματι.
> τὸν θάνατον τοῦ κυρίου καταγγέλλετε.

Further, he arraigns those who treat it as a *selfish* jollification. Against them he insists on its significance as the Sacrament of the unity of the Church, the Body of Christ. Failure to discern —and respect—this Body and this unity entails judgement. It is the same thing as despising the Church of God.

In all this the fundamental thing is the unity of the Church, the body of Christ, and the real fellowship of believers with Him and with one another in the Church. If we ask who are the people that Paul is criticising here, the kind of answer that suggests itself is that the Church feasts at Corinth were open to censure from two sides. To the devout Jewish-Christian the glaring scandal was that it was not a *kosher* table ; to Paul the most disquieting thing was the lack of a true spirit of brotherhood. His whole treatment of the complex issues in these chapters is governed by the conviction that if the spirit of the Church is right, there will be no real difficulty about settling the details of Church life and worship. We must, I think, conclude that the folk who failed to maintain the true standard were Gentile-Christians, who had carried over into their new life some of the characteristics of the cult meals to which they were accustomed in their pagan days. Paul insists on radical reform, but his reform is to be based not on Jewish dietary rules but on the true nature of the Lord's Supper as determined by its Founder in the circumstances and manner of its foundation. The reformed practice in Corinth will not be nearer to Judaism : it will be nearer to that of Christ ' in the night in which He was betrayed '.

Next comes the answer to a question about what are called ' spiritual gifts ' (xii–xiv). Paul begins, as usual, by laying down general principles to serve as a basis for the discussion of the particular case. He does it this time by setting out a series of contrasts : first, between the ' *dumb* idols ' and the God who speaks ; next, between the variety of spiritual manifestations and the one God who is behind all of them ; third, between the variety of spiritual manifestations and the unity of the Body which they all serve ; fourth, between this variety of spiritual gifts and the one supreme principle of the spiritual life, which is love.[1] What Paul is arguing in these contrasts seems to be something like this. Your spiritual life is first, last, and all the time, Christian. This means that it is founded upon God, who is the only source of spiritual power ; that it is lived in and for the Church, the Body of Christ ; that within the spiritual sphere there is a hierarchy of values, at the head of which stands love. Love is not merely the complete satisfaction of the demand of the Law (Gal. v. 14) ; it is also the crown and consummation of all spiritual gifts.

Having laid down these foundation principles Paul is now in a position to face the specific issue. It is the phenomenon known as γλωσσολαλία—' speaking with tongues '.

The usual treatment of this part of the Epistle begins by making *glossolalia* a symptom of the exuberant religious enthusiasm of Paul's Corinthian converts, and seeking its psychological roots in the mobile excitable Greek temperament. The principal evidence offered is the εὐοῖ of the Dionysiac votaries, helped

---

[1] This fourth contrast is set out in chapter xiii, which is properly understood only when it is held in its context, and studied *along with* chapters xii and xiv.

P

out by gleanings from the magical papyri. The latter need not detain us long. The complicated mess of alphabetic permutations and combinations, interlarded with battered relics of divine names, which appears in the papyri is the product of perverted ingenuity rather than religious ecstasy. It is not *glossolalia*, whatever else it may be. Nor is the Bacchic εὐοῖ. *Εὐοῖ* is the cry by whose constant repetition the votaries of the god work themselves up into a frenzy or ecstasy. The shouting is one of the causes of the ecstatic condition, not a result of it. But in the *glossolalia* of the New Testament the falling into the ecstatic state comes first, and the strange utterances are the outward sign of the inward condition. The Spirit falls upon the persons, and they speak with tongues.

Further, it would seem that the cults which tended towards the ecstatic were not native to Greece. That of Dionysus was of Thraco-Phrygian origin, for example. No doubt there were elements in the Greek temperament which made it responsive to this kind of thing, but all the evidence that can be brought forward falls far short of proving that *glossolalia* originated in Corinth. On the contrary, the phenomena described by Paul in I Cor. seem to be akin to those outbursts in the Palestinian Church, of which we read in Acts. These again have their closest analogues in the prophetic ecstasies described in the Old Testament on the one side, and in the accounts of Phrygian Montanism on the other. The most natural place to seek for the origins of *glossolalia* is not Corinth but Jerusalem.

If so, we must go on to ask when it made its way to Corinth. Most commentaries on the Epistle take it almost for granted that it is something of old standing in the community there. It is said that Paul treats the topic as one that will be quite familiar to the Corinthian Christians. The opposite seems to me to be the case. He deals elaborately with it as though it were a new thing about which the Corinthians needed detailed instruction and guidance. Moreover, Paul was eighteen months at Corinth and saw the early growth of the Church. He laid down the lines along which he wished it to develop. If the problem of *glossolalia* had arisen during that time, presumably he would have dealt with it there and then. Indeed, if his exposition of the Gospel had included this phenomenon at all, doubtless he would have given some kind of instruction about its place in the scheme of Christian values and the importance to be attached to it in comparison with other aspects of the Christian life.   The fact that at this late date he has to begin an explanation is evidence that the thing is something of a novelty in the Corinthian Church. And the fact that Paul can thank God that he has done more of it himself than the entire Corinthian community, strongly suggests that the practice has not yet reached any very imposing proportions there, especially in view of the fact that Paul himself does not appear to have gone out of his way to seek experiences of this sort.

I venture, therefore, to think that what the Apostle is dealing with in these chapters is not a surfeit of *glossolalia* at Corinth, but a demand which was being made on the Church to produce this particular fruit of the Spirit.   I suggest that the demand came from the leaders of the Cephas party, and was part of the concerted move to instil Palestinian piety and Palestinian ortho-doxy into the Corinthian Church.   Paul's converts were being told that here was something most important, indeed absolutely essential to the Christian life.   Paul had said little or nothing about it when he was with them ; what had he to say now ? That is the question that is faced and answered in these three chapters, and at the end Paul has made it clear just how important he considers *glossolalia* to be, and just how many things take precedence of it in the Christian life.

Chapter xv introduces a new problem, that of the resurrec-tion, the resurrection of Christ and the resurrection of believers. Once more it turns out that the question is mixed up with the question of Paul's status as an Apostle.

The resurrection of the Lord is vitally important.   The Gospel hangs on it.   Paul's own status as an Apostle hangs on the fact that he is a witness to the resurrection, the last witness and the least of the Apostles, unworthy of the title because he had been a persecutor of the Church.   Yet, having received the title, he claims that he has justified its bestowal by his exertions as a missionary, exertions more strenuous and more prolonged than those of the other Apostles.

There were some in Corinth who did not care for this article of the Christian Faith, just as at Athens there were some who at once dismissed it as absurd, while others preserved an open mind (Acts xvii. 32). Now the dogma of the resurrection is just about the most Jewish thing in the whole Christian Gospel. The resurrection of Jesus was an event that took place in Palestine and was vouched for by Jewish witnesses. The belief in a resurrection was a characteristically Jewish belief, which could be traced back certainly as far as the book of Daniel. If we ask who in Corinth would be likely to question the doctrine, the answer is not far to seek. It was certainly not the followers of Cephas or Paul, the first and last witnesses to the appearances of the Risen Lord. We are left with the Apollonians or those who took the name of Christ as their party name. In any case it is the intelligentsia, under whatever name. For them, no doubt, the immortality of the soul was the sound doctrine, the reasonable and philosophical creed, while the idea of resurrection was crude and barbarous. Moreover, the belief in resurrection involved a cosmic eschatology, a religious philosophy of history, and that, too, was unacceptable to the intelligentsia.

It is again noticeable how Paul in defending the doctrine is at pains to safeguard his own independence. To the resurrection of Jesus he is an independent witness. There are others of course of older standing than himself, but his testimony does not derive from theirs, though theirs may serve to corroborate his. The belief in the resurrection of believers he will defend by arguments of his own, and by the reasonableness of his arguments, and not by any appeal to the authority of the older Apostles, he will convince the doubters in Corinth.

Concerning the collection for the Saints I have little to say, and almost all of it has already been said by Karl Holl.[1] The main point, I think, is that in Jerusalem the contributions of the Gentile Churches were regarded as tribute rather than charity. Paul, at the outset of his ' Foreign Mission ' campaigns, had agreed to raise these contributions, and he cannot go back on his promise. But he does elsewhere try his hardest to produce proof, apart from the Jerusalem claim to primacy, that it is a

[1] *Gesammelte Aufsätze*, ii. 58-62.

good thing to bring gifts to the original nucleus of the world-wide Church.

We may now attempt to sum up this rather rambling discourse. The probabilities that emerge, and I do not rate them higher than probabilities, are these :—

(1) At the time when I Cor. was written Paul was engaged in a struggle with agents of Palestinian Jewish Christianity either under the direct leadership or acting in the name of Peter.

(2) This struggle had two aspects. Outwardly it was an attack by the representatives of Palestinian orthodoxy on a number of alleged abuses and laxities in the Corinthian community. Beneath this surface it was an attack on Paul himself, as the person chiefly responsible for Corinth, and a challenge to his status and authority as an Apostle.

(3) This latter fact explains why, wherever Paul finds himself forced to endorse the criticisms of the Cephas party, he is careful to find his own grounds for agreeing with them.

(4) The operations of the Cephas party look very like an attempt to establish in the Gentile churches an authority superior to Paul's, thus going behind the agreement reached at the beginning of the campaign and described in Gal. ii. What were the precise relations between Cephas and his followers at Corinth, and James and the church of Jerusalem, remains an unsolved but fascinating problem.

(5) We may hazard a guess about the nature of the ' Christ party '. It seems to stand at the opposite extreme to the Cephas party. I should be very much inclined to think that they were a group for whom Christ meant something like ' God, freedom, and immortality ', where ' God ' means a refined philosophical monotheism ; ' freedom ' means emancipation from the puritanical rigours of Palestinian barbarian authorities into the wider air of self-realisation ; and immortality means the sound Greek doctrine as opposed to the crude Jewish notion of the Resurrection. For Paul this kind of thing was a deadly peril, more deadly than the threat to his own status involved in the attacks of the Cephas party. He is forced to fight on two fronts, and his most serious difficulties—and our most difficult problems of exegesis—

arise from that fact. His solution of the difficulties may rank as one of the major triumphs of his career.

Detached Note on the Jewish use of מקום, אתרא, and ΤΟΠΟΣ as designations for places of worship.

The following references and materials may be of interest :—

Sukenik, *Ancient Synagogues in Palestine and Greece*, p. 71, n. 2.

'It is interesting to note that these [the Synagogue] inscriptions almost invariably designate the synagogues by the Hebrew, Aramaic, or Greek words for " place " (τόπος, מקום, אתרא).'

Examples : (References are given to S. Klein's *Jüdisch-Palästinisches Corpus Inscriptionum* and to J. B. Frey's *Corpus Inscriptionum Iudaicarum*).

Kafr Bir'im (Klein, p. 8), יהי שלום במקום הזה ובכל מקומות ישראל .

'Alma (Klein, p. 6), יהי שלום על המקום הזה ועל כל מקומות עמו ישראל .

'Ain Dûk (Klein, p. 3), ll. 6 f., [די]הב בהדן אתרה [ק]דישה וגו" .

'Ain Dûk (Na'aran), another inscr., l. 3. בה]דן] אתרה .

Stobi (Sukenik, pp. 79 f., Frey, i. 694), τοὺς μὲν οἴκους τῷ ἁγίῳ τόπῳ κτλ.

El Ḥammeh (Sukenik, *The Ancient Synagogue of El-Ḥammeh* p. 65), τῷ θεῷ καὶ τῷ ἁγίῳ [τόπῳ . . .

El Ḥammeh (Sukenik, *op. cit.* p. 69), . . . ἐπὶ] τοῦ ἁγίου τόπου ανενέ[ωσεν τὸ κτίσ]μα τῆς κώνχης κτλ.

See also S. Krauss, *Synagogale Altertümer*, on the names of the synagogues. The following examples are noteworthy :—

Midrash Tehillim, iv. 3, p. 42, Buber, מקום תפלתו .

Philo, *Quod omn. prob.*, c. 12, εἰς ἱερούς . . . τόπους οἳ καλοῦνται συναγωγαί.

In Flacc., c. 7 (§ 49).

Ἅγιος τόπος is used of a synagogue between Gaza and Jaffa (Clermont-Ganneau, *Rec. d'Arch. Or.*, iv. 139, No. 8), and of a synagogue in Antioch (Chrysostom, *adu. Iud.*, i. 5).

Further, Moulton-Milligan, *Vocabulary, s.v.* ; Juster, *Les Juifs dans l'Empire Romain*, I, 456-472 ; L. Robert, *Études Anatoliennes*, p. 65.

We may ask whether there are other traces of the possible use of this idiom in the New Testament. I am strongly inclined to think that Mk. vi. 11 is a case. The two accounts of the ' sacrament of rejection ' in Mk. and Q are not perfectly clear about details, but there are indications which suggest that the ceremony is to take place inside the town. This is clearest in Lk. x. 10 (Q); and Mk. vi. 11, taken by itself, is consistent with that. The interpretation will then be that the disciples are to proclaim their message in the synagogue. If they are rejected, they come out of the synagogue (τόπος) into some open space in the town and there perform the ceremony.

Lk. xi. 1 is a possibility ; though I do not know of any evidence that the synagogue was particularly used as a place for *private* devotions.

It is possible that the use of τόπος has been extended to cover Christian places of worship in I Cor. i. 2 ; II Cor. ii. 14 ; I Thess. i. 8 ; I Tim. ii. 8. The example given by Robert, mentioned above, is presumably neither Jewish nor Christian.

11.

THE CORINTHIAN CORRESPONDENCE. (2)
(1942)

I N this lecture I propose to carry a stage further the plan begun in the last, and to ask what light we can obtain on the relations between St. Paul and the Jerusalem community from a study of II Corinthians. For the purposes of this study I shall assume the truth of the hypothesis that chapters x.-xiii. of II Cor. are a part of the 'severe letter.' [1] That is to say, using the notation suggested in the last lecture, I Cor. is Cor. B (the so-called 'previous letter' being Cor. A), II Cor. x.-xiii. is part of Cor. C, and II Cor. i.-ix is Cor. D (or the greater part of it). We may dispense ourselves from the necessity of going over the detailed arguments for this partition of II Cor., since they have been stated solidly, brilliantly, and, to my mind, convincingly by J. H. Kennedy.[2]

Accordingly the starting-point for our present purpose will be a brief recapitulation of the conclusions reached in our study of I Cor. The main points are two. In the first part of the letter we have positive evidence of the existence in the Corinthian Church of a section whose rallying-cry is the name Cephas ; that is, they claim Peter as their leader. In the second half, in the discussion of particular problems, it seems a fair inference that the Corinthian community was exposed to criticism from the Jewish-Christian side, and that some at least of this criticism,

---

[1] It is clear from II Cor. ii. 9 ff. that the severe letter contained a demand for disciplinary action against a member of the Corinthian Church. No such demand appears in II Cor. x.-xiii. Therefore if these chapters are part of the severe letter, they can be only a part, and not the whole of it.

[2] *The Second and Third Epistles of St. Paul to the Corinthians*, 1900.

though certainly not all, was justified. It seems reasonable to suppose that the Cephas party were the main channel, if not the source, of the Jewish-Christian criticisms. There is, however, nothing in I Cor. to suggest that there is a crisis in the affairs of the Church at Corinth. Indeed at the end of I Cor. Paul has no idea of visiting them in the immediate future : and the visit planned and mentioned in I Cor. xvi. is part of a routine trip through Macedonia and Achaea, which is not to begin until full use has been made of existing opportunities for missionary work in the province of Asia. It is anticipated that these opportunities will keep the Apostle occupied until Pentecost, that is, until early summer. I am inclined to think that in making these plans he was looking at least six months ahead and that I Cor. was probably written in the autumn, or at latest the early winter, of the previous year. I think, too, that there is a reasonable probability that Titus was the bearer of I Cor. and that he was to supervise the arrangements for the relief fund for the Jerusalem Church. On this view a period of almost a year elapsed between the dispatch of Cor. B and Cor. D. I will devote the first part of this paper to the investigation of what happened during this period, beginning with an examination of Paul's travel plans.

The first plan made by Paul has already been mentioned. It is in I Cor. xvi. The provisions it makes are these : Paul will remain at Ephesus till Pentecost (early summer) ; then he will visit the Macedonian Churches and come on to Corinth, where he will perhaps stay the winter ; afterwards he *may* go to Jerusalem with the Relief Fund. We may notice that the plan is definite only in the earlier parts : the later stages are vague and provisional. However, the whole project was considerably modified by a second plan of which we learn in II Cor. i. 15 ff. (Cor. D). There Paul tells the Corinthians that he had intended to make Corinth his first port of call after leaving Ephesus ; thence proceed to Macedonia and, after visiting the Churches there, return to Corinth for a longer stay. After that he would go to Jerusalem. There can, I think, be no doubt that this second plan is later than that described in I Cor. xvi. The visit to Jerusalem, which in I Cor. is only a possibility, is here definitely decided upon. As in the first plan we have the intention to visit Macedonia ; only now it is postponed slightly in order to allow a preliminary visit to Corinth. Both plans assume that the work at Ephesus is, for the time being at any rate, completed ; and no provision is made for any return to Ephesus.

Two questions at once spring to the mind when we consider this change of plan. Why must a visit be paid to Corinth before the Macedonian tour begins ? And why must Paul go to Jerusalem after the round of visits ? Any answer must be conjectural ; but it seems a reasonable conjecture that affairs in Corinth were causing the Apostle some anxiety, that he hoped by a personal visit to reinforce the appeal made in Cor. B, that the main trouble arose from the activities of the Cephas party, and that he hoped by the early visit to Corinth to check it there and, by the later visit to Jerusalem, to put a stop to these intrusions into his sphere of work. There are no indications that, when Paul made this second plan, any sort of crisis had developed at Corinth. Rather, the situation may well have appeared to be one that could be dealt with by tactful friendly discussion on a personal visit. It seems to me certain that this plan, which superseded that in I Cor. xvi., was seriously intended by Paul. Was it ever carried out ?

The usual answer to this question is no. It is assumed that, before it could be put into operation, Paul received news from Corinth which so disturbed him that he undertook an immediate visit to the Church there. This visit was unsuccessful and painful to the Apostle, who returned humiliated to Ephesus. He then wrote the ' severe letter ' (Cor. C) and sent it by Titus to Corinth. After this he wound up his missionary work in Ephesus and set out for the Troad, where he could not settle to anything because of his anxiety about Corinth and the absence of news. He, therefore, went on into Macedonia and there, to his infinite relief, met Titus bringing news of a complete submission by the Corinthian Church.

It is necessary to point out that a good deal of this reconstruction is pure conjecture, without a shred of evidence to support it. There is not a word in our documents about disturbing

news coming from Corinth to Ephesus and causing Paul to under-
take a special visit to Corinth. There is not a word about a
return to Ephesus after the painful visit, not a word about
winding up the Ephesian missionary campaign after the painful
visit. I think it possible that we can get along without all these
conjectures on the assumption that Paul began to carry out his
revised plan as arranged.

Now this plan provided for a visit to Corinth at the outset.
Let us suppose that this visit in fact took place. It follows
at once that this, the first stage of the revised plan, is the painful
visit referred to later by Paul. What exactly happened on this
occasion we do not know and have no means of discovering.
It seems clear, though, that the troubles in the Corinthian community were not of a sort to yield to tactful persuasions during
a friendly visit. The Apostle left Corinth thwarted and with
the feeling that he had been ill-treated by those from whom
he was entitled to expect kindness and loyalty. It further
appears from II Cor. ii. 5-8 that a specific wrong was done by
some member of the Corinthian community, but whether at
this time or later, and whether to Paul himself or to one of his
helpers, it is not possible to say.

Paul left Corinth. In II Cor. i. 23 and ii. 1 he tells them
that he decided not to come back and gives his reasons for the
decision. It was partly for their sakes and partly for his own.
If he came again he would be compelled to deal drastically
with his opponents and that would inflict suffering on the
community which he wished to avoid. It would also cause
additional suffering to himself, and he had already endured a
good deal at their hands. So instead of a visit they received
a letter (Cor. C or the ' severe letter '), of which a part is,
I think, preserved in II Cor. x.-xiii.

Here we must pause to ask where Paul went after the painful
visit. If we suppose that he was carrying out his revised plan,
the answer is that he went on to Macedonia. The visit to
Corinth that was cancelled would then be the return visit which
had been intended to follow the Macedonian tour.[1] To go

[1] There are some small indications in the text which seem to support this
view.   [Footnote continued on page 5.

on to Macedonia would be the obvious and sensible thing to do. For if things were so bad in Corinth, it was most advisable to take steps at once to prevent a similar state of affairs from developing in the Macedonian Churches. No useful purpose would be served by a return to Ephesus.

I therefore conjecture that after the painful visit Paul went on to Macedonia as he had planned to do. If Titus had been in Corinth since the despatch of Cor. B, it is to be supposed that he accompanied Paul. Some time after this departure Cor. C was written, probably from Macedonia and at the time when Paul should have begun the return journey to Corinth. Our knowledge of this letter comes from two sources : (*a*) what Paul tells us about it in Cor. D ; (*b*) the fragment of it preserved in II Cor. x.-xiii.

(*a*) He wrote in great trouble and anguish of heart and with many tears (II Cor. ii. 4). His object was twofold : to

(i) In II Cor. i. 23 Paul says φειδόμενος ὑμῶν οὐκέτι ἦλθον εἰς Κόρινθον. The use of οὐκέτι here is more natural if the reference is to the return visit planned to follow the Macedonian trip. If Paul sitting in Ephesus had abandoned the entire plan and decided to go to Macedonia instead, we should have expected the simple οὐκ. (The textual evidence strongly supports οὐκέτι. οὐκέτι P⁴⁶ אABCD, non ultra *vg.*, nondum *r* Ambst. Aug., οὐκ FG *d e g* Ambr. Pel. pesh. cop.)

(ii) In II Cor. ii. 1 Paul says ἔκρινα δὲ ἐμαυτῷ τοῦτο, τὸ μὴ πάλιν ἐν λύπῃ πρὸς ὑμᾶς ἐλθεῖν. Here again the use of πάλιν seems more natural if it was a return trip that was abandoned.

(iii) In II Cor. ii. 3 f. Paul explains that he wrote the severe letter in order to avoid another painful visit : ἵνα μὴ ἐλθὼν λύπην ⌜ἐπὶ λύπην⌝ σχῶ. Here there is a textual point which deserves discussion. The bracketed words ἐπὶ λύπην are given by DFG *minn. it. vg Pelagius syr*ʰᵉˡ, and are commonly dismissed as an assimilation to Phil. ii. 27. As a matter of pure probability it is much more likely that some scribal eye jumped to the second λύπην than that a scribal memory jumped to Phil. ii. 27. Further the fact that Paul uses the phrase in Phil. does not debar him from using it again in suitable circumstances ; and it may be argued that the circumstances are eminently suitable. Paul had already had one experience of λύπη during the painful visit, and he was not disposed to add another on top of it by paying another visit. It may be remarked in passing that one declared purpose of the additional visit was ἵνα δευτέραν χάριν (χαρὰν אᶜBLP etc.) σχῆτε. Paul was determined that it should not be a δευτέρα λύπη. (The bearing of the passages on one another may perhaps turn the balance in favour of χαράν in i. 15.) It may be claimed that ii. 3 reads most naturally if Paul is explaining why he did not come back to Corinth from Macedonia.

demonstrate his own love to them and to test their loyalty and obedience to him (II Cor. ii. 4, 9). It appears from II Cor. ii. 5-11 that the letter tested the obedience of the Corinthians by making a specific demand for disciplinary action against a particular person who had caused pain by some wrongful act. In II Cor. vii. 12 we are told that this issue was raised in this ultimatum-like way not as a personal matter affecting the wrong-doer or the injured party (no names are mentioned) but as a sort of test case concerned with the whole relation of the community to its founder.

(b) When we turn to II Cor. x.-xiii., we find that in general it tallies with this description. By far the largest part of these chapters is taken up with the assertion of Paul's apostolic status and authority, including judicial powers (x. 1-9). He insists that he is no whit inferior to what he calls the ' super-Apostles ' (xi. 5 ; xii. 11) ; and it is clear from xi. 22-31 that these super-Apostles came from Palestine. He insists that in birth, standing, and achievements he is the equal of anyone from that quarter. In the matter of special religious experiences also he can stand comparison with any (xii. 1-10). He has in fact all the marks of an Apostle (xii. 12 f.). So far as the Church at Corinth is concerned, they owe everything to him ; and he has taken nothing from them. He preached the Gospel to them gratis (xi. 7-12), and he has not had and does not want any gain from them (xii. 14-18). The challenge to this authority claimed by Paul comes from persons at Corinth who make personal attacks on him saying that he is a strong man on paper, but only on paper (x. 10 f.), that he runs away from danger (xi. 32 f.). These persons are trying to introduce their own version of Christianity into Corinth (xi. 4), and themselves as the spiritual lords and masters of the community (xi. 13, 20)—and not without success. The time has come when he ought to be returning to Corinth for his third visit ; but he is not coming to them as they are, for if he did, there could be only one result and that disastrous (xii. 19-21 ; xiii. 1-10). Let them amend their ways while there is still time.

I think it necessary to emphasise the fact that the four chapters are of this character because this seems to me to be one of the strongest reasons for regarding them as part of Cor. C. These emphatic, even violent, assertions of his apostolic status and authority would be pointless, and indeed positively harmful, addressed to a Church which had already recognised fully the claims of the Apostle. I think it necessary too to emphasise the fact that the most serious threat to Paul's position at this time came not from within the community but from without, and in particular from Palestine. In I Cor. a name is mentioned, a Palestinian name, the name of one of the Twelve, the name of Cephas. In Galatians, which I regard as belonging to this period, Paul speaks of trouble that had broken out on a previous occasion in Antioch, and curiously enough the tension is again between Paul and Cephas, with James in the background at Jerusalem. The Galatian and Corinthian epistles are all of a piece : they all reflect the same situation of conflict between Paul and the Palestinian Church, caused, I think, by the attempts of the Jerusalem authorities, in defiance of the agreement made with Paul (Gal. ii. 9), to extend their power and influence into the churches of his foundation. I think we may find some confirmation of this view when we come to consider the results achieved by the severe letter.

Titus was sent to Corinth with this letter. Paul meantime set out on a missionary expedition in the Troad.[1] We are not told what arrangements were made with Titus. From the nature of the case they could not be other than provisional. It could not be known beforehand what would happen when he reached Corinth. He might be sent to the right about immediately and come straight back to Paul. He might, on the other hand, be engaged in protracted negotiations and discussions which might end favourably or unfavourably for Paul. Nor could Paul say beforehand how things would go in the Troad. In the circumstances we can only conjecture that some very flexible plan was made. Titus was to return to Macedonia from his mission to Corinth. If Paul was still in the Troad, he would continue and join the Apostle there. On the other

[1] The use of the article (ϵἰς τὴν Τρωάδα) would seem to favour the view that the scene of the campaign was the whole area in the N.W. corner of Asia Minor, rather than just the port of Alexandreia Troas.

hand, if circumstances caused Paul to leave the Troad earlier, he would return to Macedonia and await Titus there. Something of this sort may well have been arranged. It would seem that in the event Titus made a fairly long stay at Corinth. Paul worked on in the Troad fighting against his own anxieties about the mission of Titus. The time came when he might expect to see Titus if the mission had been an immediate success ; but there was no sign of Titus. In these circumstances concentration on missionary work became impossible. Sick with worry, Paul broke off the work and hurried back to Macedonia.[1] Here to his great relief he met Titus and received the news that the Corinthian Church had come to its senses.

It is important to get a clear picture of the nature of the submission made by the Corinthians ; and here, fortunately, we can extract a good deal of information from Cor. D (II Cor. i.-ix.) which Paul sent off to Corinth on hearing the good news. First it appears that Paul's demand for disciplinary action against a certain individual had been complied with and that what Paul regarded as adequate punishment had been meted out to him by a decision of the majority of the members.[2] This overt act was the outward and visible sign of a complete change in the attitude of the community towards Paul. This inward change is mentioned in chapter vii., and it is very significant that Paul speaks of it twice, in v. 7 and again at greater length in v. 11. I translate the whole passage (vii. 5-11) :

> For even when we came into Macedonia, our flesh had no repose, but we were troubled at every point : fightings without, fears within. But he who ' comforts those who are brought low '—God—comforted us by the arrival of

---

[1] I think it possible—not more—that the strain of this period caused a serious illness, and that this is the ' θλίψεως ἡμῶν τῆς γενομένης ἐν τῇ Ἀσίᾳ ' described in II Cor. i. 8 ff. For the view that in these verses Paul is describing a severe attack of some chronic malady, perhaps a fever, see Allo, *Seconde Épître aux Corinthiens* (1937), pp. 15-19.

[2] I agree with those scholars who think that the minority were probably strong adherents of Paul, who regarded the punishment as insufficient and were demanding a severer penalty. Paul himself did not share their view ; but, once the rights of the matter had been vindicated, was all for clemency towards the offender (II Cor. ii. 5-11).

Titus ; and not only by his arrival, but also by the encouragement he had received with regard to you, reporting to us your longing, your grief, your taking of my side, so that I was still more pleased. For if I grieved you by the letter, I do not regret it. If I was inclined to regret it on seeing [1] that that letter, even if only momentarily, grieved you, I now rejoice, not because you were put to grief but because you were put to a grief that led to repentance ; for you were grieved in godly fashion, so that you might not at all be penalised by us. For sorrow of the godly sort produces repentance which has no regrets since it issues in salvation ; while worldly sorrow produces death. For see this very thing, this being grieved in godly fashion, what earnestness it produced in you, what desire to clear yourselves, what indignation, what fear, what longing, what loyalty, what retribution ! At every point you have shown yourselves to be blameless in the matter.

I think it is worth our while to pay particular attention to the terms in which Paul describes the Corinthian change of mind in *v*. 7 and *v*. 11. In *v*. 7 he speaks of three things : their ἐπιπόθησις, their urgent desire and longing to have Paul back among them and in his rightful place ; their ὀδυρμός, their open and obvious grief at what had happened ; their ζῆλος ὑπὲρ ἐμοῦ, their enthusiastic partisanship for Paul. In *v*. 11 is a more detailed account of the change in the Corinthian community. The grief aroused by the letter made them (*a*) take the matter seriously to heart (σπουδήν), (*b*) seek some way of clearing themselves (ἀπολογίαν) ; (*c*) it made them indignant at the way in which they had been put in the wrong with Paul (ἀγανάκτησιν), and (*d*) not without reason apprehensive of the consequences (φόβον). At the same time it (*e*) renewed their desire to have Paul back in full amity (ἐπιπόθησιν), and (*f*) put

---

[1] Reading μετεμελόμην βλέπων for μετεμελόμην · βλέπω γὰρ κτλ. The omission of γάρ is supported by P⁴⁶ BD* *d vg Ambst* ; the reading βλέπων by P⁴⁶ and *vg*. Hort conjectured βλέπων on the strength of *vg* alone, as did Lachmann before him. Now *vg* has the support of P⁴⁶. Doubtless βλέπω arose from ΒΛΕΠѠ. Then γάρ was inserted to ease the awkward construction. For Ѡ in participial termination at the end of a line see P⁴⁶ at I Cor. ix. 17, ΕΚѠ . . . ΑΚѠ ; II Cor. v. 19, ΚΑΤΑΛΛΑΣΣѠ.

them on his side with an enthusiastic loyalty hitherto lacking (ζῆλον). Finally (g), this loyalty to the Apostle made them take practical steps to right the wrong done, by disciplinary action against the wrong-doer. In this way they cleared themselves of any further complicity in the matter.

If we give full value to these terms it is fairly evident that there had been a definite anti-Paul campaign in Corinth, and that many members of the Church there had allowed themselves to be seduced from their loyalty to Paul by it. I have no doubt that the originators of the attack came from Jerusalem, and I strongly suspect that they claimed the authority of Peter. I think that they probably found tools as well as dupes in the Corinthian community, and that the wrong-doer whose punishment Paul demanded in the severe letter was perhaps a sort of Corinthian quisling, who had hastened to identify himself with the spiritual new order that was to be established among the Gentile Christians.

All that had now been swept away and proper relations between Paul and the Corinthian Church were established more firmly than ever.

On Paul's side, too, there is a notable change which we should not overlook. When the question of parties and loyalties first raised its head he dealt with it by way of eloquent appeal against taking sides. ' For all things are yours, whether Paul, or Apollos, or Cephas, or the world, or life, or death, or things present, or things to come ; all are yours, and you are Christ's, and Christ is God's.' All the missionaries are at the service of the community. The Church was not made for the Apostles, but the Apostles for the Church. Paul is ready to efface himself, as no doubt the others are too, for the sake of the Church, which belongs to Christ, who belongs to God. So Paul. His appeal, we may suppose, had the effect that gestures of appeasement so often have—of cooling the enthusiasm of his own supporters and encouraging his opponents. The result was to precipitate a crisis in which he found himself unable to cope with the opposition for lack of support in the community ; so we get the frustrations and humiliations of the painful visit. As a result appeasement was dropped and the severe letter

Q

was written. It did its work and now Paul can rejoice, and does rejoice aloud, in the fact that he has so many loyal and enthusiastic supporters in Corinth.

The thoroughness of the change of heart at Corinth appears in another and subsidiary way (vii. 13-16). Paul is intensely pleased at the impression made on Titus by his reception in Corinth : how they received him with fear and trembling and complete submission. It appears that the new attitude to the Apostle was extended to his lieutenants also. Paul says that he had led Titus to think that the Corinthians would turn out to be better than they seemed when the severe letter was being written, and the expectation had not been disappointed. We may perhaps infer that Titus himself had had an unfortunate first experience of the Corinthians, which the words of Paul and later the acts of the Corinthians themselves had been able to correct.

The result of Paul's severe letter and Titus' visit is thus a personal triumph for the Apostle, who overcame at a blow all the opposition that had been organised at Corinth and reasserted his position as the Apostle of the Corinthians—and the Gentiles generally. Out of all this strain and tension, fear and anxiety, followed by sudden relief and reassurance, joy and gladness, comes the last letter in the series. In it, as A. D. Nock well says, ' Paul sets forth his deepest reflection on the Christian ministry in its relation to those who hear its message and to those whose minds are closed, in relation again to the ministry of the law. Suffering is of the essence of this vocation.' [1] We may add that these reflections are not mere theorising about the nature of the Christian ministry, but all brought to the touch-stone of recent and searching practical experience. And this is borne out most strikingly by the very structure of the letter, where the profound exposition of the ministry of reconciliation is set in the framework of a detailed explanation of Paul's former plans and why they were altered and of his future plans and all the ins and outs of the raising of the relief fund for the Jerusalem Church.[2]

[1] *St. Paul*, p. 202.

[2] It is really very remarkable how this long excursus suddenly begins at ii. 14, when Paul is describing how he broke off his missionary campaign in the

[*Footnote continued on page 12.*]

The subject of the Jerusalem relief fund is dealt with in Cor. D, viii.-ix., chapters which are not free from difficulties and obscurities. Indeed they seem to reflect a certain embarrassment on the part of the writer himself. He was never quite at his ease when he was dealing with the financial side of the work, a characteristic which is probably to be put down to his proud and sensitive nature. He hated asking for money, even for other people ; and the letter to the Philippians shows how difficult it was for him to accept gifts, even spontaneous and unrequested gifts, in an easy and gracious manner. It would take too long to deal at all adequately with the various points that arise in these two chapters, and I must be content to state summarily what seem to me to be the most probable conclusions.

I am inclined to think that Titus had been the bearer of Cor. B (I Cor.) and had begun the organisation of the collection at Corinth on the lines suggested in that letter. It is quite possible that in the troubles that broke out in Corinth the finances of this fund had a place, and even that insinuations were made reflecting on the integrity of Paul and Titus. Something of this sort may well lie behind the indignant protests of II Cor. xii. 14-18 (Cor. C). Now that relations between Paul and Corinth are once more as they should be, Titus is sent again as the bearer of Cor. D to resume the work of the collection (II Cor. viii. 6). Paul hopes that by the time he himself arrives in Corinth the fund will amount to something worthy to stand beside the generous contribution already made by the Churches of Macedonia. And that is as far as the letters take us in the reconstruction of events at the close of the Ephesian period.

It may be asked how the reconstruction here proposed tallies with the narrative of Acts. The Ephesian ministry occupies chapter xix. of Acts, of which the first twenty verses cover a period of about two years and a quarter. There we

Troad and returned to Macedonia. The excursus continues to vii. 4, and Paul resumes at vii. 5 the narrative which had been broken off at ii. 13. With almost any author but Paul we should begin to wonder whether the text was in order.

(I should perhaps add, at this point, that the passage vi. 14-vii. 1 does not seem to me to be in place where it is. It is possible, as some scholars have thought, that it is a surviving fragment of the ' previous letter,' Cor. A.)

are told (*vv.* 21 f.) that Paul made travel plans according to which, after a tour through Macedonia and Achaea, he would go to Jerusalem. Thereafter he was determined to see Rome. He accordingly sent two of his lieutenants, Timothy and Erastus, to Macedonia, while he himself stayed some time longer in Asia.[1] After this comes the account of the Ephesian riot (Ac. xix. 23-41). This story is introduced by the phrase ἐγένετο δὲ κατὰ τὸν καιρὸν ἐκεῖνον, a time reference which is probably not so precise as it looks. It is significant that the only other occurrence of the term is at Ac. xii. 1 (κατ' ἐκεῖνον δὲ τὸν καιρὸν) where it introduces Herod's execution of James and arrest of Peter into the context of the famine-relief visit of Paul and Barnabas, a visit which took place some two years after the death of Herod. We must therefore not assume that because the story of the Ephesian riot is introduced at this point in the narrative, it happened at just this stage in the course of events. It may have happened at any point in the Ephesian ministry, though a late date is perhaps more likely than an early one.

The account of the riot is followed by the statement (Lake and Cadbury's translation) :

> After the disturbance had ceased Paul sent for the disciples, and with exhortation and farewell departed to go to Macedonia. And he went through those districts and exhorted them with much discourse and came to Greece (Ac. xx. 1 f.).

This adds little or nothing. It tells us that the author of Acts, having inserted the story of the riot at this point, is now under the necessity of making Paul start out again from Ephesus,

---

[1] αὐτὸς ἐπέσχε χρόνον εἰς τὴν Ἀσίαν. The preposition is noteworthy and also, as Blass noted, the use of the term Asia. Acts does not say that Paul remained behind at Ephesus, but that he stayed some time in Asia ; and εἰς suggests that the time was spent in visits to parts of the province other than Ephesus. But the information is of the vaguest kind and really tells us nothing beyond the fact that there was some activity in the province of Asia in the period after Paul's decision to end the Ephesian ministry and his final departure for Macedonia and Achaea. This may well be an echo of the fact attested by Paul himself in II Cor. that he conducted a mission in the Troad during this period. In any case Acts knows nothing of a painful visit to Corinth with a subsequent return to Ephesus.

though in xix. 22 he seems already to have left for travel in Asia. The conclusion of the whole matter is that the author of Acts knew much less than we do about events at the end of the Ephesian ministry. He knew of a travel plan made by Paul which resembles in certain respects that announced by Paul in I Cor. He knew in a vague way that between the decision to close the Ephesian ministry and the final journey through Macedonia to Corinth, there had been a period of time spent in Asia. He knew that eventually Paul did go to Corinth via Macedonia. These bits of information are not inconsistent with the reconstruction based on Paul's own statements, which I have attempted in this paper.

I will end with a few remarks on the long passage in Cor. D (ii. 14-vii. 4), in which Paul sets forth his convictions about the Christian ministry, which for him is a ministry of reconciliation. The first thing to be said is that Paul does not mean by this a ministry of compromise or appeasement. The reconciliation which he has in mind is reconciliation to God on God's terms as laid down once and for all in the Gospel. It would consequently be a mistake to suppose that Paul in Cor. D is any less ' anti-Jewish ' than in earlier statements of the case. His convictions about the Law and the Gospel may be less violently stated in Cor. D than in Galatians (or for that matter, Philippians), but they are not less strongly held ; and if a right-wing Jewish-Christian would have got fewer shocks from Cor. D, he would have got no more comfort. The truth seems to be that in Cor. D the heat and bitterness of the controversy is, for the time at least, over ; and we are now on the way towards the calm and considered statement of the case which Paul was able to give a few months later in the letter that we call Romans. But it *is* the Law and Gospel issue that is and has been the central issue all through, the question whether or not Christianity was to be just a movement within the framework of Pharisaic Judaism or a universal religion which fulfilled and, in fulfilling, superseded Judaism. What Paul thought on this question can be seen as clearly in II Cor. as in any other of his letters of this period.

Only it is vital to our understanding of the controversies

of this period that we should constantly remember that Pharisaic Judaism was always a vast deal more than the meticulous .cultivation of an elaborate system of legal casuistry. Pharisaic Judaism expressed itself in the book of Daniel and in the *Psalter of Solomon* as well as in the legal subtleties of the *Mishnah*. It had its organisation as well as its code, its devotional life as well as its book of rules. From this point of view reception into the commonwealth of Israel was a real condition of salvation. The messianic hope was the hope of the triumphant vindication of Israel ; and it is that hope that is expressed in the canticles at the beginning of Luke's gospel ; it is that hope that is expressed in the question addressed by the Eleven to the Risen Lord at the beginning of Acts : ' Lord, dost thou at this time restore the kingdom to Israel ? '

Paul's acceptance of Christianity means the giving up of all this, a fact which finds expression in more than one place in the letters of this period, and in particular in II Cor. v. 16. I feel sure that Baur [1] and those who followed him were right in thinking that Paul, when he speaks of ' knowing Christ κατὰ σάρκα ' means holding a this-worldly view of the nature of Messiahship. If so, we may argue that in this passage Paul is maintaining that the true Messianic task is universal reconciliation of man to God. He remarks in passing, ' If I ever believed that the Messiah had merely to exalt Israel to world-dominion, I no longer hold that view.' Out of all the storm and stress of the Ephesian period one thing had come out clear, and that was the crucial thing for the young Church. Paul had cleared up once and for all the relation between the Gospel and that complex structure of beliefs, hopes, and practices which was the Pharisaic Judaism of the first century A.D.

---

[1] Baur, *Vorlesungen über N.T. Theologie*, p. 131 : ' κατὰ σάρκα erkannte er Christus, solange er nur die nationaljüdische Vorstellung von Messias hatte, und das Wesentliche dieser Vorstellung war, dass der Messias keines solchen Todes sterben sollte, wie der Tod Jesu war.' In this connexion I would draw attention to an admirable discussion of II Cor. v. 16, by F. C. Porter, in the *Journal of Biblical Literature*, xlvii. (1928), 257-275, in which he argues convincingly that to know κατὰ σάρκα means to know selfishly, regarding what is known from the point of view of our own selfish interests. Nationalistic messianism could certainly be regarded as just that in a generalised and intensified form.

12.

ST. PAUL'S LETTER TO THE ROMANS—AND OTHERS.
(1948)

THE twentieth chapter of the Acts of the Apostles describes the events which followed the termination of St. Paul's Ephesian ministry. We are told that after taking leave of the disciples he set out for Macedonia, where he carried out a preaching tour through the province while making his way to Greece ('Ελλάς—the only occurrence of the word in the New Testament). Greece here probably means the Roman province of Achaea, and that in its turn may be taken to mean Corinth. The Apostle stayed in Greece for three months ; and it is fairly safe to assume that these were the winter months, which were unsuitable for travel. At the end of the three months he set out for Syria in accordance with plans which he had previously made.[1] It appears from Acts xix. 21 f. that he had framed a further project : after the visit to Jerusalem he must also see Rome. In Rom. xv. 14-33 he gives a fresh statement of his intentions, which confirms the plans already outlined in the Corinthian letters and in Acts, and adds further particulars. The journey to Jerusalem is imminent, if indeed it has not already begun.[2] Paul has serious misgivings, which events later more than justified, about the outcome of the visit. He is doubtful about the reception that he and his gift will have from ' the Saints ', and he expects to be in danger from ' the un-believers in Judaea ', that is, from the active Jewish opponents of Christianity in Palestine, of whom he had formerly been a

---

[1] I Cor. xvi. 1-9 ; II Cor. i. 15 f. ; Ac. xix. 21 f.

[2] Rom. xv. 25. νυνὶ δὲ πορεύομαι εἰς ʼΙερουσαλήμ. Here πορεύομαι may mean ' I am going ' or ' I am on my way '. Cf. Ac. xx. 22.

leader and in whose eyes he was an apostate of the worst kind.[1]
He nevertheless hopes that by the prayers of himself and his
friends he may come through and be able to carry out his plan
of visiting Rome. There is one new feature : after Rome he
proposes to start a missionary campaign in the far west. Spain
is to be the scene of these new labours.[2]

All these data combine harmoniously to fix the time and
place of the composition of Romans. It clearly belongs to the
period of three months in Greece (Ac. xx. 2 f.) The controversies with members of the Corinthian church, which had
caused Paul so much anxiety and grief during the Ephesian
ministry, were now a thing of the past. The fundamental
issues remained, of course, and on these Paul had not changed.
But it was now possible to state the issues and set forth the
essential truth of the matter without the heat and bitterness that
had marked the earlier stages of the dispute. And this in fact is
what Romans does. The first eleven chapters are devoted to a
full-dress debate on the question which lay at the root of most
of the troubles of the Ephesian ministry, the question, Can one
be a good Christian without embracing Judaism ? To this Paul's
answer is that the real question, and the only question for Jews,
is, Can one be a good Jew without embracing Christianity ? The
remainder of the didactic part of the document, xii. 1-xv. 13, is
mainly occupied with the discussion of points that had arisen in
the Corinthian correspondence. That is to say, Romans is the
calm and collected summing-up of Paul's position as it had been
hammered out in the heat of controversy during the previous
months. It is a positive and constructive statement of his understanding of the Gospel.

An absolute dating of Romans is not possible. It involves
forward reckoning from the date of Gallio's proconsulship at
Corinth and back reckoning from the date of the replacement of
Felix by Festus in the procuratorship of Judaea. The former
date can be fixed within a year or so ; the latter is more doubtful.
This much, however, can be said : that the trial of Paul before
Gallio is unlikely to have taken place earlier than the summer of

---

[1] Rom. xv. 30 ff.   [2] Rom. xv. 23 f., 28.

A.D. 51. The earliest probable date for the beginning of the
Ephesian ministry would then be 52 ; and this would mean that
the three months' stay in Greece could hardly be earlier than
the winter of 54-55. The latest date possible for the super-
session of Felix would seem to be 61. This is the date defended
by Eduard Meyer ; but it is far from commanding universal
assent.[1] Meyer places the three months' stay in Greece in the
winter of 58-59, which is as late as it can well be put. Within
those limits, then, late 54-early 59 the composition of Romans
must fall. There seems to be a slight balance of probability in
favour of the earlier end of this period.

But the real problems concerning Romans have not to do
with date or place of origin but with destination. Put in its
simplest form the question is this : Is the Epistle to the Romans,
in the form in which it appears in our Bibles, from i. 1 to xvi. 27,
a single composition made by St. Paul expressly for the Christian
community in Rome and sent to them entire and complete as it
now stands ? Of course this general question only arises because
a number of particular questions have emerged in the course of
detailed study of the text of the document. They are concerned
mainly with the first and the last two chapters.

The first seventeen verses of chapter i form the longest and
most elaborate introduction to any Pauline epistle. We have
first the prescript, a single sentence extending over seven verses
(1-7) heavily encrusted with doctrinal embellishments, so that it
becomes a miniature exposition of the Faith in itself. Then
comes a second long passage (8-17) forming the transition from
the prescript to the first main theme of the epistle. In both
prescript and transition passage we have explicit mention of
Rome. In verse 7, which forms the second item of the prescript
formula, we read πᾶσι τοῖς οὖσιν ἐν Ῥώμῃ ἀγαπητοῖς θεοῦ,
κλητοῖς ἁγίοις. In verse 15 Paul expresses his readiness καὶ
ὑμῖν τοῖς ἐν Ῥώμῃ εὐαγγελίσασθαι. These clear references to
Rome are supported by the great mass of the MSS. and other
witnesses to the text ; but there are a few dissentient voices. In

---

[1] Ed. Meyer, *Ursprung und Anfänge des Christentums*, iii. 51-54. Cf. K. Lake
in *The Beginnings of Christianity*, v. 464-467, for a statement of the case for the
date 55.

i. 7 we have the variant πᾶσι τοῖς οὖσιν ἐν ἀγάπῃ θεοῦ offered by the Graeco-Latin MS. G. The Latin of G (g) supports this reading in the omission of the reference to Rome, and offers alternative renderings of ἀγάπῃ : *in caritate uel dilectione dei.* The omission of 'Ρώμῃ is also attested by a marginal note in MS. 1908 stating : τοῦ ἐν 'Ρώμῃ οὔτε ἐν τῇ ἐξηγήσει οὔτε ἐν τῷ ῥητῷ μνημονεύει. That is, somebody who has written a commentary on Romans does not mention the words ' in Rome ' either in his exposition or in the text which he expounds. This commentator appears to have been Origen. The first stage of the corruption of the text is, then, the substitution of ' all who are in the love of God ' for ' all who are at Rome, beloved of God '. The next stage is the attempt to restore the reference to Rome in the corrupted text. This takes two forms : (a) *omnibus qui sunt Romae in caritate dei,* the reading of two Vulgate MSS., Fuldensis and Langobardus, of Pelagius,[1] perhaps also of Ambrosiaster, and of the Latin side (d) of Codex Claromontanus ;[2] (b) *omnibus qui sunt Romae in dilectione dei,* the reading of the two Vulgate MSS. Amiatinus and Ardmachanus.[3] These are rather obvious attempts to repair the damage that had been done when the reference to Rome was cut out. In i. 15 G again omits the reference to Rome by dropping τοῖς ἐν 'Ρώμῃ, and in this it is supported by its Latin side (g) which omits *qui Romae estis.* In D and d we get the following text :

καὶ ἐν ὑμῖν ἐν 'Ρώμῃ εὐαγγελίσασθαι
et in uobis in Roma euangelizare.

[1] A. Souter, *Pelagius's Expositions of Thirteen Epistles of St. Paul : Text* (*Texts and Studies,* IX. 2), p. 9.

[2] On this cf. H. J. Vogels in *Amicitiae Corolla,* p. 283. ' Das Wort *romae* ist in einem Vorgänger von d eingefügt worden.'

[3] On *dilectio* and *caritas* as renderings of ἀγάπῃ see Hans v. Soden, *Das Lat. N.T. Afrika z. Z. Cyprians,* 67 ff. He points out that *dilectio* is the regular rendering in Tertullian and probably the earlier of the two in African use. It also seems to be the first choice, *caritas* being used in many cases merely for variety. On the other hand in the Vulgate *caritas* is the normal rendering in all N.T. books except the Fourth Gospel, which has *dilectio.* In a later study, *Der lat. Paulustext bei Marcion und Tertullian,* in *Festgabe für Adolf Jülicher,* he shows (p. 249) that the Latin version of Marcion's *Apostolikon* translated ἀγάπῃ by *dilectio.*

Here again we have what appears to be patchwork.[1] These repairs in D*d* go back to the sixth century, which is the date of the MS., and were probably already made in an ancestor of the MS. These and other facts mean, as Corssen[2] showed, that the three bilingual MSS. DFG should be regarded as descendants of a common ancestor from which the references to Rome in chapter i were absent.

Three conclusions follow from the examination of the text of Rom. i. 1-17 : (*a*) that the omission of the references to Rome is ancient ; (*b*) that it is wrong—the context, particularly verses 8-17, imperatively demands a particular reference to a well-known community not founded by Paul or hitherto visited by him ; (*c*) that we have to do not with accidental loss but with deliberate excision—if ' in Rome ' were missing in verse 7 or verse 15 it might be accident ; but its absence in both places strongly suggests design. But who, it may be asked, would want to cut out the Roman address, and why ? One answer, which has received considerable and I think undeserved acceptance is that the object was to turn a particular epistle into a general epistle ; by removing the local reference, to make the document more catholic.[3] In support of this view appeal is made to the Muratorian Canon ; but that document gives no real support : all it says is that letters addressed to individual churches have a message for the universal church, of which it is said *una tamen per omnem orbem terrae ecclesia diffusa esse dignoscatur* (ll. 55 ff.). Furthermore the theory does not explain why the generalising process was applied only to Romans, and possibly Ephesians, while all the other Pauline letters are left in their scandalous particularity.

The case of the letter to the Ephesians may or may not be relevant : it should, however, be briefly noticed at this point. Here we have another case where the textual authorities do not agree about the address of the letter. The great mass of the witnesses, including the versions, favour Ephesus as the destination. The minority is divided. On the one side P⁴⁶B*ℵ*, the

---

[1] See Vogels, *op. cit.* 283 f.   [2] *ZNW* X (1909), 1-45, 97-102.
[3] See, for example, Wendland, *HBNT*, I. 3, 351 n. 3. Lietzmann, *HBNT : An die Römer*, p. 27.

corrector of 424, Origen, and Basil omit any local reference : on the other the Marcionite *Apostolikon* contains the epistle under the title ' To the Laodiceans '.[1] Of these three possibilities it may be said that ' Ephesus ' is probably wrong—the internal evidence of the epistle is against it—and probably very early, seeing that it appears in all the versions. Secondly the authorities for the omission of a place-name are in the main Alexandrian : the earliest of them, Origen and P[46], take us back to the third century. Thirdly the Marcionite address to the Laodiceans goes back at least to the second century. We are left with questions to which no certain answers can be given. Is the omission of a place-name a piece of higher criticism by someone who saw the objections to ' Ephesus ' (or ' Laodicea '), or is it the primitive text (and so probably evidence that Ephesians was a circular letter)? Is ' Ephesians ' a very early bad guess or does it reflect the fact that the circular letter ended its travels at Ephesus ? What had Marcion before him? Did he displace ' Ephesus ' in favour of ' Laodicea '? Or fill in a blank space with ' Laodicea '? Or was ' Laodicea ' already there ?

We do not know, but we may try to guess. My guess, for what it is worth, starts from the fact that these problems of address are peculiar to Romans and Ephesians, and that it is at Rome and Ephesus that Marcion received two great and humiliating rebuffs. It is conceivable that Marcion may have considered that the two churches that had contemptuously rejected the one man who really understood St. Paul had thereby forfeited their status as recipients of a letter from the Apostle. This is no more than a conjecture ; and it is time now to turn to the consideration of other factors in the problem of Romans. In view, however, of the fact that so many of the clues lead back to Marcion, it may be worth while to keep the conjecture in mind.

The second main group of problems is concerned with the last two chapters of Romans. On these, a very full and careful statement of the progress of research down to 1929 was given

---

[1] There is a careful discussion of this problem by E. Percy in his *Die Probleme der Kolosser- und Epheserbriefe*, 449-466.

by Schumacher.[1] The fact that there is a problem was perceived as early as the eighteenth century by Semler ; and the
debate has continued ever since. Since Schumacher wrote
matters have been further complicated by the discovery of the
Chester Beatty Papyrus of the Pauline Epistle (P[46]), and my
chief concern is to reconsider the problem of the last two chapters
in the light of the new evidence furnished by P[46]. We may begin
by setting out the essential facts.

First, the structure of the Epistle. After the prescript
(i. 1-7) and the transition paragraph (i. 8-17), both of which we
have already discussed, we come to the first main topic, Judaism
and Christianity, which occupies i. 18-xi. 36 and concludes with
a doxology (verses 33-36). This is followed by the second main
section dealing with practical problems of Christian Ethics.
This extends from xii. 1 to xv. 13, and is concluded by a benediction (verse 13). The remainder of chapter xv, verses 14-33
is occupied with personal matters, details of Paul's missionary
activity in the past and his plans for the future. It is clearly
addressed to the Roman community, and it ends with a short
benediction (verse 33). Chapter xvi begins with a commenda-
tion of one Phoebe, deaconess in the church at Cenchreae near
Corinth (verses 1-2). Verses 3-16 and 21-23 are taken up with
greetings to various named persons and greetings from others.
The two sets of greetings are separated by a passage in which
the recipients are solemnly warned against false teachers. This
passage seems to presuppose some personal acquaintance of the
Apostle with those to whom it is addressed. It closes with a
blessing (verse 20b) whose position is not certain. It appears in
the MS. tradition in three places : here at the end of the warning
passage ; as verse 24 after the second list of greetings ; and,
finally, after the doxology (verses 25-27). Along with the
varying positions go slight differences of wording. Without
attempting at the moment to solve the problem of the proper place
of this last benediction it may be remarked that these numerous
full closes occur in the places where we should expect to find

---

[1] R. Schumacher, *Die beiden letzten Kapitel des Römerbriefes* in *Neutestamentliche Abhandlungen*, edited by Meinertz, xiv. Band. 4 Heft. Münster i. W.
1929.

them : xi. 33-36 ; xv. 13, 33 ; and xvi. 20 or 24 or 27. Whatever views we may hold about the unity of the document, these
are the logical places for major pauses.

But this sensible and natural division is crossed by another,
which has left its mark in the textual tradition of the Epistle.
This second system is marked by the position of the final doxology
τῷ δὲ δυναμένῳ ὑμᾶς στηρίξαι . . . . ᾧ ἡ δόξα εἰς τοὺς αἰῶνας
ἀμήν. It is widely held that this doxology is an interpolation
originating in Marcionite circles, though not the work of Marcion
himself. With this opinion I am inclined to agree. But whether
it be genuine or not, it seems to be intended as the concluding
word of the text. Now this doxology appears in three different
places in the textual tradition of Romans : at the end of chapters
xiv, xv, and xvi. In two of these cases it comes where there is a
real full close already in the text, namely after xv. 33, at the end
of the personal statement to the Roman community ; and at the
close of the second set of greetings in chapter xvi. The position
after xv. 33 is attested by the Chester Beatty Codex, P⁴⁶, the
first and, so far, the only witness to this position. The position
at the end of xvi is supported by the leading Alexandrian MSS.
אBC as well as by the Sahidic and Bohairic versions, the Vulgate,
the Peshitta, the Latin version of Origen's commentary and the
Athos MS. (1739) based on the Greek Origen, Ambrosiaster, and
Pelagius. The position at the end of chapter xiv is supported
by the common run of later (Byzantine) MSS. along with L,
the Harklean Syriac, the Gothic, Chrysostom, and Theodoret.
The essence of this position is that it is not one of the natural
logical pauses in the epistle. The insertion of the doxology
after xiv. 23 produces a break in the continuity of the text. It
is very unlikely that any thinking person with the complete text
of Romans as far as xv. 13 before him would have thought of
putting the doxology at xiv. 23. The natural inference is that
when the doxology was attached to xiv. 23, it was attached to a
form of the text which ended at that point.

This conclusion is confirmed by other pieces of evidence.
There is first the table of contents in the Codex Amiatinus of
the Vulgate. This divides the epistle into 51 sections of which
the fiftieth quite clearly refers to the last paragraph of chapter

xiv. (verses 13-33), and the fifty-first to the doxology. This capitulation is older than the MS. in which it appears ; for this MS. gives the complete text of Romans with the doxology at the end of chapter xvi. Again in the Codex Fuldensis of the Vulgate we have an even more remarkable capitulation, or rather one and a half capitulations. The first one covers chapters i to xiv in twenty-three sections : it implies probably a form of the text from which the last two chapters were absent. It tells us nothing about the doxology. Having covered fourteen chapters in this way in twenty-three sections, the capitulation now goes back to the beginning of chapter ix and gives sections 24 to 51 of the capitulation of Amiatinus. To the evidence of these tables we can add that of three MSS. of the Vulgate—in Gregory's notation 1648 and 1792 (both of Munich) and 2089 (of the Monza Chapter Library). In these the text ends at xiv. 23 and is followed by a short benediction and the doxology. It is to be noted that this is all Latin evidence.[1]

To this we can add some further facts and inferences. It is a fact that the Graeco-Latin MS. G does not have the doxology in any of the three places ; and it is practically certain from the researches of Corssen that the ancestor from which DFG all descend did not have the doxology anywhere. Corssen has also made it probable that this ancestor of DFG, which he calls Z, had a ' Western ' text in chapters i-xiv, and one with a considerable number of peculiar readings in the last two chapters. From this fact he inferred that behind Z lay a MS. which had the short text of Romans (i-xiv) without the doxology.

How did it come about that a text ending at xiv. 23 existed? It cannot be the work of the author ; for he would not have cut the text in the middle of an argument, and he himself shows that the proper place for a cut would be at xv. 13. We must suppose that some other hand was responsible ; and we are not left to guess whose hand it was. We have the direct assertion of Origen that it was Marcion who cut the last two chapters of Romans.[2]

---

[1] The Capitulations are printed in full in the great Oxford edition of the Vulgate New Testament, vol. II, pp. 44-61. For the details regarding the three MSS. of the Vulgate see Schumacher, *op. cit.* 15.

[2] For the text of Origen and a full discussion of its interpretation see Schumacher, *op. cit.* 3-10.

Tertullian can also be called as a witness that Marcion's text of Romans ended at xiv. 23 or thereabouts. Origen quotes xiv. 23 and tells us that Marcion from that point *usque ad finem cuncta dissecuit.* How much is *cuncta*? No doubt for Origen it meant the whole of the last two chapters, for he was acquainted with a text of Romans similar in extent to that in our Bibles. It was natural to assume that the difference between the text known to Origen and the text of Marcion represented the extent of Marcion's cut. But it is not at all certain that the text on which Marcion operated was Origen's text. The fact is that we know what was left when Marcion had finished his work on Romans : we can only guess what was there when he started. Harnack was of the opinion that at this point Marcion had before him a text from which the last two chapters were already absent.[1] This seems to me to be very unlikely.

The whole question is set in a new light by the publication of the third century Codex of the Pauline Epistles (P^{46}).[2] Here we have the oldest Greek MS. of Paul ; and it gives the doxology at the end of chapter xv, that is, at the end of the personal notes addressed to the Roman church. The clear implication is that there was once—at an earlier date than the date of P^{46}—a form of the text which omitted chapter xvi.

Now more than a century before the discovery of P^{46} the hypothesis had been put forward by David Schulz that Rom. xvi is no part of what St. Paul wrote to Rome but is a fragment of a Pauline letter to the Ephesian church.[3] This hypothesis had been accepted on internal grounds by many scholars ; but it remained a conjecture unsupported by MS. evidence. Now the required testimony was provided by the oldest known

[1] Harnack, *Marcion* (1921), 145* f.

[2] This MS. belongs part to Mr. Chester Beatty and part to the University of Michigan. The part of Romans that concerns us is in the Michigan portion. It was published by Professor H. A. Sanders in 1935 (*A Third-century Papyrus Codex of the Epistles of Paul*). Plate III of this edition gives a facsimile of the page containing Rom. xv. 30-33 ; Doxology ; xvi. 1-3. The complete text of the Pauline corpus as given by the Michigan and Chester Beatty leaves was published by Sir Frederic Kenyon in 1936. (*The Chester Beatty Biblical Papyri. Fasc. III Supplement. Pauline Epistles.*)

[3] Schumacher, *op. cit.* 63. He gives the reference to *Theol. Studien und Kritiken*, 1829, 609 ff.

MS. of the Epistles.   The natural inference to be drawn is that
we are here in the presence of the form of text that was sent to
Rome in the first instance.   But, if Harnack is right, ' Marcion
did not edit his Apostolikon in Pontus or Asia, but in the west.
The text that lay before him was thus the text of the Roman
community shortly before the middle of the second century.' [1]
In that case we are justified in supposing that what Marcion
removed from the text of Romans was what we now know as
chapter xv.   Chapter xvi he could not touch, for it was not there :
it formed no part of the text known at Rome in the second
century.   This view is consistent with the evidence from western
patristic sources.   We have no quotation from Rom. xv-xvi in
Irenaeus, Tertullian, or Cyprian.   There is, however, an indication in the Muratorian Canon which suggests a possible acquaintance with Rom. xv.   There an explanation is being offered of
the absence of any account in Acts of St. Paul's missionary
journey to Spain.   The explanation is not that it did not take
place, but that Luke was not present when the Apostle set out,
and therefore did not report the departure.   The point is that
the Muratorianum uses the uncommon form Spania instead of
Hispania, and that Σπανία is the word used by Paul in xv. 24
and 28 in describing the plans for his future activities.

On the assumption that Marcion removed chapter xv, and that
only, we have to attempt to discover some motive for the excision.
Here I venture to suggest that the same motive that I have
already put forward to explain the removal of local references in
Rom. i. 7, 15 and Eph. i. 1, will serve to explain the removal
of the personalia in Rom. xv. 14-33.   It remains to find a
reason for breaking off at xiv. 23 the argument which runs naturally on to xv. 13.   If we may judge from Marcion's treatment of
other parts of Romans, particularly his omission of chapter iv,
with its detailed appeal to the Old Testament story of Abraham,
and of most of chapters ix-xi, with their frequent appeals to the
Old Testament, we may perhaps suppose that he found the
repeated quotations of Old Testament texts in xv. 1-13 uncon-
genial, as well as the idea (xv. 4) that ' whatsoever things were

[1] Harnack, *op. cit.* 127*.

R

written aforetime were written for our learning, that through patience and through comfort of the scriptures we might have hope '. Moreover, it may be considered that from the Marcionite point of view the statement of xiv. 23 that ' whatever is not of faith is sin ' makes a more decisive conclusion to the argument than anything the Pauline continuation can offer.

If the argument up to this point is sound certain conclusions seem to follow, which are not without importance for the textual criticism of the Pauline epistles. First of all we must regard all MSS. which present the doxology after xiv. 23 as at least open to the suspicion of having a Marcionite streak in their ancestry.[1] This may seem to be a surprising conclusion in view of the fact that so many of these MSS. belong to the Byzantine or Koine group. We must, however, bear in mind that in many cases the streak in question may be no more than the insertion of the doxology at that point. Further, as the major part of Marcion's activity consisted in excisions, it is quite possible that a text originally Marcionite, in the process of having its omissions supplied, might also be revised in other respects and so brought into closer agreement with a different type of text. It has also to be remembered that at the time when Marcion was active the number of MSS. of the Pauline corpus was small, and probably very small. Consequently his Apostolikon may easily have been the source from which many copies were taken simply because there was no other text available.

The second conclusion is that we should regard P[46] as offering in chapters i-xv the form in which the epistle was received at Rome ; and, what is perhaps more important, its text should be taken as descended from the pre-Marcionite Roman text of the letter. It may not be a very pure example of the text. It has suffered the interpolation of the doxology and the addition of chapter xvi. But at any rate it has a pre-Marcionite Roman base. This makes it a very important and valuable witness.

Thirdly we should note that P[46] has chapter xvi attached after the doxology. In view of the fact that P[46] comes from Egypt, and that it is the Alexandrian textual witnesses that testify to the longest form of text by having the doxology at the end of chapter xvi, and further that our earliest patristic writer

---

[1] See *Additional Note*, p. 19 f.

to show certain knowledge of chapter xvi is Clement of Alexandria, it may be permissible to guess that this last chapter was added to the pre-Marcionite Roman text underlying P⁴⁶ in Egypt. In favour of such a hypothesis it may be noted that the text of chapter xvi in P⁴⁶ seems to stand nearer to the B type than does the text of other chapters of the epistle.

So much for the text. What can be deduced from these facts about the history of the letter? The first thing that emerges is that in the second half of the second century the document was circulating in three forms : the Marcionite, which had no reference to Rome and ended at xiv. 23 ; the Roman, which ended at xv. 33 ; and the full text of sixteen chapters which was in circulation in Egypt and was known to Clement of Alexandria. It is our view that Marcion produced his text from the Roman by the removal of chapter xv and of the references to Rome in i. 7 and 15. If we eliminate Marcion from the reckoning we are left with two forms of text : a Roman of fifteen chapters and an Egyptian of sixteen. Our problem is to account for the existence of these two types of text. It is here that the hypothesis that chapter xvi is a letter, or part of a letter, to Ephesus comes in.

This hypothesis had been the subject of much debate from its first suggestion by David Schulz in 1829. It is not necessary to go over all the ground again. The arguments are stated in the Introductions to the New Testament and the commentaries on Romans.[1] The major points are that chapter xvi contains a large number of greetings to Paul's friends. It is unlikely that he had so many personal friends—some of them intimate friends —in the Roman church which he had never visited. Further, those in the list, who are otherwise known, are connected with Asia and Ephesus. Again the exhortations in xvi. 17-20 read very oddly if they are taken to be addressed to a church to which Paul was a stranger : they are very natural things to say to a community which he had founded and in which he had worked for several years. On the other side comes Lietzmann's acid

[1] For a clear and fair statement of the case before P⁴⁶ came on the scene, see Dodd's *Commentary on Romans* (1932), pp. xvii-xxiv.

comment on the theory that Rom. xvi is a letter to Ephesus : ' A letter consisting almost entirely of nothing but greetings . . . is a monstrosity '.[1] There is further the fact that a detailed study of the names in chapter xvi leads to the conclusion that they *could* have been the names of members of the Roman church in the first century. Professor Dodd concluded (p. xxiv) ' It is clear that the arguments for Rome and Ephesus respectively come far short of proof one way or the other. As the burden of proof rests upon those who would set aside the tradition in favour of a conjecture, we may be content to accept chap. xvi (except the doxology) as an integral part of the epistle.'

That was certainly a fair summing up of the argument in 1932. In 1935, however, came the new evidence of P[46] to set the whole matter in a new light. The position of the doxology in this MS. was a clear enough indication that Romans had once existed in a form which ended where the upholders of the Ephesian theory said it ought to end. They could now buttress their conjecture by the evidence of the earliest known MS. of the Pauline corpus. This means that the Ephesian theory now has a stronger claim than ever before to the most serious consideration. Suppose that it is true.

We must then suppose that Paul prepared a letter (Rom. i-xv) and sent it to Rome. At the same time a copy was prepared to be sent to Ephesus. It may be assumed that this Ephesian copy would include the personalia of Rom. xv. 14-33 ; for these, though primarily intended for the Roman Church, nevertheless contained information about Paul's plans which would certainly be of interest to the Apostle's friends in Ephesus. As all this was given in i-xv it was unnecessary to say much more in the added paragraphs. Consequently all that we have in chapter xvi is an introduction of Phoebe, who may be regarded as the bearer of the letter to Ephesus ; the greetings to Paul's friends in the province of Asia; and the exhortation of verses 17-20, which has points of contact with Paul's address to the Ephesian elders at Miletus.[2] Any further information that was

---

[1] *HBNT. An die Römer*[3], 129.
[2] Acts xx. 17-38. Compare Rom. xvi. 17 f. with Acts xx. 29-32.

asked for at Ephesus could doubtless be supplied verbally by the bearer of the letter.[1] Naturally the covering note (xvi) and the Roman letter (i-xv) were associated from the beginning and presumably they formed a single document, which was preserved as such in the archives of the Ephesian community. From Ephesus copies reached Egypt at an early date, and the sixteen chapters were well known to Clement of Alexandria as well as to the translators of the Sahidic version.[2]

Meanwhile the Roman letter (i-xv) made its way to its destination. It was doubtless preserved in the archives of the Roman church, and a copy of it may have been known to the author of the Muratorian Canon. From this Roman text Marcion, in the first half of the second century, prepared his text ending at xiv. 23. This became the standard text of the Marcionite communities, which were strongest and survived longest in Syria.[3]

The rest of the history of the text is concerned largely with the intermixture of these types of text. P[46] itself is one of the earliest examples : a Roman text supplemented from the Ephesian text current in Egypt. Another mixture is represented by AP 533 where the doxology appears in the Marcionite position and the Ephesian.

Returning now to Paul at Corinth, we may ask one final question concerning the motive for the writing of the letter. So long as the letter was thought of as a simple letter to Rome the obvious answer to the question was to the effect that it was a rather elaborate and detailed statement of faith offered by the Apostle as evidence on which the Roman church might give him a friendly reception and set him forward on his Spanish

---

[1] Such verbal supplements to the written document are contemplated in Col. iv. 7 ff. and Eph. vi. 21 f.

[2] For this transmission of Christian material from Asia to Egypt we have striking evidence in the John Rylands Library. The Rylands fragment of John (P. Ryl. Gk. 457) is proof that the Ephesian Gospel had reached Egypt within a few decades of its composition ; and this evidence is confirmed by the British Museum papyrus, P. Egerton 2, containing a fragment of an apocryphal gospel, which clearly is dependent on John, and equally clearly was in existence within a few decades of the composition of John.

[3] It may be noted that it is in this area that evidence is strongest for the existence of the doxology in what may be called the Marcionite position, after xiv. 23.

missionary enterprise. But this answer needs reconsideration in the light of the conclusions so far reached in our discussion. It seems to me that we must begin from the facts (a) that the text of Romans was produced at Corinth, and (b) that it was sent both to Rome and to Ephesus.

(a) With regard to the Corinthian origin, we have to note that the document was produced immediately after the close of a period of bitter and violent controversy over matters affecting the church at Corinth and the churches of Galatia, and in all probability the Macedonian churches too. The central issue in this controversy was that of the relation between Judaism and Christianity, Law and Gospel. This issue is hotly debated in Galatians and in Philippians iii, more calmly in 2 Cor. iii-vi ; and finally it is discussed at length in a careful and judicial way in the first eleven chapters of Romans. These chapters may fairly be regarded as Paul's considered judgement on the whole issue. Now when we turn to the text of these chapters and study the argument in detail it is difficult to avoid the impression that we have here the report of a real debate. Again and again Paul is answering objections and meeting criticisms of his position. Are these imaginary objections and hypothetical criticisms ? Or are they points which were actually made in real debate ? I am inclined to think that we have here a record made by Paul and his clerical helpers of a real discussion. The order and arrangement of the account is probably Paul's own ; but the materials used in putting it together may well have come in large part from the actual debate.

This impression is confirmed when we turn to the sections dealing with Christian practice (xii. 1-xv. 13). Chapter xii takes up the question of unity within the church and stresses afresh the organic conception of the Christian community, a very necessary idea at Corinth where the church had been rent by party divisions. Chapter xiii. 1-10 deals with the relation of the church to the civil power, a matter that had arisen in another connexion in I Cor. vi. Chapter xiii. 11-14 touches on matters dealt with at greater length in I Cor. xv. And finally xiv. 1-xv. 13 rediscusses the problems which were earlier considered in I Cor. viii-x.

These facts seem to me to lead to the conclusion that we should think of our document primarily as the summing up of the positions reached by Paul and his friends at the end of the long controversy whose beginnings appear in I Corinthians and—if the Ephesian dating of Philippians is, as I think it is, right—in Philippians iii. Having got this statement worked out to his own satisfaction, Paul then decided to send a copy of it to his friends in Ephesus, which he did not intend to visit on his way to Jerusalem (Acts xx. 16). This copy would be available for the information of all the churches of Asia. At the same time he conceived the idea of sending a copy to Rome with a statement of his future plans. It might be permissible to guess that a written record may have remained in Corinth, though that, I think, is not necessary on the assumption that the substance of what is now in Romans had been gone over in discussion with the members of the Corinthian community. The situation then is that the Corinthian church has had the Apostle's summing up by word of mouth ; the church in Syria and Palestine may expect to hear it in the same way in the near future. The church in the province of Asia and the church in Rome will receive it in writing. Looked at in this way Romans ceases to be just a letter of self-introduction from Paul to the Roman church, and becomes a manifesto setting forth his deepest convictions on central issues, a manifesto calling for the widest publicity, which the Apostle did his best—not without success—to give it.

Additional Note (p. 14).—I should add that where, as is probably the case in the ancestor of DFG, we have a text ending at xiv. 33 without the doxology, we have a very early form of the text, as it was current in Rome in the second century. In this connexion it is significant that P[46], which I regard as the primary witness for the Roman form of the Greek text of Romans in chapters i.-xv., shows a far higher degree of agreement with DFG against ℵABC in Romans than in any other Epistle. The figures as worked out by Sir F. Kenyon are given in the following table :—

	P[46] with ℵABC	With DFG
Rom.	89	51
Heb.	79	20
I Cor.	143	29
II Cor.	60	11
Eph.	47	5
Gal.	40	5
Phil.	23	6
Col.	20	3

13

THE PROBLEM OF
THE EPISTLE TO THE HEBREWS.
(1949)

THE Epistle appears in our Bibles with the superscription, ' The Epistle of Paul the Apostle to the Hebrews ' (A.V. and R.V.). I propose to substitute for this,

' The Epistle of Apollos to the Churches of the Lycus Valley '. The original heading is a guess and so is this, but I hope to show that a number of converging lines of argument make it a fairly probable guess. I take first the external evidence ; but before doing that we must ask whether letter is the correct name for the document.

Hebrews has no epistolary beginning (just as the Epistle of James has no ending) ; but it has an ending which, if genuine, shows that it is a letter and not a sermon. The words, ' I exhort you the more exceedingly to do this, that I may be restored to you the sooner ' (xiii. 19), show that the author is not present with the recipients of his message.

Further there are indications within the letter that it is not a ' general epistle ' addressed to the Church at large. The writer has in view a definite group ; this is clear from such passages as xiii. 18 f. ; x. 32-34 ; vi. 10 ; v. 11-vi. 8, all of which point to a community known intimately, and over a period of time, to the author ; one, moreover, in which he has a lively and personal interest.

It is the more curious that there is no introductory matter, and the possibility must be kept in mind that this has been lost. Such loss might be due to accident or design. Against accident is the fact that the letter seems to begin at the beginning of its argument ; and it seems unlikely that accidental mutilation would have made the cut so neatly. It is possible that the address was suppressed. If it was, there was presumably some reason why. But we have no means of knowing or even making a guess.

The current title, πρὸς Ἐβραίους, is not the address : most probably it is a guess. But it must have been made at an early stage since the Epistle is known under this title in all MSS. and versions, and to the Alexandrian school and Tertullian. This means that the title was in use by the end of the second century. The name ' Hebrews ' would mean one thing in Palestine and another outside. As the addressees are Christians, it would mean, if the document was sent to Palestine, Aramaic-speaking Jewish Christians, natives of the land as opposed to Greek-speaking ' Hellenists ', i.e. Christian Jews of the Diaspora. If sent to a community outside Palestine it would naturally mean Christians of Jewish extraction whether Aramaic- or Greek-speaking. Early Fathers mostly preferred the former alternative ; but the latter possibility cannot therefore be excluded. There is no guarantee that the originator of the title held the patristic view ; nor are we bound to follow blindly. Indeed there is nothing to show that the originator of the title did anything but what we must do—make more or less probable inferences from the contents of the Epistle itself.

In Alexandria, so far as we can get back, Hebrews was regarded as an Epistle of Paul. It was certainly so regarded by Clement of Alexandria (Eus., H.E., vi. 14. 2 ff.) and probably also by his teacher Pantaenus (Zahn., Einl., ii. 122 f.). The problem for the Alexandrians was to account for the difference in style between Hebrews and the accepted Pauline Epistles. This was done by supposing, for example, that Paul wrote it in Hebrew or Aramaic and that Luke translated it into Greek. Origen was more fully aware of the difficulty and while he tries to defend the tradition of his own church, he cannot conceal the fact that he is dubious about the Pauline authorship (Eus., H.E., vi. 25. 11-14). He suggests that the thoughts are Paul's and the expression of them due to a scholar of the Apostles. He thus tacitly abandons Clement's translation theory. He also mentions Clement of Rome and Luke as supposed authors.

On the other hand, whatever may have been the doubts and hesitations of the Christian scholars of Alexandria, there is no doubt that Hebrews was accepted as Pauline in the Egyptian Church and included among the letters to Churches from a very early date. The position of Hebrews in the Canon of the New Testament has been the subject of an elaborate and detailed study by Professor W. H. P. Hatch in the *Harvard Theological Review* (xxix (1936) 133-151) from which it appears that there are three different positions for the Epistle: (i) among the letters to Churches; (ii) after II Thess., i.e. at the end of the letters to Churches; (iii) after Philemon, i.e. at the end of the Pauline corpus. It is of interest to consider the witnesses to these different positions; and we may begin with the third position, after Philemon. It is fairly obvious that in this case Hebrews has been added as an afterthought to a collection already closed; and it is significant that the most important witnesses to this order come from the West (D f and the Latin Vulgate. The Syriac versions, pesh. and hcl., also have this order; but, as Hatch points out, in Syria it replaced an earlier arrangement in which Hebrews followed Romans). Now we know independently that it was in the West that the resistance to accepting Hebrews as Pauline was most determined and prolonged. We should therefore be inclined to suppose that our third position originated in the West and spread from there to Antioch and so to the Syriac-speaking Churches. The second position, after II Thess., has as its leading witnesses the principal authorities for the so-called 'Neutral' or Alexandrian text (‎א ABC, Athanasius, Cyril of Alexandria, etc.). Hatch thinks that this arrangement originated in Alexandria when the revision which produced the B‎א text took place, probably early in the fourth century.

Older than either of these arrangements is the first order, in which Hebrews is placed among the letters to Churches. The exact position varies: it is after Romans in the Chester Beatty Codex (P⁴⁶), the oldest known MS. of the Pauline corpus, and in the Syrian Canon of about A.D. 400 ; it is after II Corinthians in the MSS. of the Sahidic version and in the Sahidic translation of the 39th Festal Letter of Athanasius, where Athanasius' order as given in the Greek has been altered to agree with the Sahidic Canon ; it was after Galatians in the archetype of B. The important point here is that the leading witnesses for a place among the major Pauline letters are Egyptian. The evidence of the MSS., versions, and early Fathers all points to the conclusion that full recognition of Hebrews begins in Egypt and spreads from there to Syria and eventually to the West. The earliest Syriac evidence agrees with the Old Egyptian in classing Hebrews with the major Pauline Epistles.

(1) W. Bauer (*Der Apostolos der Syrer*, p. 28) accepts Zahn's demonstration that the original order of books in Ephrem's († 373) commentary on the Paulines was Gal. I and II Cor. Rom. Heb. (Zahn, *NKZ.* xi (1900), 798 f.).

(2) The Syriac Stichometry (Lewis, *Studia Sinaitica.*, i. pp. 11-13).

(3) Theodore of Mopsuestia († 428) appears to have had a similar order (*Comm.* on Gal. iv. 24 (Swete I., p. 76) and preface to Philemon, quoted in Swete's note *ibid.*). On Gal. iv. 24 he says ' et hoc in epistola illa quae ad Hebraeos est interpretantes ostendimus euidentius '. In the preface to Philemon he mentions, ' Epistolae quae ad Rom. et Cor. et Hebraeos.' Theodore's order seems to have been Rom. I and II Cor. Heb. Gal.

(It may be noted that here the position of Heb. is fixed— after II Cor. It is Gal. that is the variable factor. In Ephrem and the Stichometry it stands first in the group of five Epistles ; in Theodore it stands last.)

The Syrian Church entertained no doubt about the Pauline authorship of Hebrews. It is cited as Paul's by Ephrem († 373), Rabbula († 435), Titus of Bostra († *c.* 375), Apollinarius († *c.* 390), Diodorus of Tarsus († *c.* 394), Chrysostom († 407), Theodore of Mopsuestia († 428), Nestorius († *c.* 440), Theodoret († 458). Proofs are given by Bauer, *op. cit.*, pp. 25 ff.

On the other side in the Churches of the West the Epistle was well known from an early date ; it is quoted in I. Clem. But, up to the middle of the fourth century it was not accepted as Pauline or included in the N.T. canon. Irenaeus [1] and Hippolytus [2] do not seem to have any tradition as to its author.

Tertullian (c. 220) and the author of a treatise wrongly attributed to Origen [3] ascribe Hebrews to Barnabas the apostle.

The result is that between 180-260 there were three prevailing views : (1) Paul (Alexandria), (2) Barnabas (Tert.), (3) An unknown author (Iren. Hipp.). Zahn argues that (3) is the common root of (1) and (2)—in other words that (1) and (2) are guesses : and that the author was really not given in any reliable tradition. Zahn himself adopts (2).

After the middle of the fourth century the Alexandrian—now the Greek—tradition broke down the Western attitude and led to the recognition everywhere of Hebrews as Pauline and a genuine part of the N.T. This is a triumph of Alexandrian guesswork, for the Epistle is surely not by Paul. We must reject the Alexandrian guess, and make a better if we can. In framing our hypothesis we shall have to depend very largely on the evidence supplied by the document itself ; and I hope to show that this internal evidence gives reliable indications of the date of the document, of its probable purpose, and of a possible author and destination.

1. *Date.* We have a reasonably well fixed terminus ad quem in the fact that the Epistle is quoted in *I. Clem.* (c. A.D. 96).

On the assumption that the personalia at the end are part of the original document, we can push the date still further back. The statement in xiii. 23 implies that Timothy is still in active missionary work and capable of travelling in the interests of the Gospel. Now Timothy was probably born about A.D. 20-25, so that when *I Clem.* was written he would be, if still alive, about 70-76 years old, a somewhat advanced age for active missionary

---

[1] On Iren. see C. H. Turner in *N.T.S. Iren.*, 226 f. It seems certain that Irenaeus neither ascribed the Epistle to Paul nor reckoned it in the N.T. canon.

[2] On Hippol. see R. H. Connolly in *JTS*, xlvi. 198 f. That Hippolytus denied the Pauline authorship is expressly stated by Photius, *Bibliotheca*, 121. Gaius also rejected the Pauline authorship. See Eus., *H.E.*, vi. 20, who says that even in his (Eusebius') day some Romans denied Heb. to Paul.

[3] This work entitled *Tractatus Origenis de libris SS. Script.*, was published by Batiffol in 1900. It is certainly not by Origen. By some authorities it has been assigned to Novatian or one of his followers. See Zahn, *Einl.*³, ii. 118 f., 124 ; Moffatt, *Introd.*³, 437 f.

work.   We may, therefore, on the strength of Heb. xiii. 23 push
the date back to about 80-85.   As we do not know when Timothy
died we cannot make any more progress along this line.

We have also a fixed terminus a quo, if we can show, as I
think we can, that the author of Hebrews was acquainted with
Romans.   This would give a date about 55 as the earliest possible.

We are thus left with a period 55-85 as that within which the
Epistle must most probably fall.   Can we narrow these limits
any further ?   I think that we can if we look carefully at the
argument of the Epistle as a whole and particularly at the part of
it which is developed in chapters v-x.

The Argument of the Epistle.

The theme of the Epistle is set out in the opening words.   It
is an interpretation of the history of Israel in terms of God's
purpose, now fully and finally realised in Jesus Christ.   For this
purpose it is of course assumed that the Church is continuous
with the old Israel of the O.T.—a position which the writer shares
with St. Paul.   In Christ there has been a divine intervention in
the fullest sense.   The creative, sustaining, and redeeming
activity of God has been manifested to the world in the person of
Jesus crucified and exalted, and now supreme over every power in
the universe (i. 1-4).   This supremacy the author now proceeds
to demonstrate.

A. *Jesus is superior to the Angels* (i. 5-14).   The proof is
obtained by taking texts from the O.T. and interpreting them in a
Messianic sense, at the same time comparing them with texts
referring to angels.   It is argued that these groups of texts show
that the angels are lower in status than the Messianic Son.
Their functions are of an interim, preparatory, and subordinate
character (*v.* 14).   In particular they proclaimed the Law which
is inferior to the Gospel (ii. 1-4).   Furthermore, their authority
does not extend into the coming order of existence ($\tau\grave{\eta}\nu$ $o\emph{i}\kappa o\upsilon\mu\acute{\epsilon}\nu\eta\nu$
$\tau\grave{\eta}\nu$ $\mu\acute{\epsilon}\lambda\lambda o\upsilon\sigma\alpha\nu$ = עולם הבא), where, as may be again shown
from Scripture, Christ is supreme (ii. 5-8a).   It is true that this
supremacy is not yet very obvious ; but that is part of the divine
plan.   The humiliation and suffering of Jesus are there in order
that he may carry through his redemptive work (ii. 8b-18).

B. Jesus is superior to the great historic leaders of Israel.
He is superior to Moses. Proof from Scripture. Moses was a
faithful servant. Jesus is the Son (iii. 1-6). Moreover, if we
look at the O.T. history, we can see how Jesus is superior to other
heroes besides Moses—Joshua and David for example. For the
perfect state called in the Bible 'Rest' is a reality from the beginning. It is offered by God to his people. Yet scripture shows
that Moses was not able to bring the people into it because of their
unbelief, which he could not overcome (iii. 7-19). And it is
clear that Joshua succeeded no better, for the promise is still
unfulfilled and the invitation still open in the time of David
(iv. 1-13). But what they could not achieve has been achieved
by Jesus the Son of God, and so made possible for us (iv. 14-16).

This achievement of opening a way of access to God through
humiliation and suffering is best understood if we think of Jesus
as our great High-priest. That is to say, for our author the
supreme good, which is groped after in the O.T. and found in
Christianity, is essentially a religious good ; and its achievement
depends not on bringing it into existence—as though it were not
already there where God is — but in removing those obstacles—
ἀπείθεια, ἁμαρτία, etc.—which hinder men from ' entering into
the Rest '. The messianic task is one of atonement—making
men at one with God, and therefore the messianic office is
priestly. The delineation of Jesus as the supreme High-priest
thus occupies the central place in the argument (chaps. v-x).
The main thesis is that in this high-priestly office,

C. Jesus is superior to the High-priests of Judaism in the nature
of his office, in himself, and in the effectiveness of his ministration.

(1) The nature of the office. Called by God from among men to
act on behalf of them in divine things (v. 1-10). Thus
Aaron was called (*v.* 4) and thus Christ. The proof that the
Christ is called to the high-priestly office is Ps. cx. 4.
' Thou art a priest for ever after the order of Melchizedek.'
Jesus in the days of his flesh acted in this office and by
his own self-sacrifice became the αἴτιος σωτηρίας αἰωνίου.
(Here the author inserts a long piece of exhortation
(v. 11-vi. 12) suggesting that if they find his argument

unintelligible, the fault is in themselves, and calling them to new zeal and consecration.)

(a) This Melchizedek priesthood is connected with another firm promise of God, that to Abraham. (The two hang together and as Paul worked out the one in Galatians so our author will work out the other.) (vi. 13-20.)

(i) This Melchizedek was contemporary with Abraham and acted as priest for him receiving tithes. He was no ordinary priest but the description in Genesis shows him to have been the prototype of the perfect High-priest to come (vii. 1-3).

(ii) Abraham recognised his superiority (α) by paying tithes to him, (β) by accepting his blessing (vii. 4-8).

(iii) In a sense the unborn Levi was subordinate to Melchizedek when Abraham paid the tithes (vii. 9 f.).

(b) The levitical priesthood on the other hand is connected with the Mosaic Law. They fail and fall together (vii. 11-25).

(i) If the levitical priesthood were effective what need for the Melchizedek priesthood ? With the levitical priesthood goes the Law also (vii. 11 f.).

(ii) The Law prescribed priests from Levi : Jesus sprang from Judah. So the Law is abrogated (vii. 13-17).

(iii) And this because the Law had proved weak and ineffective (vii. 18 f.).

(iv) The true priesthood is confirmed by divine oath. The levitical priesthood lacks this (vii. 20-22).

(v) The levitical priesthood constantly changes hands. The Melchizedekian priest is ' for ever ' (vii. 23-25).

(2) *Character.* The Law contemplates a high-priest who knows sin. The true high-priest is sinless (vii. 26-28).

(3) *Effectiveness of ministration.*

(a) The two priesthoods are connected with the two covenants, the old covenant of Sinai and the new covenant spoken of by Jeremiah (ch. viii.).

(i) The old covenant had its order of worship and its outward furniture of devotion. But all this was merely an earthly copy of the real spiritual thing as is proved by Moses' being shown the pattern of the Tabernacle when he was on Mt. Sinai (viii. 1-5).

(ii) Christ introduces a better form of worship corresponding to the new covenant (viii. 6-12).

(iii) The fact of the new covenant shows that the old is obsolete (viii. 13).

(b) The purpose of both priesthoods is the same—to make atonement (chs. ix, x.).

(i) Hence the culminating point in the old ritual was the annual service of the Day of Atonement. But the very nature of the service showed its insufficiency. Only the High-priest had access to the Holy of Holies. And the ritual had to be constantly repeated. The worshippers were not perfected by the worship, which merely pointed the way to what should one day supersede it (ix. 1-10). Now Christ has come with a better ritual, the sacrifice of himself ; and has opened the way into the true Holy of Holies—heaven itself, the very presence of God—for those who by him are cleansed from all the defilement that separates them from God and unfits them to enter into his presence (ix. 11-14).

(ii) He is thus the mediator of the new and better covenant (as Moses was of the old). By his death he has delivered men from the transgressions of the old so that they can now receive the promise as heirs of an eternal heritage (ix. 15).

(iii) As a sacrifice was necessary under the old regime, so also under the new (ix. 16-22). But whereas the old sacrifice had to be repeated, Christ's one sacrifice is sufficient (ix. 23-28). More than that, the old sacrifices were really ineffective. The blood of bulls could not really cleanse away sins. Jesus comes into the world to offer not animal sacrifices but the oblation of a will wholly devoted to God's will. This is effective and so the new covenant replaces the old (x. 1-18).

D. Exhortation to lay hold of this great salvation while there is still time (x. 19-25) ; and to sin no more lest a worse thing befall them (x. 26-31). Let their own former enthusiasm spur them on to new efforts (x. 32-39). The whole secret of the religious life is that it is a life of faith—that trust in God which expresses itself in obedience to his will and hope of the fulfilment of his promises. This faith is exemplified in the saints and heroes of Israel who carried on bravely in their own day of partial fulfilment, though they could not receive the whole promise then, because God's plan was more comprehensive and included us also (ch. xi.). That plan has now been completed in Jesus and it is for us to follow their example and his footsteps. If that means loss and suffering, interpret these trials as the fatherly discipline that proves you to be the sons of God (xii. 1-13). Cultivate the Christian virtues and do not despise your heritage (xii. 14-17). It is something far greater than the old covenant for which the old heroes suffered so much (xii. 18-19). Cherish kindness, purity, unselfishness, contentment. God is with you : what more do you need ? (xiii. 1-6). Follow Christ even if it means obloquy and being outcast (xiii. 7-17).

Greetings and blessings and personal messages (xiii. 18-25).

We have seen that Hebrews was probably written between 55 and 85. That period is divided about the middle by the great catastrophe of the fall of Jerusalem. On which side of that event does Hebrews lie ? It is—as has often been pointed out—precarious to argue from the present tenses in descriptions of Jewish ritual that they imply that the Temple is still standing. For (a) the same phenomenon occurs in the Mishnah (c. A.D. 200) and in Josephus [1] ; and (b) the author of Hebrews argues from the arrangements of the Tabernacle, not of Herod's Temple. But while this is so, there is a further and weighty argument which we can now adduce. As we have seen the whole point of the argument of Heb. v.-x. is that the levitical priesthood with all its ritual has now been superseded by the Melchizedekian High-priesthood of Christ. To support this proposition our author brings forward all kinds of arguments and performs the most amazing feats of exegesis. Surely the clinching argument would have been this : ' That God has no further use for the old priesthood and ritual is conclusively shown by the fact that he has permitted the Temple to be destroyed and its services to be

---

[1] See Thackeray, *Josephus, the Man and the Historian*, 99.

S

brought to an end '. It is difficult to see how the writer, who shows such ingenuity in drawing support for his thesis from the most unlikely places, could have missed this argument, if it were there to be used. That he does not use it I take to be a strong indication that he was writing before A.D. 70, quite possibly before the outbreak of the Jewish revolt in 66. This consideration narrows down the period of writing to 55-70.

That, I think, is as far as we can go in fixing the date with any degree of certainty. In what follows I shall bring in some other factors and attempt to be more precise ; but I must admit that this further construction is, and probably must remain, no more than a moderately attractive hypothesis. Any nearer determination of the date depends on bringing in considerations of authorship and destination. I will deal first with the question of destination.

2. *Destination.* I suggest that the Epistle was written to the Churches of the Lycus Valley, two of which, Colossae and Laodicae, we know by name in the Pauline letters.[1] The main reason for thinking this is that the conditions implied in our document seem to answer to the conditions in those Churches at some time during the period 55-70, i.e. during the period in which I think the letter must have been written. We have independent evidence concerning those conditions in Paul's letter to the Colossians. The trouble in the Lycus Valley Churches is thus summarised by Bishop Lightfoot in his *Commentary on Colossians*, p. 71.[2]

' 1. A mere glance at the Epistle suffices to detect the presence of *Judaism* in the teaching which the Apostle combats. The observance of Sabbaths and new moons is decisive in this respect. The distinction of meats and drinks points in the same direction (ii. 16 ff.). Even the enforcement of the initiatory rite of Judaism may be inferred from the contrast implied in St. Paul's recommendation of the spiritual circumcision (ii. 11).

---

[1] On the Lycus Valley and its Churches see Lightfoot, *Colossians and Philemon*, 1-70 ; W. M. Ramsay, *Cities and Bishoprics of Phrygia*, i. 1-121 ; A. H. M. Jones, *Cities of the Eastern Roman Provinces*, 73-76.

[2] For a very full recent discussion of the ' Colossian heresy ' see Ernst Percy, *Die Probleme der Kolosser und Epheserbriefe*, 137-178.

'2. On the other hand a closer examination of its language shows that these Judaic features do not exhaust the portraiture of the heresy or heresies against which the Epistle is directed. We discern an element of theosophic speculation, which is alien to the spirit of Judaism proper. We are confronted with a shadowy mysticism, which loses itself in the contemplation of the unseen world. We discover a tendency to interpose certain spiritual agencies, intermediate beings between God and man, as the instruments of communication and the objects of worship (ii. 4, 8, 18, 23).' Lightfoot makes two main points : a hankering after Jewish religious observances and a doctrine of intermediaries between God and man.

Now the central argument of Hebrews (v.-x.) is just that the whole Jewish ritual system is superseded by the High-priestly work of Christ. That is, the central argument of Hebrews is a complete answer to the first main point in the Colossian heresy.

More than that, the argument of Heb. i.-iv. is concerned to prove the uniqueness and supremacy of Christ as against all other intermediaries. The Epistle begins with the argument that Christ is superior to the angels (i.-ii.). There the proof is obtained by taking texts from the O.T. and interpreting them in a messianic sense, at the same time comparing them with texts referring to angels. The comparison always works out to the disadvantage of the angels : they regularly come out with a lower status than the Messianic Son. Their functions are of an interim, preparatory, and subordinate character (i. 14). In particular they proclaimed the Law, which is inferior to the Gospel (ii. 1-4). Furthermore their authority does not extend into the coming order of existence, where, as can be shown from Scripture, Christ is supreme (ii. 5-8).

Similarly Christ is superior to the other great intermediary Moses (iii. 1-6) ; and to anybody else you like to name. In effect the author says to his readers, ' You seek mystical communion with God and contemplation of the unseen world ? The Old Testament itself shows that neither angels nor men can give it (iii. 7-iv. 16). No being, heavenly or earthly, can give you what you are seeking except Christ.'

Thus Heb. i.-iv. is a detailed answer to the second main point in the Colossian heresy ; and so Heb. i.-x. is a complete refutation of the Colossian heresy as that heresy is described by Lightfoot.

One minor point of agreement between Hebrews and Colossians may be added.   Lightfoot draws attention to the distinction of meats and drinks as pointing to the Judaising character of the Colossian heresy.   In Col. ii. 16 the Apostle exhorts his readers not to let any man judge them in matters of meat and drink, and in verses 20 ff. he protests against their subjecting themselves to ordinances which say ' Handle not, nor taste, nor touch ', with reference to goods which exist to be used and used up. Heb. xiii. 9 reads : ' Do not be carried away by varied and novel doctrines ; for the good thing is to have one's heart strengthened by grace, not by foods wherein those who walked had no benefit '.   That is, we already know all about a dietary discipline that was of no real advantage to those who submitted to it.   The reference in both Hebrews and Colossians may well be the same whether we take the dietary restrictions to be Jewish food laws or pagan mystical asceticism.

I therefore think that the Epistle to the Hebrews may have been sent to the Churches of the Lycus Valley to meet the same peril as is combated by Paul's to the Colossians.

3. *Author.* By whom was it sent ?   I conjecture Apollos for the following reasons: (1) He has the qualifications for writing a letter of this sort.

Our knowledge of Apollos depends on :

(a) Primary authority : the mentions by Paul in I Cor. i. 12 ; iii. 4, 5, 6, 22 ; iv. 6 ; xvi. 12.   To these add Tit. iii. 13— if, as P. N. Harrison argues (*Problem of the Pastoral Epistles*, 115-118), Tit. iii. 12-15 is a genuine note written by Paul to Titus between the ' severe letter ' and II Cor. while Titus was at Corinth.

(b) The narrative in Acts xviii. 24-28, and the mention in Acts xix. 1.

Ἀπολλώς (shortened form of Ἀπολλώνιος) probably was an Alexandrian Jew.   Acts xviii. 24 describes him as ἀνὴρ λόγιος . . . δυνατὸς ὢν ἐν ταῖς γραφαῖς. Λόγιος may mean either *learned* or *eloquent*. Phrynichus, the Atticist, says that *learned* is the proper sense of the word ;

from which J. H. Moulton inferred that *eloquent* was
what Luke meant by it. Δυνατὸς ἐν ταῖς γραφαῖς—
mighty in the Scriptures, can, of course, only mean at this
period the O.T. In the N.T. the phrase δυνατὸς ἐν is
peculiar to Luke. (Lk. xxiv. 19, δυνατὸς ἐν ἔργῳ καὶ
λόγῳ—of Jesus ; Acts vii. 22, δυνατὸς ἐν λόγοις καὶ
ἔργοις αὐτοῦ—of Moses ; and the present passage).
LXX parallels are Judith xi. 8, δυνατὸς ἐν ἐπιστήμῃ ; Ps.
xxiii. (xxiv.) 8, δ. ἐν πολέμῳ ; Eccles. xxi. 7, δ. ἐν γλώσσῃ;
and *Ps. Sol.* xvii. 42, δ. ἐν πνεύματι ἁγίῳ. In *Sotah*
14a R. Simlai (*c.* 250) calls Abraham, Isaac, and Jacob
' mighty in knowledge of Torah and in the fulfilment
of the Commandments ' (עצומים בתורה ובמצות)—the reference being to Is. liii. 12 where עצום is rendered in
LXX by ἰσχυρός. Parallels from profane Greek writers
in Wettstein *ad* Lk. xxiv. 19. It is clear that Luke means
us to gather that Apollos had a masterly knowledge of the
O.T. It may be conjectured that he was also a skilled
exegete after the Alexandrian manner of Philo on the
Jewish side and Origen later on the Christian. The
allegorical method was characteristic of Alexandrian
exegesis. Acts further states that Apollos was κατηχημένος
τὴν ὁδὸν τοῦ Κυρίου. On κατηχημένος cf. Cadbury, in
Beg. Chr., ii., 508 f. The word implies *oral* instruction or
information. It is a question whether τοῦ Κυρίου here
means ' Jehovah ' or ' Jesus '. Probably the latter in contrast to δυνατὸς ἐν ταῖς γραφαῖς. Apollos knew the essence
of Judaism from book-study and he had learned something
about Christ and the Gospel orally. It may be conjectured
that τὴν ὁδὸν τοῦ Κυρίου here means the way of life set
forth in the teaching and by the example of Jesus : roughly,
the ' Ethics of the Sermon on the Mount '. With this
goes the statement that he knew only the baptism of John,
i.e. a baptism of repentance as a prelude to this new way
of life. He further knew and could recount τὰ περὶ τοῦ
Ἰησοῦ, i.e. the main outlines of the story of Jesus. For

what Luke understood by this phrase see Luke xxiv. 19 ff. It is to be noted that all this, even backed by the spiritual fervour of Apollos, was not regarded as a *Gospel*. What Apollos was preaching when Priscilla and Aquila found him was still not the Gospel. He knew Jesus the Prophet of Nazareth, colleague and successor to John the Baptist, and with John leader of a prophetic and spiritual revival within Judaism. The something more, that made Apollos into a Christian missionary instead of a Jewish revivalist, was communicated by Priscilla and Aquila ; and Luke describes it by saying that they took him in hand and ἀκριβέστερον αὐτῷ ἐξέθεντο τὴν τοῦ θεοῦ ὁδόν (J. H. Ropes om. τοῦ θεοῦ). We can only conjecture what is implied in this ; but it is a fairly safe guess that it is what is given in *v.* 28, εἶναι τὸν Χριστὸν Ἰησοῦν. In other words what Apollos' previous preaching had been meant to lead up to, and prepare the Jews for, is now seen by him to be something already accomplished. The Kingdom has come ; the Messiah has appeared. Jesus is not another forerunner like John preparing the people for the coming Messiah and his Kingdom. He *is* the Messiah : and the Kingdom has come in him and his followers. In place of a Johannine repentance-baptism in preparation for a future Kingdom we have the Christian rite of incorporation into a present Kingdom.

With this new message Apollos went from Ephesus to Corinth bearing a letter of introduction to the community there ; and began to work among the Jews, using his O.T. scholarship as a means to convince them of the truth of his new faith (xix. 27 f.). Some of the terms used by Luke to describe the work of Apollos are of special interest. Συνεβάλετο. This word is peculiar to the Lucan writings (Ev. 3 ; Ac. 4) in the N.T. its meanings are :

Act. lit. ' throw together ', and hence :—

(*a*) To discuss, confer, arrange a matter.

(*b*) To meet with, fall in with.

Middle. To make a contribution, help, assist.

(See the exx. in Moulton and Milligan, *Voc.* s.v.)

διὰ τῆς χάριτος. Should this be taken with πεπιστευκόσιν or with συνεβάλετο ? For (1) cf. Ac. xv. 11. διὰ τῆς χάριτος τοῦ Κυρίου Ἰησοῦ πιστεύομεν σωθῆναι. For (2) cf. Ac. iv. 33 ; vi. 8 and Luke ii. 40, 52 ; iv. 22. As a rule if Luke means the grace of God or Christ, he says so explicitly. Therefore we are justified in taking the second alternative and regarding χάρις in this case as a certain quality about Apollos, a spiritual gift possessed by him, through which he was able to be of real help to the Corinthian Christians.

διακατηλέγχετο. He not only beat them in argument —he completely floored them. And he made a regular business of it (εὐτόνως) ; and he did it publicly (δημοσίᾳ). Apollos ought to be the patron saint of the Christian evidence societies ; the father of apologetics.

Such vigour and eloquence doubtless had their effect in two ways : (a) by strengthening the conviction of some who were already members of the Church ; and (b) by securing the conversion of others, perhaps from Judaism. The result would be a section of the Corinthian community who could own Apollos as their father (or step-father) in the Gospel. Here doubtless we have the Apollos party at Corinth : simply the people who had been either converted by him or who being already Church members had fallen under the spell of his personality and his eloquence.

(2) He has the local connexion and interest. In Acts he makes his first appearance at Ephesus.

(3) Hebrews shows great familiarity with the characteristic thoughts and expressions of Paul as we find them in Corinthians and Romans. And the period when Corinthians and Romans were written was the time when Apollos was in close touch with Paul.

(4) The attitude on second repentance in Hebrews might be traced back to the austere teaching of John the Baptist.

And now I really launch out into the deep.

What is the relation between Hebrews and Colossians ? Here I make very tentative suggestions.

I suggest that Hebrews is prior to Colossians, and re-construct the story in this way.

Apollos has an interest in the Churches of Ephesus and the neighbourhood. News is brought to him possibly at Corinth about the new departures in the Lycus Valley. This letter is his attempt to counter the new teaching by showing the sufficiency and finality of Christ.

When the news about the Colossian heresy was later conveyed to Paul at Rome, a copy of Hebrews was sent along with the news. This would account for several facts.

(a) The fact that Hebrews is known at a very early date in Rome, *and is known not to be by Paul.*

(b) That it is known to Irenaeus ; but its authorship is not known.

(c) That it is known to Tertullian, and supposed by him to be the work of Barnabas. I should think that (b) and (c) arise out of (a).

(d) It would account for the somewhat advanced Christ-ology of Colossians. We assume a general and dominant Pauline influence perhaps too readily, and sometimes overlook the possibility that Paul may have been influenced by others. May it not be the case that Paul in Colossians has been influenced by Heb. i.-iv ?

(e) It would account for the belief in Egypt that Hebrews was Pauline. For the first collections of the Pauline corpus were made in Asia Minor and—if Harnack is right—Corinth. An important letter like Hebrews attached to such a collection, and having nothing to show its authorship, would naturally be reckoned in with the rest.

14.

THE LETTERS TO THE
THESSALONIANS.
(1953)

RECENTLY the authorities of the Greek Orthodox Church celebrated the nineteen-hundredth anniversary of the bringing of the Christian faith to their land by St. Paul. It is an event that deserved to be celebrated; for it is one of the momentous things in the history of mankind. Somewhere about the same time that the new faith came to Macedonia, it must also have arrived in Rome, perhaps a little earlier; and that, too, was an event which was destined to have great consequences. It is interesting to compare the two arrivals of Christianity in Europe. We know who brought it to Greece; we can fix the date with reasonable precision; and we can at least draw up an outline account of the reception given to the first missionaries. On the beginnings of the Church in Rome we are much less well informed. We do not know who first brought the good news; we do not know when it arrived or how it was received. We do know that when Paul wrote to Rome, in A.D. 55 or a year or two later, there was already a Christian community there. We may suppose that in the constant coming and going between the capital and the provinces it was inevitable that before long Christians should arrive in the city, brought there by business interests or by the nature of their work [1] or simply by the normal operations of the

---

[1] Thus, for example, one of our oldest Christian private letters (*B.G.U.*, I. 27, ii/iii A.D.) is from a certain Irenaeus, one of the crew of a grain-ship plying between Egypt and Italy. While his ship was lying in port, he had taken the opportunity to go to Rome and visit the Christian community there. It is interesting to note that the term used for the Church is ὁ τόπος, on which see the note in my Corinthian Chapter (Ch. 10). We can readily imagine Christians

slave-market. There is nothing to suggest that the foundation of the Roman community was part of an organized missionary campaign such as St. Paul conducted in Greece.

The story of how this campaign began is told in Acts xv and xvi. The Conference at Jerusalem, which had laid down the terms on which Jewish and Gentile Christians should have table-fellowship, was over. Paul and Barnabas, accompanied by two leading members of the Jerusalem community, Judas Barsabbas and Silas, had returned to Antioch and delivered the letter from the Conference. After a time Judas and Silas, or Judas alone,[1] returned to Jerusalem, while Paul and Barnabas stayed in Antioch teaching and preaching. The narrative of Acts goes on to tell how Paul suggested to Barnabas that they should revisit the South Galatian churches founded on the first missionary journey. The plan fell through because of a disagreement over Mark, whom Barnabas wanted as travelling companion and Paul did not. In the end Barnabas took Mark and went to Cyprus, while Paul, accompanied by Silas, took the overland route into Asia Minor.[2]

The activities of Paul and Silas are described in Acts xvi. 1-5, very summarily indeed. We hear of visits to Derbe and Lystra and of the circumcision of Timothy, who was at this time added to Paul's staff. Many students of Acts and the Pauline epistles have felt a serious difficulty here in view of Paul's emphatic repudiation of circumcision in his letter to the Galatians.[3] I think that the difficulty is greatly reduced if we

arriving in Rome at an earlier period in similar ways. Tertullian (*Apol.* 42) bears witness that Christians in his day were engaged in trade and shipping as well as in agriculture.

[1] Acts xv. 33 ff. The text is in some uncertainty. The Western and Byzantine evidence in verse 34 asserts that Silas stayed in Antioch by his own choice. This statement is absent from the B text. It may be that it is a later insertion to pave the way for the announcement in verse 40 that Paul took Silas with him on the second missionary campaign. On the other hand, the statement that Paul took Silas is strange, if Silas had left Antioch for Jerusalem. If it is another Silas that is meant in verse 40, it must be said that he is very abruptly introduced.

[2] Acts xv. 36-41. It is worth noticing that what in fact happened was that the places visited on the first journey were divided for the second. Cyprus, which Barnabas took on the second trip, had been the first place to be evangelized in the previous campaign.

[3] Gal. v. 2 ff.

can accept the interpretation of the second chapter of Galatians which I proposed in 1940,[1] namely, that the issue of circumcision was not raised as a matter of principle till a much later date, when Paul was at Ephesus during the third missionary journey. On the second journey Paul was still trying to work through the synagogues of the Dispersion ; and it was surely desirable from a practical point of view that he and his lieutenants should be qualified to address the synagogue congregations. So long as Timothy was uncircumcised he was disqualified from taking any active part in the synagogue service. It may well have seemed *at this time* that the operation was a small price to pay for the advantages that would accrue to the missionary enterprise.

We are told that the findings of the Jerusalem Conference were communicated to the churches ; and that, as a result of the visit by the missionaries, the churches were strengthened in the faith and increased in number daily.

As we read this account of the second journey through South Galatia we get the impression that it is being hurried over. Either the writer is in haste to come to new developments of his theme, or, possibly, Paul himself was in a hurry to break new ground, his restless spirit demanding new worlds to conquer for the Kingdom of God. However it may be, the fact is that in three verses Paul is transported from South Galatia to Troas in the north-west corner of Asia Minor ; and Troas marks a turning-point in the story second only to Antioch in importance.[2] For it is here that Paul has the dream in which he sees a Macedonian who begs him to " come over into Macedonia and help us ".[3] He and his associates interpret the dream as a call from God to extend the work of evangelization to Macedonia.[4]

---

[1] Cf. Chapter 9 above.   [2] Acts xvi 4 f.

[3] Lake and Cadbury remind us that the question has been raised how Paul knew that he was a Macedonian ; and say that " to ask this is contrary to the psychology of dreams ". As to the psychology of dreams I say nothing : I would say that to ask this is contrary to common sense. If someone comes to me and says " Come over into Scotland and help *us* ", I shall assume that he is a Scot, without requiring that he wear a kilt and play a selection on the bagpipes to prove his identity. And in most cases I shall expect my guess to be correct.

[4] Acts xvi. 9 f.

It is at this point that the first large stretch of narrative in the first person plural begins : " And when he saw the vision, immediately we began planning how to get away to Macedonia, concluding that God had called us to bring the gospel to them." This " we-section " continues as far as verse 17, when the party is at Philippi. From that point the third person is used until we come to xx. 6, again at Philippi, where the first person is resumed. There is a good deal to be said for the hypothesis that the person who speaks in this " we-section " is left behind when Paul leaves Philippi and remains in that neighbourhood until he is rejoined there by Paul in xx. 6.

The narrative of the journey from Troas is simple and straightforward. The sea passage with a favourable wind took two days and the party landed safely at Neapolis, the modern Cavalla, where they could join the great Roman trunk road, the *Via Egnatia*. From Neapolis they went to Philippi, and there the usual procedure in Pauline missionary work was followed. He began with the synagogue and converted a seller of purple-dyed wool from Thyatira, who entertained the missionaries in her house. In Acts xvi. 24 her name is given as Lydia ; but it has been suggested by Johannes Weiss [1] that this was a second name arising from that fact that Thyatira was a Lydian city, and that possibly the lady's personal name was Euodia or Syntyche.[2] After the story of Lydia the narrative of Acts goes on to describe how Paul exorcised an oracular spirit from a slave-girl, thus depriving her owners of a valuable source of income. They take action, and Paul and Silas are beaten and imprisoned. During the night there is an earthquake : the jailer and his family are converted, and next morning the prisoners are released. Paul makes formal protest at having been beaten, a punishment which ought not to be inflicted on a Roman citizen. This, we are told, caused some alarm among the Philippian magistrates, who came and asked them to do the city the favour of leaving it without delay. So they left, with the nucleus of a church established at the Thyatiran wool shop. As we know, this church grew and flourished, and remained the most con-sistently faithful to the Apostle of all his foundations. They

[1] *Das Urchristentum*, p. 211.   [2] Cf. Phil. iv. 2.

sent gifts to him from time to time; and, as we can see from the letter to the Philippians, they were very dear to him.

From Philippi the missionaries followed the Egnatian way through Amphipolis and Apollonia to Thessalonica, the modern Salonika. Here again Paul begins in the synagogue and makes converts, particularly among the adherents, that is, those Greeks who found the God of Israel more like their idea of what a God should be than any of the numerous occupants of their own Pantheon. For three Sabbaths Paul had had access to the Jewish congregation before opposition began to develop. Once aroused it no doubt quickly came to a head and before long a crowd, organized by the Jews, was demonstrating in front of the house where Paul and his friends were lodged. Failing to find the missionaries, they seized their host, Jason by name, and some of the converts, and brought them before the city magistrates alleging that the new religion was in fact revolutionary propaganda aimed at the overthrow of the Empire. The magistrates acted cautiously and contented themselves, for the time being, with binding Jason and the others over not to harbour seditious persons.[1] This left the Thessalonian Christians with no alternative but to rid themselves of the incriminating evidence, in this case Paul and his assistants, as quickly and as quietly as possible. Accordingly Paul and Silas were sent away under cover of darkness to Beroea, a city lying about fifty miles to the west of Thessalonica on the road to Athens.[2]

At Beroea the starting-point for the work was again the synagogue; and here the response was enthusiastic, many converts being made. But news of their success came back to Thessalonica; the synagogue authorities there took action and disturbances began in Beroea. Paul had to move on leaving Silas and Timothy behind. His Beroean escort brought him to Athens and returned home with instructions to Silas and Timothy to follow and report to their chief as quickly as possible.[3]

In Athens Paul saw the whole apparatus of Greek religion displayed in the most impressive form. He saw entire and complete those temples and statues of which the battered and broken remains are still among the wonders of the world. The

[1] Acts xvii. 1-9.   [2] Acts xvii. 10.   [3] Acts xvii. 11-15.

sight filled him with horror. He began a campaign for monotheism in the market-place and for Christian monotheism in the
synagogue. In the market-place he found plenty to argue with
him. The philosophically minded were prepared to talk about
the nature of ultimate Reality endlessly ; but as soon as Paul
proposed to bring into the debate more particular matters such
as Jesus and the resurrection, they became acutely aware of the
" scandal of particularity " and concluded that it was not a
genuine thinker that they were dealing with, but just another
agent of some Oriental cult. In the end Paul appeared before
the Areopagus and made a statement which is recorded in
Acts xvii. 22-32. The results of this effort in Athens were
disappointing and Paul later moved on to Corinth,[1] where he
carried on an active and successful ministry for some eighteen
months.

In his first letter to the Corinthians he reminds them that he
came to Corinth in deep depression ;[2] and it is open to us to
think that his loss of confidence was due, in part at least, to the
comparative failure of his effort at Athens. But not to this
alone. Athens was his fourth attempt in Europe. In the first
three his activities had been cut short just when he was getting
a church well started ; while at Athens his presentation of the
gospel in a manner likely to be acceptable to a cultured and
philosophical audience had fallen flat. It would not be tried
again. He tells the Corinthians, " I made up my mind that
among you my one and only subject would be Jesus the Messiah,
and a crucified Messiah at that ". We may perhaps think also
that the polemic against the wisdom of this world in the early
chapters of First Corinthians gains added point from his own
experiments with it at Athens.

The letters to the Thessalonians belong to this period of
Paul's life. They were written after his departure from Thessalonica and before his departure from Corinth. Our first task
is to see whether we can give approximate dates to these events.
The one secure link with secular chronology is the fact recorded
in Acts that Paul was brought before Gallio, the proconsul of
Achaea. It is possible on the basis of inscriptions and other

---

[1] Acts xvii. 32-xviii. 1.   [2] 1 Cor. ii. 1-5.

evidence to date the proconsulship of Gallio with considerable confidence.[1] The most important piece of evidence is the well-known inscription from Delphi giving the decision of the Emperor Claudius on some local dispute which had been referred to him by the proconsul Gallio. The document is dated in the 12th year of the Emperor's tribunicial power, that is, sometime between 25 January 52 and 24 January 53. It is also in the period between the 26th and 27th acclamations of Claudius as *imperator*. It is known from other sources that the 27th acclamation took place before 1 August 52, how long before we cannot say. The 26th acclamation *may* have fallen in Claudius's 11th year : if so, it must probably have been late in the year since four others would have to be fitted in before it. It follows that the Delphi case was considered in Rome and the decision issued between the latter part of 51 and 1 August 52 at the outside. More probably the limits should be narrowed to the period February-July 52. Further, Gallio must have been in office before the date of the decision, since it was he who had dealt with the case in its preliminary stages and had referred it to the Emperor. Now if Gallio took office in 52, arriving at Corinth in early summer, there is perhaps time for him to have completed the first hearing, prepared a report and sent it to Rome ; than for the report to have gone through the usual channels, for the Imperial decision to have been taken and transmitted from Rome to Gallio ; all before the 27th acclamation which occurred some time before 1 August. There is perhaps time ; but at best it would be a tight fit. If, on the other hand, Gallio arrived at Corinth in the early summer of 51 there is ample time for all the coming and going. I therefore think that there is a slight balance of probability in favour of the view that Gallio was in office from the early summer of 51 to the early summer of 52, assuming that his proconsulship lasted one year.

If we now make the further assumptions that the charge against Paul was made near the end of his stay in Corinth and near the beginning of Gallio's term of office, we get the early

[1] The relevant texts are given and discussed by Kirsopp Lake in *The Beginnings of Christianity*, v. 460-4.

summer of 51 as the date of the hearing ; and by reckoning back eighteen months from this point we come to late 49 or early 50 as the date of Paul's arrival in Corinth. This means that the events described in Acts xvi. and xvii. will be assigned to the year 49. The letters to the Thessalonians will fall somewhere within the period of two years between the summer of 49 and the summer of 51.

From the letters themselves we learn that in spite of hostility and ill-treatment the Apostles had made a good beginning with the building up of the church at Thessalonica. They had put their hearts into the work and they had had their reward in that the gospel was taken up and held fast by their converts in spite of strong opposition and even persecution. In 2 Thess. ii. 9 Paul mentions that during his stay at Thessalonica he earned his own living working at his trade, so as not to be a burden on the brethren. He was thus able to rebut the charge, which was made against him by opponents, that he was out for gain.[1]

But these are not the only facts to emerge from the study of the letters. We learn from 1 Thess. ii. 17-iii. 5 that the narrative of Acts is anything but complete. As we have already seen, when Paul left Beroea, Silas and Timothy remained behind ; and the Beroean escort who had accompanied Paul to Athens brought back a message to them to follow Paul *to Athens*. Now Acts makes no mention that this instruction was ever carried out : Silas and Timothy do not reappear on the scene in Acts until xviii. 5, when Paul is already in Corinth. There would seem to be two possibilities. Either Paul left Athens so soon that Silas and Timothy had not time to overtake him there ; or they did come to Athens and the fact is not recorded in Acts. A consideration of 1 Thess. ii. 17-iii. 5 suggests that the second alternative is to be preferred. In this passage Paul says :

But we, brethren, being bereaved of you for a short season, in presence, not in heart, endeavoured the more exceedingly to see your face with great desire : because we would fain have come again unto you, I Paul once and again ; and Satan hindered us. . . . Wherefore when we could no longer forbear we thought it good to be left behind at Athens alone ; and sent Timothy, our brother and God's minister in the gospel of Christ, to strengthen and encourage you in the matter of your faithfulness ; so that no one should be shaken by these afflictions ;

[1] 1 Thess. ii. 5.

for you yourselves know that hereunto we are appointed. . . . For this cause I also, when I could no longer forbear, sent that I might know your faith, lest by any means the tempter had tempted you, and our labour should be in vain.

From this it appears that Timothy, and probably Silas also, did come to Athens as instructed ; and further that, while Paul was still at Athens, Timothy was sent on a mission to Thessalonica. It is therefore presumably the return from that errand that is recorded in Acts xviii. 5 at Corinth. It is also clear that Paul had good reason to be anxious about the welfare of the Thessalonian community. The Christians there were suffering persecution, and there was the ever-present danger that their faith might break down under stress of loss and suffering. Moreover, even when Timothy was able to bring good news of them, it was clear to Paul that their faith was by no means perfect : he says that he wishes he could be with them in person to make up their deficiencies in this respect.[1]

Now it is surely probable that if Paul felt as strongly as he says he did about Thessalonian affairs, he would not only send Timothy, but also send with him a letter containing his own personal message. As long ago as the seventeenth century Hugo Grotius maintained that this was done and that 2 Thess. was the letter in question.[2]   In more recent times the thesis of the priority of 2 Thess. has been defended again and again : I mention two of the latest defenders : J. C. West, who discussed the problem in the *Journal of Theological Studies*,[3] and Johannes Weiss, who dealt with it in his *Urchristentum*.[4]   It seems to me to offer the best explanation of the facts. Before giving the reasons for holding it, we may consider the alternatives.

The Tübingen School rejected both Thessalonian epistles as spurious. Modern critical opinion on the Continent has tended to accept 1 Thess. and reject 2 Thess. The reason is that when you have read the first letter, the second appears like a pale ghost of its neighbour. As Johannes Weiss puts it,[5] " the majority of critical scholars are doubtful of the genuineness of

[1] 1 Thess. iii. 10.
[2] *Annotationes in Novum Testamentum*, i (Amsterdam, 1641), 1032-42 ; ii (Paris, 1646), 651.
[3] " The Order of 1 and 2 Thessalonians ", *J.T.S.*, vol. xv (1914), pp. 66-74.
[4] *Das Urchristentum*, pp. 213-23.   [5] Op. cit. p. 217, n. 2.

T

2 Thess. ; for, since they only read it in the shadow of 1 Thess., it appears to them as an insignificant and empty copy of 1 Thess.". So Jülicher in the seventh edition of his *Introduction* decides after considerable discussion that on the whole the best way of dealing with 2 Thess. is to cast it out of the authentic Pauline corpus. He may be regarded as a typical representative of the school referred to by Weiss.

The second alternative was proposed by Harnack in a paper read before the Berlin Academy in 1910. His thesis is that the likenesses between the two letters may be explained if we suppose that they were written at about the same time to two different addresses in Thessalonica. 1 Thess. was sent to the Gentile section of the Thessalonian church : 2 Thess. was written almost immediately afterwards for the Jewish Christian section of the same community. This view was adopted by Kirsopp Lake and fully discussed by him in his important work *The Earlier Epistles of St. Paul*.[1]   Its chief weakness is that it puts too great a strain on the imagination. It is more than difficult to see how Paul, who lays such great stress on the unity of the Church, should have consented to recognize a cleavage of this sort by writing two letters to two sections of one Christian community. Further, there is no sign in the letters themselves of any such intention. They are both addressed to the Thessalonian church as a whole. And there is no sort of real evidence that any division of the kind suggested existed at Thessalonica. The evidence rather seems to point the other way. For example, 1 Thess. ii. 13-16, which on the two-addressee hypothesis is intended for the *Gentile-Christian* section in Thessalonica, speaks in a very appreciative way of the churches in Judaea and practically congratulates the readers of the letter on having been imitators of these Jewish Christians.

We may now turn to consider the view that both letters are genuine, and that 2 Thess. was written first. The arguments on which Weiss rested his case are as follows.

[1] Pp. 61-101.   This view is still held to be the most probable in *An Introduction to the New Testament* by K. and S. Lake (1938), pp. 131-6. There the view is taken that 2 Thess. was somewhat later than 1 Thess., and was written to the Jewish Christians in Thessalonica after " Paul had received some communication which made him realise that 1 Thessalonians was not quite satisfactory ".

1. The Thessalonian community had to endure a good deal of persecution for their faith. These trials and tribulations are at their height in 2 Thess. : they are spoken of as past in 1 Thess.

(a) The troubles are present in 2 Thess. At the very beginning of the letter, immediately after the opening salutations, Paul speaks of conditions in Thessalonica. He commends the growing faith and love that are manifest in the life of the community and then goes on :

And so we on our part are boasting about you in all the churches of God for your steadfastness and faith in all your persecutions and in the afflictions which you are enduring. It is evidence of the just judgement of God that you should be adjudged worthy of the kingdom of God, for which you are suffering (granted that God holds it right to repay with affliction those who are afflicting you, and to grant rest with us to you who are at present afflicted, which he will do when the Lord Jesus is revealed from heaven . . .).[1]

Here the contrast is between the trials which the Thessalonians are at the moment enduring and the very different lot which will be theirs at the Parousia. Then the situation will be reversed : those who are now being harried will receive their reward in the kingdom of God, and those who now reject the gospel and persecute the believers will receive dire punishment. In the meantime the faithful must continue faithful ; and the missionaries pray constantly for them that they may be worthy of their high destiny.[2]

They must be faithful : they must also be imperturbable. Whatever excited members may say in ecstasy or in the heat of preaching or teaching, even if documents come purporting to be from Paul himself, the Thessalonians are to keep their heads. The Parousia has not come and will not come before the powers of darkness have had their last fling. Before the real Parousia there must be a Satanic imitation of it, the revelation of the lawless one with all the apparatus of bogus signs and wonders. This will precipitate the end. The Lord Jesus will slay the pretender with the breath of his mouth.[3] Come what may the recipients of the letter can rejoice, as its writer does, in the knowledge that they have received and responded to the call of God and that their future is safe in his hands.[4]

---

[1] 2 Thess. i. 4-7. [2] 2 Thess. i. 11 f. [3] 2 Thess. ii. 1-12.
[4] 2 Thess. ii. 13-iii. 5.

Next comes a particular warning made necessary by the fact that some members of the Thessalonian church have been carried off their feet by the expectation of an imminent Parousia, and have abandoned their normal life with its tasks and responsibilities. They are living in idleness waiting for the end ; and they expect others to supply their needs while they wait. Paul's direction is that they must work and earn their own living, and that nothing is to be done by the community to encourage members in lazy and parasitic ways of life.[1] The letter closes with a note of authentication and blessings.

Read thus in its own light, and without asking about its relation to 1 Thess., it is a remarkably vivid picture that is presented : the picture of a young community on tip-toe of expectation, looking eagerly for the great divine intervention that is to end the existing order and usher in the better world which has been prepared for the faithful. The hope of this golden age just round the corner makes it easier to put up with the eccentricities of some members, and to bear the insults and injuries which are the daily portion of the young church. The letter deals simply and directly with these points. Regarding the Parousia it says that the end is not yet ; and therefore the members of the church must carry on with their ordinary duties and bear their persecutions with patience and fortitude.

(b) When we turn from this simple note to 1 Thess., we are at once conscious that we have before us a more deliberate and carefully thought out letter. After the usual opening salutations it embarks on a detailed survey of the history of the church in Thessalonica from its first beginnings to the moment of writing. In the first chapter we have words of praise and thanksgiving for the remarkable progress made by the church, progress which is well known in Christian centres throughout Macedonia and Achaea. The second chapter is mainly concerned with Paul himself. Verses 1-12 give an account of his missionary work in Thessalonica with a good deal of emphasis on the purity of its motives and the unselfishness of its methods. Paul stresses the fact that when he was with them he was self-supporting, maintaining himself by working at his own trade. Then

[1] 2 Thess. iii. 6-15.

we have four verses on the relation of the Thessalonian community to the original Jewish-Christian community in Palestine : Macedonian Christianity is modelled on Judaean ; and relations appear to be completely friendly. The only hostility to the spread of the gospel in lands outside Palestine comes from pagans or unconverted Jews. Paul's indignation with the latter is readily understandable when we remember that his missionary strategy, which was to use the synagogues of the Dispersion as landing-beaches for his assault on paganism, had been thwarted by the action of the synagogues themselves. Verses 17-20 explain, in somewhat cryptic terms (" Satan hindered us "),[1] why Paul had not been able to pay another visit to Thessalonica, though plans had been made for it at least twice. Instead he had sent Timothy to strengthen and encourage them in their loyalty to their religion,[2] so that none of them should be shaken [3] by the troubles they were going through, since such things are involved in being a Christian. At a still earlier stage, when he was still with them, he had warned them of what he and they would have to bear ; and his predictions had been fully justified by the event, as the Thessalonians knew only too well. After this short digression Paul returns to the situation as it appeared to him when he was at Athens. At length his anxiety became

[1] I Thess. ii. 18. Various explanations, none entirely free from objection, have been offered of the meaning of the phrase. They are admirably summarized in Frame's note in his commentary, p. 121. If we are not to leave the reference indefinite, we may perhaps think of some illness of Paul, comparing 2 Cor. xii. 7. See E. B. Allo's Commentary on 2 Cor. (Études Bibliques), pp. 313-23. The objection that it is unlikely that Paul, Silas, and Timothy would all be ill at the same time is met by the consideration that a visit by all three might well have to be postponed if the senior and most important member of the party fell ill.

[2] I think that ὑπὲρ τῆς πίστεως ὑμῶν refers to the faithfulness of the Thessalonian Christians to their profession, as in 2 Thess. i. 4 where it is set alongside ὑπομονή.

[3] The verb used here, σαίνεσθαι, has provoked much discussion and a good deal of conjectural emendation. There is a small amount of evidence that it can mean " to be disturbed ". Bauer (Wörterbuch [4] s.v. σαίνω) cites Sophocles, Ant. 1214 παιδός με σαίνει φθόγγος and Diog. Laert. 8, 41 οἱ σαινόμενοι τοῖς λεγομένοις ἐδάκρυον. To these examples Mr. H. Chadwick, in J.T.S. (N.S., vol. i (1950), pp. 156 ff.), adds from the recently recovered Dialogue of Origen with Heraclides, τὰ μὲν περὶ πίστεως, ὅσα ἔσηνεν ἡμᾶς, συνεξετάσθη, " all the questions about the faith which disturbed us have been examined ". This seems to be enough to justify the rendering adopted in the text.

unbearable ; and, since he could not go to Thessalonica himself, he sent Timothy to find out whether they were still faithful,[1] or whether the tempter had seduced them and brought the labour of the missionaries to nothing.[2]

It is clear that the afflictions described here are things that were happening some time before the writing of the present letter. In ii. 14 ($\dot{\epsilon}\pi\dot{\alpha}\theta\epsilon\tau\epsilon$), similarly, the persecution is something past, and apparently not continuing into the present. In iii. 4 it is something they had been duly warned about before it happened : then it happened, and now they know by their own experience what is involved in being a Christian in a pagan world. But nowhere in 1 Thess. is there anything to suggest that the persecution is still in progress. On the contrary, the passage,[3] in which Paul speaks of Timothy's return and report and of his own feelings on receiving it, suggests very strongly that the Thessalonian community is for the moment free from outside interference. This is borne out by the fact that the Apostle's further counsels and exhortations all have to do with the internal discipline of the church and not with resistance to external enemies.

The trials and persecutions, which are a present threat in 2. Thess., are a thing of the past in 1 Thess. The inference is that 1 Thess. is the later document.

2. The internal difficulties of the Thessalonian church are in 2 Thess. a new development of which the writers of the letter have just heard. In 1 Thess. they are referred to as completely familiar to all concerned.

(a) In 2 Thess. iii. 11 ff. it is said :

We are informed that some of you are behaving irresponsibly, busybodies [4] very busy doing nothing. Such persons we urge with all the authority that we have under the Lord Jesus Christ to settle down quietly to work and earn a

[1] I take $\pi i\sigma\tau\iota\nu$ in verse 5 to mean " faithfulness " as in verse 2.

[2] 1 Thess. iii. 1-5.

[3] 1 Thess. iii. 6-10, followed by a blessing in verses 11-13.

[4] $\pi\epsilon\rho\iota\epsilon\rho\gamma\alpha\zeta o\mu\dot{\epsilon}\nu o\nu s$. There is a play upon words in the Greek, which I have tried to represent in the translation. Theophrastus describes $\pi\epsilon\rho\iota\epsilon\rho\gamma\iota\alpha$ in *Char.* xiii. His $\pi\epsilon\rho\iota\epsilon\rho\gamma o s$ is a fool, a fussy and inept meddler in other people's affairs. At a later time other and more reprehensible qualities came to be attached to the word. For these see Farquharson's commentary on Marcus Aurelius, vol. ii. pp. 490 f.

living for themselves. And you brethren who are already behaving properly—
keep it up ! If anyone refuses to obey this written instruction of ours, let him be
a marked man, have nothing to do with him, that he may be shamed (into obedience). Do not regard him as an enemy, but warn him as a brother.

All this is news which the writers of the letter have just
learned about the troublesome minority at Thessalonica ; and
they give immediate instructions how the matter is to be dealt
with. They also remind the members of the community that
when they were at Thessalonica founding the church there,
they had inculcated the virtues of honest work, both by precept
and example [1] ; but they do not refer to any earlier letter, as we
might expect, if 1 Thess. had preceded 2 Thess.

(b) When we turn to 1 Thess. we find references to the
disorders dealt with in 2 Thess. ; but they do not suggest that
the disorders are a new thing. On the contrary, they allude to
them as matters already well known to both the readers and
the writers of 1 Thess. When the writers say, " we exhort you
brethren, warn the irresponsible ", the full force of the exhortation is not appreciated unless we have in mind the things said in
2 Thess. iii. 11 ff. The same applies to the injunctions in 1 Thess.
iv. 10-12. In this passage the writers refer to a specific injunction which they had previously given (καθὼς ὑμῖν παρηγγείλαμεν,
verse 11). It may well be that this is a reference to the injunction of 2 Thess. iii. 12 (τοῖς δὲ τοιούτοις παραγγέλλομεν, καὶ
παρακαλοῦμεν ἐν Κυρίῳ Ἰησοῦ Χριστῷ).

The data concerning the internal difficulties at Thessalonica
are best understood if we take 2 Thess. to be the earlier letter
of the two.

3. The emphasis on the autograph closing greetings as a
mark of genuineness in any letter claiming to be from Paul
is pointless except in a first letter. The passage runs :

The greeting of me, Paul, in my own handwriting. This is the mark (of
genuineness) in every letter (of mine). This is the way I write. The grace of
our Lord Jesus Christ be with you all (2 Thess. iii. 17 f.).

That the warning against spurious letters purporting to come
from the Apostle was not superfluous is clear from 2 Thess. ii. 2,
where Thessalonians are warned against allowing themselves to

[1] 2 Thess. iii. 6-10.

be misled by such forged documents. The statement in iii. 17 was fully discussed by O. Roller.[1] After careful consideration of similar passages in 1 Cor. xvi. 21 ; Gal. vi. 11 ; Col. iv. 18 ; Phil. v. 19, he concludes that the purpose of the note is to draw attention to the fact that there is no change of handwriting such as would appear if a secretary wrote the main body of the letter and the Apostle added only the concluding greetings. If Paul himself wrote the whole of 2 Thess. the purpose of the note in iii. 17 is to say : " This is my handwriting. I may not always write the whole letter myself, as I have done in this case ; but I always write the closing greeting at least, and it will be in this handwriting. No letter without it is genuine." This intimation is very much to the point, if 2 Thess. is the first genuine letter of Paul to come to the Thessalonian church—they had already had at least one that was not genuine. The question may well be asked, why the Thessalonians should accept the document and the handwriting as Paul's merely because it claimed to be his. To this the answer will be that if, as has been suggested already, Timothy was the bearer of the letter, its authenticity would be independently guaranteed. The already known messenger authenticates the first letter : the already known handwriting will authenticate any future communication.

4. The statement (1 Thess. v. 1) that the Thessalonians have no need to be instructed about times and seasons is very much to the point, if the readers are already acquainted with the contents of 2 Thess. ii., where the time of the Parousia is dealt with at some length and in considerable detail.

So far I have taken the points made by Weiss, elaborating and adding to them where necessary. I now go on to some further considerations.

5. In 1 Thess. iv. 9-v. 11 we have a series of three didactic sections each introduced by the formula " Now concerning . . . ".[2] This formula is familiar to us from 1 Cor. There it occurs six times, beginning with vii. 1, περὶ δὲ ὧν ἐγράψατε,

---

[1] *Das Formular der Paulinischen Briefe* (1933), pp. 187-91.
[2] These are : iv. 9 περὶ δὲ τῆς φιλαδελφίας, iv. 13 περὶ τῶν κοιμωμένων, v. 1 περὶ δὲ τῶν χρόνων καὶ τῶν καιρῶν.

which makes it clear that the Apostle is replying to points raised in a letter from the Corinthians to him. An exact parallel from outside the Bible is to be seen in the letter of the Emperor Claudius to the citizens of Alexandria [1] dated A.D. 41, less than a decade before the writing of 1 Thess. Here the Emperor says (ll. 52 f.) " Concerning the requests which you are anxious that I should grant I decide as follows ". The decisions follow. In line 66 we find, " Concerning the matter of the Senate . . . ", followed by an intimation of the steps being taken. We may therefore surmise that in 1 Thess. Paul is replying point by point to questions raised at Thessalonica and communicated to him either in a letter or verbally by Timothy. Now if 2 Thess. was taken to Thessalonica by Timothy, we should expect that the three points now to be dealt with will have arisen from statements made in 2 Thess. Let us see if this is the case.

(a) Concerning love of the brotherhood,[2] you have no need of anyone to write to you ; for you yourselves are taught by God to love one another. What is more, you are putting it into practice in your treatment of all the brethren in Macedonia. But we urge you, brethren, to achieve even more, to make it your ambition to live quietly, to mind your own business, and to work with your own hands,[3] as we instructed you ; that your behaviour may win the respect of outsiders and you yourselves be independent.[4]

In this passage the words " as we instructed you " may well be, as suggested above, a reference to the specific instruction given in 2 Thess. iii. 12. If that is so, the passage as a whole may be the answer to supplementary questions arising out of the whole passage 2 Thess. iii. 6-15. It may be, for example, that the strong measures proposed for dealing with the irresponsible minority were thought to be somewhat drastic, not least by the minority themselves. What becomes of the love of the brotherhood if members of it are to be treated in this way ? The

---

[1] P. Lond. 1912. The text of this important document was published with introduction, translation, and commentary by H. I. Bell in the volume *Jews and Christians in Egypt* (1924), pp. 1-37.

[2] Cf. F. W. Beare, *The First Epistle of Peter* (1947), p. 84 : " φιλαδελφία does not mean ' brotherly love ' in general, but quite specifically ' the love of the (Christian) brotherhood ', the mutual love which binds together the children of God in one family ".

[3] Cf. M. Aur., i. 5, where these two things come in the reverse order : τὸ αὐτουργικὸν καὶ ἀπολύπραγμον.   [4] 1 Thess. iv. 9-12.

answer is that the Thessalonian community has shown, and is showing, that it understands very well what love of the brother-hood means, both within its own circle and in the wider field. There is, however, room for improvement ; and that will come when it is realized by all that genuine love of the brotherhood includes not being parasitic on the brotherhood.

(b) The second section begins, " We do not wish you to remain ignorant, brethren, concerning those who are at rest, that you may not grieve as others do who have no hope ". It then goes on to explain that Christians who die before the Parousia will not be at any disadvantage when the Lord returns. On the contrary, they will have a certain priority : they will be raised from the dead first, and then those Christians who are still alive will be caught up along with them to meet the Lord in the air.

It seems clear that this is the answer to a question which must have run something like this : " What about the good Christians who die before the Second Coming ? " Then we must ask in what circumstances such a question would be most likely to be asked, and surely the answer is that it would be when the Thessalonians had been told by Paul that the Parousia, which they were so eagerly expecting, would be deferred to the indefinite future. But this is precisely what is done in 2 Thess. ii. 1-12. The situation may be reconstructed thus.

There is at Thessalonica a young and enthusiastic community living in daily expectation of the dawning of the day of the Lord. They are being persecuted by enemies outside and troubled by eccentrics within. The question soon comes to be why the Parousia does not happen, and that carries with it the danger that being disappointed on this head the members will come to think that the whole gospel is a fraud or a delusion. The delay of the Parousia threatens the very existence of the community.

The statement in 2 Thess. ii. 1-12 meets this danger by saying what the " Little Apocalypse " in Mark xiii says : οὔπω τὸ τέλος—" the end is not yet " [1]. Before the Parousia there will be one last convulsive effort of the kingdom of Satan to assert

---

[1] Mark xiii. 7.

itself in the world : there will be a Satanic parousia, which will be tricked out with bogus signs and wonders and will lead many people astray. Then, and not till then, the genuine Parousia will take place and the power of evil be finally destroyed.

This answer, if accepted, clearly resolves the difficulties created by the delay of the Parousia ; but it does so at the price of raising new questions. Among them is the question, " What about the brethren who may never live to see the delayed Parousia? Where is their share in the good time that is coming?" This question is answered in 1 Thess. iv. 13-18. Those who have died in faith before the Parousia will be raised from the dead to share in it along with those who are still alive. Read in this way and in this order the two passages make perfect sense and illuminate one another.

(c) The third section [1] is headed " Concerning the times and the seasons ". Here again it is possible to frame the kind of question to which the statements in the section give an answer. And it is another supplementary question which would naturally arise out of the teaching on the delayed Parousia given in 2 Thess. A community waiting for an imminent Parousia is not greatly concerned about premonitory signs : it is the thing itself that is looked for. But if the thing itself is postponed and the watchers are told to expect something else first, then they are likely to ask for further details. The natural retort to " the end is not yet " is " how long then?" " What will be the signs that events are beginning to march, and when may we expect to see them?" Paul's answer is that no time-table can be drawn up. " The Lord will come like a thief in the night." [2] This also favours the hypothesis that 2 Thess. preceded 1 Thess.

If this conclusion is well established we may reconstruct the order of events somewhat as follows.

A.D. 49 Paul sets out on the second missionary campaign, in the course of which he crosses from Asia Minor into Macedonia and there founds churches, including one at Thessalonica. After leaving the city he comes to Beroea and later goes on to Athens.

---

[1] 1 Thess. v. 1-11.
[2] 1 Thess. v. 2. This is the Q teaching on the final consummation, on which see my book *The Sayings of Jesus* (1949), pp. 114-48.

From Athens he sends word to Silas and Timothy to join him there. Later they arrive, probably bringing news of the trials and problems at Thessalonica, which they would no doubt have heard of at Beroea. They may even have brought a letter from the Thessalonian church to Paul, though we have no positive evidence for this. From Athens Timothy is sent to Thessalonica bearing 2 Thess. What Silas does at this juncture is unknown. All we know is that Paul went from Athens to Corinth alone.

Winter 49/50 Paul arrives in Corinth from Athens. Later he is joined by Silas and Timothy, the latter bringing a report on conditions at Thessalonica and a number of questions raised in the minds of the Thessalonian Christians by the message of 2 Thess. Paul then sends 1 Thess., partly to express his joy at the good news brought by Timothy and partly to deal with the questions that had been put to him. This letter should perhaps be dated early in A.D. 50.[1]

---

[1] The question may be asked, why if 2 Thess. 1 Thess. is the correct order, the two letters appear in the order 1 Thess. 2 Thess. in the New Testament. The most probable answer is in one word—size. There seems to be a tendency to put the longest letters first in the Pauline corpus.

I. INDEX OF PROPER NAMES

279

II. INDEX OF SUBJECTS

III. PATRISTIC REFERENCES

IV. INDEX OF BIBLICAL REFERENCES:
OLD TESTAMENT:

287

NEW TESTAMENT